Travels
with a
Brompton
In the Cévennes & other regions

Sue Birley

CRANTHORPE
—MILLNER—
PUBLISHERS

Copyright © Sue Birley (2022)

The right of Sue Birley to be identified as author of this work has been asserted by her in accordance with section 77 and 78 of the Copyright, Designs and Patents Act 1988.

All rights reserved. No part of this publication may be reproduced, stored in a retrieval system, or transmitted in any form or by any means, electronic, mechanical, photocopying, recording, or otherwise, without the prior permission of the publishers.

Any person who commits any unauthorised act in relation to this publication may be liable to criminal prosecution and civil claims for damages.

First published by Cranthorpe Millner Publishers (2022)

ISBN 978-1-80378-027-6 (Paperback)

www.cranthorpemillner.com

Cranthorpe Millner Publishers

To the Modestines of this world: patient little plodders who know a good snack when they see one

Chapter 1
Introduction

On pondering the title of this volume, the quick-witted reader will lose no time in grasping the allusion to a book by Robert Louis Stevenson, *Travels with a Donkey in the Cévennes*. In 1878 Stevenson, for reasons best known to himself as winter with its long nights was drawing near, set off on a walking tour of the Cévennes mountain range in southern France, and the book he wrote about it made him famous for the first time. We toured the area in summer, and it rained, a lot. With a small donkey to carry his luggage, he (and she) walked from Le Monastier to St-Jean-du-Gard, often camping out in the open and popping over Mont Lozère on the way, though I think this last was *sans* donkey. I hope she was taking a well-earned day off at the time. Le Monastier is near the Lot river in the Haute-Loire *département,* and St-Jean-du-Gard is, as its name suggests, in the Gard, on the river Gardon. Mont Lozère, a mighty granite *massif* (altitude 1699m) lies a little to the east of his route and is pretty rugged.

The addition to my book's title of the words 'and other regions' might be self-explanatory, given the chapter headings, but why a Brompton rather than a donkey? Indeed, what *are* a Brompton?

Modestine, the name of Stevenson's donkey, is introduced to the reader as a 'diminutive she-ass' and there can be few better adjectives to describe a Brompton, which is a bicycle, a small bicycle, a *very* small bicycle. It is a very small, folding bicycle, for just as Modestine would prepare for sleep by tucking her legs under her tummy and her head into her chest, the Brompton can tuck various bits into itself, though for carriage rather than sleeping purposes. It is thus one of the few bicycles that can be transported with ease throughout the railway system, particularly the French railway system, enabling its rider to explore many regions of France she would have found difficulty in reaching otherwise.

It is not the sort of bicycle usually associated with tours of France, and nothing like the type of machine associated with *the* 'Tour de France'. Examples of the latter beast and its tough and sinewy rider are to be met everywhere at weekends in the French countryside, and they can present quite a danger to the unwary. They seem to hunt in packs and whereas cars can usually be heard coming (the advent of the silent electric car is something to be dreaded), racing bikes are quiet and deadly, and delight in swooping past with a mere whisker to spare. The riders are prone to shout very loudly indeed at times; they did this one day when, rounding a downhill corner, they encountered an Englishman[1] and his Brompton blocking the road in admiration of a particularly pretty hedgerow flower. Happily, my husband did as they asked ("get out of the ****ing way") otherwise our Brompton travels might have come to a sadly premature end.

The similarities between those French bicycles and our own are so faint that I once found myself thinking that it was like trying to compare a racehorse and a donkey. One does not choose a donkey for speed, but it is often used as a beast of burden and a Brompton is sturdy and will carry considerable weight without complaint. Another thought that has often come to me – as I trudge up the long passes that are abundant in the south of France, footsore and weary and hoping the holes in my shoes won't let in too much rain when the next storm comes but at least knowing they will let it out again – is that a walking holiday could be more easily accomplished without a bicycle in tow. Later chapters will show that we do often seem to end up on *foot*paths, if we are that lucky, and it is quite likely that some of the people we meet are thinking along similar lines, wondering if there is a practical reason for the bicycle.

But if I do occasionally wonder if the main reason for bringing my Brompton is to carry my luggage on its back rather than mine, it's not a bad one, and it was for this same

---

[1] Dr David Anthony Haydon Birley, henceforth referred to as Dahb. I was once disturbed at work by a cold caller wanting to speak to Dr Dahb Birley. Reader, I married him in 1974.

reason that Stevenson bought little Modestine. He treated her quite shockingly, by the way, in a manner in which I would never treat a donkey or even a bicycle. Hitting a donkey on her face was a caddish thing to do, and hitting a bicycle is rather futile. My Modestine rewards my care of her by carrying me down the hills (if I get on before she takes off), whereas Stevenson had to walk up *and* down dale, and serve him jolly well right.

This book does go into some detail of the regions of France in which we have taken many a happy holiday, but it is perhaps primarily about the Brompton bicycle and the way it has enabled us to enjoy our French sojourns. Firstly, however, I will attempt some description of the fun and games we had trying to have cycling holidays before we discovered the existence of such a useful and portable animal as the Brompton.

**

We are not, of course, the only ones to suffer from the vagaries of the French railways. I remember meeting a French couple at Tours station, as we all waited for one of the few trains that day that would accept bicycles; they joined us in moaning about their own railway system. More recently we met a German couple who had felt quite annoyed at having to drive into France to enjoy a cycling holiday, because it was so difficult to travel by train. I think they were quite glad they had done when they saw the size of our wheels!

Edward Enfield, father of the comedian Harry, has written in highly entertaining fashion of the trials and tribulations of putting a bicycle onto a French train[2]. "Any contest between French Railways and the bicycle," he writes, "is such a complicated subject that it needs a special chapter to itself. The principle, so far as there is a principle, is that the French Railways system is hostile to bicycles, but the employees, being French also, are in favour of them."

Reading this reminded me of a cycling trip a friend and I once took in Somerset. On the train back from Taunton, the guard cheerfully made room for our bicycles (this was in the pre-Brompton days) by flinging sundry Red Star parcels to the other side of the van to the merry tinkling sounds of the contents shattering.

Enfield continues: "The employees therefore make it possible to do things which the system declares to be impossible." We once tried to alight, with large bicycles, from a train at a station with a short platform, Dilton Marsh,

---

[2] *Downhill all the way: cycling through France from La Manche to the Mediterranean* (1994). A subsequent book, *Freewheeling through Ireland: travels with my bicycle* (Summersdale 1996), has a picture of a donkey and a bicycle on the cover, which is only fitting.

near Westbury in Wiltshire. The conductor (I beg his pardon – the 'train manager') asked the driver to shove the train along a bit so that we could get off safely as we had, of course, managed to put the bicycles in the wrong part of the train – a 50:50 chance of that on a train with only two carriages.

"French Railways, or SNCF," trills Enfield, "have a London office in Piccadilly which is staffed by nice people who will gladly tell you what you would like to hear, which is that there is no problem about taking the bicycle on a French train." I have certainly found that I have been able to tell the staff in the Piccadilly office a lot more about bicycles and SNCF than they have been able to tell *me*.

"If pressed, they will tell you that there may be a little occasional delay because not all French trains have guard's vans and the only place for a bicycle is a guard's van. Which trains have guard's vans and will take bicycles, and which have not and will not, is a closely guarded secret concealed in special timetables that they do not possess."

A similarly closely guarded French secret that readers might like to know of is the existence of a left-luggage office at Lille-Flandres station if I might for a moment wander off the point. Don't try looking for help at Lille-Europe, though. And I'm sure things have changed at Lille-Flandres as I realise, I wrote that some time ago.

"Going off the point a minute" was a favourite saying of a favourite geography tutor of mine. It heralded all sorts of wonderful anecdotes, and we would tuck our toes into our armchairs, so to speak, and prepare for delicious nuggets of information which had little to do with the matter in hand.

Back to the knotty problem of getting bicycles on trains: Enfield once found that when 'they' said he could put his bicycle in the train, 'they' meant just that, and he had to take off all the luggage and panniers and lift the machine four feet into the air to reach the van. Perhaps his crowning achievement, however, was to be sold a ticket for the train and then to find that the line had been closed and the train had become a bus. (*Service dessert* on a timetable does not mean deserted by all and sundry or even a set of crockery but is an abbreviated assurance that there will be a bus instead of a train, i.e., *Un service d'autocars dessert ces localités*.) Fortunately, he was able to put his bicycle into the bus's luggage compartment, as I believe people do on National Express though not on most British rail replacement buses I've been on.

Dahb and I have also had jolly times trying to put our bicycles on the train, and indeed to keep them there. When travelling from Greece to Yugoslavia just before the death of Tito, the bicycles, which were big things we had bought on Crete, were made very welcome but some helpful person decided at around 2am that we would naturally want to leave the train at the border crossing, and obligingly popped the bicycles onto the platform. Luckily Dahb was in the corridor chatting to a Yugoslav in their only common language, French, and spotted the error, leaping off the train and leaping back on it, *mit* bikes, before the train continued on its way.

Later during that trip, which was a journey from Central Africa to Wiltshire, not all by cycle, we took a train from Trieste into Venice, having paid about £3 each for our tickets. The guard then came along and demanded the equivalent of £20 for the bicycles, at which point I suddenly discovered I could understand very little Italian, apart from the words for 'I do not understand' and the guard eventually gave up trying to charge for the bikes. Having spent a couple of days in Venice, where we stayed in a hotel near the station as we couldn't get the cycles on a *vaporetto* to go to the youth hostel, the next part of the journey involved sending the bicycles on ahead. We waited a day and a half in Tours for them to catch up; we have since been told horror stories of bicycles taking weeks and weeks, so obviously got off rather lightly, and Tours is an interesting city, luckily. And to be fair to myself, my Italian is fairly skimpy, having been mostly gleaned from opera *libretti*.

Once we decided to visit the Auvergne and to take our 'big bikes' on the Portsmouth-Ouistreham ferry, followed by a train from Caen to Clermont-Ferrand. What innocent souls we were! There was one train a day from Caen with bicycle space, and it left at 6.30am, so having missed it we cycled about 25 miles to the next stop, St-Pierre-sur-Dives, and caught a train the next day. It didn't take us very far – Le Mans, perhaps – and trying to discover which trains we could take from there and when we could take them was somewhat challenging, even though my French is plumper than my Italian. In the end, I threw in the towel and asked the information staff to list all the trains permitting bicycles, and we simply cycled the bits in between, reaching the north of the Auvergne about two days before we had to start the return journey. It was still a lovely holiday, and we returned to the Auvergne twelve years later (plus Bromptons), but it was some years before we revisited the Allier and the Berry areas, which are very attractive and previously unknown to us, and visited by us earlier only because they were the parts of the country that had to be cycled through rather than traversed by train.

Another time we decided to travel *without* bicycles and hire them when we got there. We travelled on the overnight train to Arles (this was before Eurostar), intending to rent cycles at the station. It used to be quite easy to do this but unfortunately on this occasion a large group had got there first, mopping up all the station bicycles and of course all the shops were shut. They always were in those days as we usually travelled on a Saturday, arriving in the evening, and then had to go through Sunday and Monday before most shops opened up again. With the advent of Eurostar and retirement, this isn't always the case.

However, we could do without shops, apart from cycle shops, so we pottered happily around Arles for the day, having first taken a bus out to a village (Fontvieille of Daudet's windmill fame) where *VTT*s, all-terrain bikes, could be hired. But they had no carrier racks, and we really dislike carrying luggage on our backs. It quite defeats the point of cycling.

The next day we were able to hire *VTTs* for the day from an Arles hotel, and spent a day exploring the Camargue. The Camargue is usually described as hot and dusty – if only! It poured and poured with rain and so one day we must return and see where we went. We nearly clogged up the shower in our own hotel trying to get the sand off our persons, as *VTTs* are not only carrier-less but also mudguard-less. The hiring hotel, however, was very relaxed about the messy machines we handed over and even offered us a shower for ourselves.

But at last it was Tuesday, the shops were open again and we hired rather feeble-looking touring bicycles with racks (Dahb suggested not saying how far we intended to take them) and we then spent a happy five days in the Luberon, a glorious part of France we keep returning to.

After all these vicissitudes, it was with huge interest that we read of a new bicycle which claimed to solve all the problems of travelling by train (as difficult by now in England as it was in France). Enter the Brompton, the true hero of this story or should I say heroine? Ah yes, enter Modestine, at a brisk trot!

**

I am sure you would like to know more about my Modestine, who has just so briskly trotted in and whose namesake carried Stevenson's luggage, as well as about Bromptons in general. We tend to refer to the designer of this magnificent velocipede as Mr Brompton but in fact his name is Andrew Ritchie, and he filed the original patent in 1979. He gave it the name Brompton because he could see the Brompton Oratory from his bedroom, which doubled as a workshop in the beginning. He clearly knows about bicycle engineering but was working as a gardener when he started to build his invention.

On the Brompton Wikipedia page there is a photograph of Mr Brompton holding one of his products and looking rather like a French horn player in an orchestra, just about to empty the dribble from his instrument into the path of a passing viola player, of which I am often one. The Brompton folds in three and has 16-inch wheels which is the main reason it causes hilarity as we tackle impassable passes and ford unfordable fords etc. My school Latin master used to talk like this and what with all rivers being called the Flumen, and Latin hangman at the end of term, he did make classes rather fun.

As production increased, Mr B moved it from his bedroom and further west to wild and woolly Greenford. About 40,000 bicycles are produced each year which makes it all the more amazing that, apart from commuters on the train to London, we have spotted only two on our travels. One belonged to an elderly Frenchman we met in Alsace. He had bought it in

Paris but had no luggage, so presumably wasn't going far. The other was being ridden at speed in Lyon by a man in a suit and we were too far away to be able to hail him and start a discussion, which he probably wouldn't have appreciated, being a commuter on his way to his home and, doubtless, a *verre* of *quelque chose*.

In reviews of folding bicycles, the Brompton usually comes up tops. This is not surprising – I don't think I've come across a cycle that folds as well but it is of course at the expense of wheel size. A close competitor, though, is the German-made Birdy. I recently met a violinist who rode his Birdy, violin on his back, from Bristol to Swindon for a rehearsal, returning by train. He conceded that the Birdy was slightly bulkier but he found it a better ride than the Brompton. I'm glad we have a British cycle, though. I've nothing against foreigners, often being one myself, but I do think we should all make our own things if we can.

Anyway, we find our Bromptons very comfortable and very stable, as long as the back wheel is tied up to the rest of the bike. The first stage of the three-stage folding process is to kick the back wheel under the bicycle so that the carrier is on the ground and the Brompton is in the 'parking position'. To park the bicycle the luggage is taken off, but if the wheel is not secured it will try and park, failing because of the luggage and causing considerable problems. In the Limoges rush hour I was somewhat inconvenienced trying to walk across a busy road by Modestine obviously feeling exhausted by the train journey and deciding to park herself in the middle of the crossing when the lights had just gone green for the traffic. That was on our first Brompton trip, and we now see the need for a bungie wrapped round the stem and luggage rack, preventing any unwanted parkings.

Another tricky thing is manipulating the folding pedal. When I bought Modestine and brought her home from Warlands of Oxford (a *proper* cycle shop), I ended up with a large hole in my shin owing to my not very skilful handling of the pedal. Naturally Modestine wouldn't dream of doing such a thing deliberately and I think I've got the hang of it now, 25 years later. Warlands cycle shop has twice done really thorough overhauls of the bicycles.

When we bought our Bromptons in 1993, the choice of gearing was between a one, a three-speed and a five-speed Sturmey Archer. Nowadays the bicycle comes in one-, two-, three-, or six-speed gearing options, with higher or lower gearing available and even derailleurs. I do sometimes look wistfully at newer Bromptons and the six speeds, but it *is* only one more gear, and I *am* somewhat attached to Modestine. We opted for a three-speed (his) and a five-speed (hers), the idea being that he was slowed down a bit to enable her to catch up, preferably at the next bar.

An excellent book about the history of and technical information on the Brompton is that written by David Henshaw and published by Excellent Books. Here you will also learn about The Folding Society and A-B magazine, all about folders!

So that, for now, is the Brompton. I have entitled the book *Travels with a Brompton in the Cévennes and other regions,* but it has to be admitted that the Cévennes are not a region, politically or administratively speaking, but a range of hills or mountains. I am not sure when a hill becomes a mountain, but the peaks are pretty uppish. The area, including the limestone Causses, was granted national park status in 1970 and forms part of a UNESCO Heritage Site.

I probably could have called my book *Travels in the Cévennes and other impossible mountains* but somehow 'regions' tripped off the tongue, and we do tend to think of our holidays in terms of regions and *départements*. In the French Revolution the country's provinces were replaced by 83 *département*s (now 96 on the mainland and 5 overseas), each with a *chef-lieu* (sort of county town) that could be reached in no more than a day's journey by horse (surely by Brompton, had it existed) from any point in the *département*. Very egalitarian if you were rich enough to own a horse. These divisions stuck, and were often named after rivers, e.g., Loire, Seine-Maritime and Tarn. I will use the French word, *département*, as the English 'department' might suggest holidays spent shopping.

In the 1980s the French government decided to add another layer of government, the region. This was really just an amalgamation of *départements* but was given its own council and powers, including some taxation, and a regional capital. Some were big, some were quite small. So you had, for example, Basse-Normandie (Calvados, Manche and Orne *départements*, capital Caen) and a little one, Alsace (Bas-Rhin and Haut-Rhin, capital Strasbourg). Then blow me down, just as everyone had got to grips with this, they changed the regions again so that as from 2016 there are now 13 instead of 22. Bourgogne and Franche-Comté were merged to form a region imaginatively named Bourgogne-Franche-Comté. Aquitaine, Poitou-Charentes and Limousin, formerly a very small region, became Nouvelle-Aquitaine, Aquitania being the Roman name for the 'watery' province in the south-west of Gaul, and imagination really took flight in the merging of Midi-Pyrénées and Languedoc to form Occitanie, the historical name of the broader region and linked to the Occitan language. Will demands for independence follow?

Fortunately, the *départements* remain the same so we can still play our favourite game of spotting where the cars come from as the registration plate includes the number of the *département*, though in smaller figures than before. It's alphabetical on the whole, so Ain is 01, Jura 39 and Val-d'Oise 95. Belfort is 90 for historical reasons. We delight in spotting 'foreigners' who might live two miles away in the neighbouring *département* and just be visiting to do some shopping. What is really thrilling is spotting a car from central Paris (75) and we carry a map and list so that we can determine where all the visitors come from. Sad, I know, but another excuse to prolong café stops.

There is another thing about the Brompton: she can be electrified. We had a friend of indifferent health who rode her battery-assisted Brompton to her work with ease. We realise that one day we might be glad of such help and have thought occasionally of hiring an electric bike for a day to see how we got on. There is an e-bike hire shop in Bonnieux, in Vaucluse, which might be the place as it's a village always worth visiting. I remember a not-so-young Dutch lady cycling in the Verdon gorges with little apparent effort, up a hill Modestine and I had plodded up on foot, and it turned out that she had hired an electric bike. Last year in Alsace we met quite a lot of people on electric cycles and although something in our Puritan souls revolts against this, these were probably people who would otherwise be travelling by car, so it can't be a bad thing.

Now I have mentioned that the Bromptons carry our luggage, but how? And how do we manage two bikes and all our luggage, going from train to train? Yes, we have a carrier over the back wheel (a commuter is unlikely to need this owing to the excellent front pannier system which allows a lot of weight to be carried), but with a 16-inch wheel a pannier couldn't be more than about 6 inches deep, and there is the problem of carrying it when transporting the folded bicycle. So we thought about it, and on the train journey we do this: we pack our heaviest stuff in the front panniers and I carry both of those. Dahb carries both the Bromptons, and we each carry a small rucksack containing our clothes, which is strapped to the back carrier when cycling. In the good old days when we still camped, Dahb would strap the tent to his rucksack and walk merrily along knocking out passers-by with gay abandon. The tent would then be strapped on his back carrier and we somehow or other got sleeping bags and (as we got older and less tough) sleeping mats in the rucksacks as well as our clothes. As soon as we reach a major station such as Paddington, St Pancras or Lille we play hunt the luggage trolley (at Lyon they'd all been stolen). This is getting more and more difficult as everyone has wheely suitcases and the stations don't provide as many trollies as they did. It really is worth doing, though, especially if we have a long wait. It makes it look as though we are carrying vast amounts of luggage but of course most of it is our mode of transport.

Dahb is always proud of the fact, and goes on about it, that he's persuaded me not to bring any cosmetics. As I haven't used cosmetics since I was an opera singer in the 1980s, I think this is a little unfair, but we must let our men have their fun. Please note, he's the one who insists on bringing talcum powder. We really pare down our clothes packing, relying on washing stuff as we go, and we do occasionally ride along with washing strapped to the back in an attempt to get it dry. Sometimes we're carrying very little as we're wearing everything – I refer later to freezing in Provence in midsummer owing to the *Mistral*. This is a strong, cold and dry wind that blows through southern France, from the north along the lower Rhône valley towards the Mediterranean.

We do *not* take a fortnight's supply of clean handkerchiefs.

An old friend of ours took himself and his bicycle (not a folder) to the south of France for a couple of weeks and he lent us his diary on return. We were entranced to read that he had taken 24 ironed handkerchiefs – he actually stipulated the ironed bit. Now I am not a great ironer. I bought a new iron in 2015 and used it for the first time just after New Year in 2018 and that was only for some sewing. We like the crumpled look, deeming it makes us look more friendly.

Following the example of some Canadian cyclists we met in Burgundy I aim to take two brollies, but occasionally find Dahb has decided to save space by leaving his behind. The next time he does this and has to mend a puncture in the rain in a rural desert, I will use my brolly for myself, and he can just jolly well get wet.

We carry lots of plastic bags as everything (except the brollies) has to be well waterproofed, especially our evening clothes (trousers rather than shorts). Good shoes are needed as we do a lot of walking. The anoraks and waterproof trousers need to be where they can be got at quickly. Most of Dahb's luggage weight is made up of bicycle tools, which can be really vital items, and as well as spare inner tubes he carries one spare tyre on top of the rucksack as there are not many 16-inch tyre shops on most routes.

We took our Bromptons to Cornwall for a few days and alighted from the train at Bodmin Road, properly called Bodmin Parkway but it was Bodmin Road when we lived in

Cornwall in the 70s, so there. The train drew away and as we put ourselves together we realised we didn't have our spare tyre. I then had a puncture on the way into Lostwithiel, the sound of which must have been heard for miles, and we needed to replace the tyre. We decided we must have left it at our home station of Swindon and rang the national lost property number and yes, there it was, in Swindon. Dahb and the lost property person arranged for it to be brought down on the next day's midday train to Par, a Sunday at that. We walked there from the Golant youth hostel, where we were staying, and sure enough, there it was, having been carefully looked after by the guard. I accosted him at one end of the train and of course the tyre was at the other end, but he didn't seem to think anyone should be in a hurry about the train moving on again. We then walked round the coast back to Fowey with a 16-inch tyre strapped to our day rucksack which must have puzzled people somewhat.

Back to Bromptoning in France. A typical day, not that there is one, will go like this. We will have breakfast if it is available although this is sometimes delayed until about teatime. We don't usually bother with mid-morning coffee unless there wasn't any breakfast or it's raining, but often there is nowhere to get coffee anyway. In our camping days we carried a small cooker and instant coffee so at least we could get something unless we ran out of coffee or water or the matches got wet.

What is absolutely essential is our midday beer, a cool French *pression*, on the dot of 12 or earlier depending on availability. Occasionally this isn't possible until teatime in which case it starts merging into our evening beer without which we can't possibly start thinking about dinner. Now Dahb, on reading one of my chapters, commented that I made it sound as if we drink only beer. He didn't mean as opposed to water (I do drink a lot of that, carrying it in an old bottle) but he thought I ought to confess that we also drink wine. Of course we do – it's the only way to get the flavour of the region. We go for the local stuff if it exists and often in *pichets* so that we can have different wines – I tend to drink white or pink whilst Dahb goes for the red. By the way, I have found – after years of research, some of it purporting to be PhD work on Anglo-French politics – that a 25cl *pichet* of rosé is the perfect recipe for a good night's sleep. So when I say dinner, or talk of lunch rather than picnic, assume that it is accompanied by wine. We are quite abstemious with our picnics, not drinking anything but water usually. But ideally we will have had a cold beer *apéro*. And we don't always manage to buy food for a picnic but might find a roadside restaurant in which case lunch (and wine) is a must.

Most of this book relies on the diaries I write as we go along. I note these are getting more fulsome as the years pass, which is probably a reflection of the fact that I write them over coffee/beer/tea/beer and am looking for an excuse not to start going up a huge hill in the midday sun just after an alcoholic drink, which is how it usually seems to be. I don't think I wrote one, or can't find it, for the holiday that started and finished at Grenoble, but it is amazing how much we find we can remember by looking at the map. Dahb is almost world famous for his inability to remember things but he is good on things geographical.

A word about the maps we use. Our first cycling trip in France was at the end of our trip home from Malawi, when we cycled, on bikes bought in Crete, through quite a bit of Europe. In Greece we had problems getting larger-scale maps, resulting one day in finding we had twenty more miles and another mountain pass to go before reaching anywhere likely to offer accommodation, which luckily it did. When we got to France we used the yellow Michelin maps, 1:200,000 scale or 1cm to 2km. Later we discovered the *Serie Verte*, which is now blue, and these were much more the thing being 1:100,000. Still, although they show what's needed, e.g., whether a road is a road or a mule track, I don't think they're a patch on our beautiful 1:50,000 Ordnance Survey maps, which can be read like a picture book. Recently we've discovered the Michelin 1:150,000 which are nearly up to the standard of the 1:100,000 *Serie Verte* and a lot cheaper.

Lately we have been able to buy maps of a whole (old) region, which are useful for planning, and we also take a map of all France. Some of these, the Michelin for example, are a bit annoying as they don't show railways, so we must try and replace our ancient Hallwag which did and also showed the larger campsites. This map, made in Germany, is still very useful although it won't show the latest bypasses and motorways. We don't always have sufficiently up-to-date *Serie Verte* maps. We once aimed for a lovely looking road gently descending to Cahors only to find we were parallel to a new motorway. Still, at least we weren't actually *on* the *autoroute*.

A recent visit to Upton upon Severn prompted us to visit The Map Shop there, a vital resource we learned about once home from Malawi. We used to telephone for maps (any map) and almost before putting down the phone the map would pop through the letter box. Now transactions are done online, they are no less efficient.

And we would not be without our Michelin Green Guides. Although aimed at motorists and liable to suggest an attraction is five minutes away, which would be a good hour for us, they are very informative and we love to book into a town and follow the green walking route in the book, secure in the knowledge that a suitable bar will not be far away, usually. Publications we miss are the regional hotel, *chambre-d'hôte* and camping guides. (We usually talk of 'Campings' since we saw a sign saying that.) These not only indicated whether a settlement was worth aiming for in having suitable accommodation but also gave the population and the altitude. Neat. Nowadays we book ahead on-line being frightfully modern folk who carry a mini iPad.

How much route planning do we do? This is very variable. Sometimes we have a specific aim, sometimes we follow a likely-looking road and hope there is something at the end of it. Sometimes it depends on the weather and one thing we are careful about nowadays is to get ourselves sorted out at the weekends. We have had some near misses on Saturday nights owing to the annoying habit of the French of sallying forth and staying in their own hotels, so we now aim to find somewhere on Friday, stay at least two nights and leave on Sunday or Monday when the beds are freed up again, unless the hotels close on Mondays.

There we have it. The reasons for buying folders and for buying Bromptons in particular – oh, I haven't discussed why we always go to France. Well, it's not far, we speak the language well enough and we just love it. Dahb occasionally whinges about it, saying we should go to Italy sometime. I reply "Fine, you arrange it" and somehow the next holiday is in France again. And no doubt will be for ever and ever.

Chapter 2
First Forays

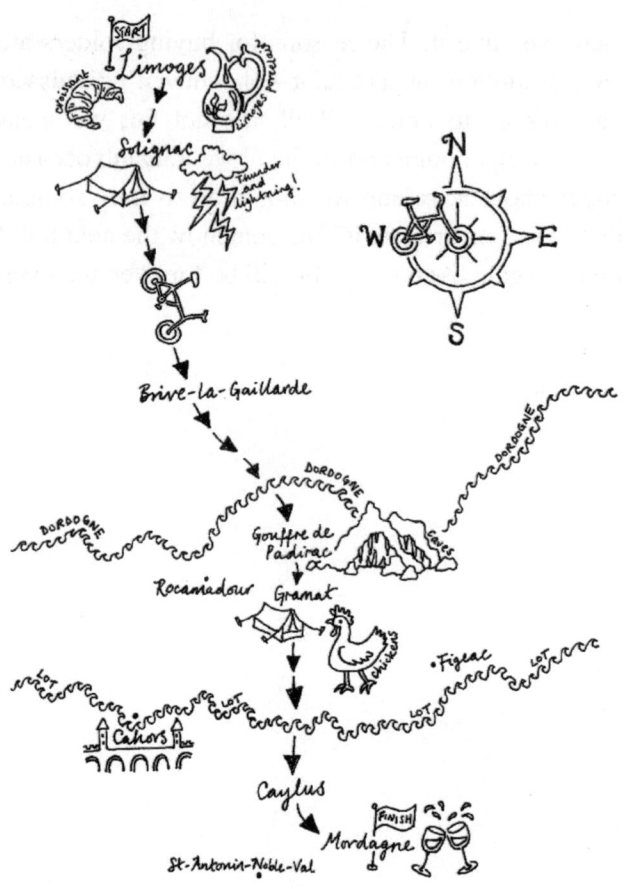

Our first Brompton foray, in 1993, started in the Limousin region and finished in Midi-Pyrénées. Limousin is now part of the Nouvelle-Aquitaine region with Aquitaine and Poitou-Charentes, and Midi-Pyrénées has joined Languedoc to form Occitanie. Our destination was Mordagne, location of a family house in Tarn-et-Garonne, near Caylus and not very far south of Cahors. It was to be a shortish trip on the road, after which we would spend a few days in Mordagne and return by train, the Bromptons being taken home by Dahb's parents who had travelled down by car.

So this was not so much a regional holiday as a linear one: we started at Point A and just kept going until we got there. And we cheated massively at the end, travelling unencumbered on the train while the bikes swanked it by car. Point A was Limoges, about 180km from Mordagne, and getting there in pre-Eurostar days was a bit of a heave, even with Bromptons. We took the overnight ferry from Portsmouth to Ouistreham and had no trouble picking up the train from Caen, thanks to the folders. It took quite a while to cycle into town from the ferry as we had not yet found, or they had not built, the cycle track linking the two. But we had time for breakfast on the terrace of the station café.

Unusually for us we were cycling in August, not our preferred time of year but the owners of the house are academics, so August was when they were there. We were rather worried about the heat, but it turned out to be quite comfortable and we have been much hotter in Provence in June (and a jolly sight colder). We also wondered if there would be hordes of people everywhere but apart from one or two hot spots, we seemed to find some quiet routes. Even crossing the Dordogne river wasn't too busy; it was lunchtime which probably made a difference to the amount of traffic on the road.

There were quite a lot of changes, and a small local train was so crowded that we had the bicycles between our seats and our feet on them, rather crowding out a lovely lady who found it all very amusing. One change involved waiting for an hour and a half at Vierzon, a town in the Cher *département* we had passed through on our trip to the Auvergne in 1990. This was a crafty thing to do as there was an excellent station restaurant and lunch could be eaten at tables on the platform. We arrived at Limoges about 5pm, the journey having taken 22 hours. Nowadays it can be done in seven and a half.

A word about Limoges, although we didn't stay long. It was Limousin's regional capital and lies at a ford on the river Vienne which had its uses in olden times. Since the 12th century the town has been famed for its enamelware though it is perhaps better known for its china, produced in Limoges since the late 18th century.

It was rush hour, not a great time to try and get out of Limoges but we needed to and eventually did. I have mentioned our discovery that the Brompton will try and park itself in the middle of the road if not kept firmly in check and Modestine did just that in the middle of Limoges. We eventually found ourselves in the quieter environs and made for the village of Solignac to the south. So quiet were the environs we could find no sign of any campings. There was a Turismu, but it was 6.30pm so it was closed, not unreasonably. We asked a young woman who was chatting with a friend, and she said she was *desolée* but there was nowhere to camp in the area. Turismu, by the way, is what tourist information offices are called in Portugal and we think it's a lovely name.

Shortly after this, however, she came up to us and said that we were very welcome to camp in her garden. We accepted this offer with gratitude and after telling us where she lived (up a hill of course) she went off home and we nipped into a shop to buy a picnic supper and were just settling down to the drink we felt was necessary for tackling the hill (wonky logic if there ever was any) when a stranger accosted us. It was the husband, who had been told the news and had popped down to pick us up. We hurriedly gulped down the beers, feeling slightly guilty for some reason, and piled selves and Bromptons into his large estate car and took the easy way up the hill.

Not only did they offer us the use of their lawn for our tent, but they insisted on us joining them for dinner, and wined and dined us at a garden table until quite late into the evening. He was delighted to have the chance to practise his English, but I was able to practise my French on the wife as she didn't speak the former. Then they insisted we use their bathroom – possibly a hint but altogether it was a very hospitable welcome for our first Brompton trip. I wish I could remember their names. He forced us (like the poor geese) to eat *foie gras* and extolled its praises. I still don't know why it's considered to be a gourmet item – I consider it to be an uninteresting food produced by disgusting methods.

Overnight it thundered and lightninged and generally chucked it, but we were snug and dry in our tent and by the time we thought we ought to crawl out the weather was clearing. There was no sign of anyone: he had gone off to work and the wife and young son, who had stayed up very late, never got up early, apparently.

We passed by the Gouffre de Padirac, a 103m deep chasm with a subterranean river system on which it is possible to take boat trips. Édouard-Alfred Martel (1859-1938), whose name will crop up in future chapters, was a lawyer and a fan of Jules Verne who decided to do his own exploring underground. Known as the father of speleology, he first explored Padirac in 1889. It is the most visited cave in France, and we decided not to go in as the car park was full of coaches. This was the first evidence on our trip of mass tourism (we went near but not *to* Rocamadour) and it does have its upsides in the form of ice-creams and lollies for thirsty wayfarers.

Our final night for this trip was spent at a delightful campings near Gramat, a small town in the Lot *département*, which was near enough for us to be able to nip into town for the evening meal. This was proper camping *à la ferme*. There were very few other people, if any, and the shower block was a converted pigsty or something, with a three-quarter door, nice and airy but with a well-working shower. There were several strange-looking but friendly chickens wandering about – strange because they were bare-necked and probably related to vultures. Perhaps owing to the heat in this part of the world it is the custom to keep the hens cool by plucking their neck feathers.

There was also a huge slab of stone, supported by other stones, so that the field had the air of being the scene of Aslan's sacrifice. Or perhaps it was where the chickens ended their days. However, the best thing about this campings was the imaginative use of one of the barns, which doubled as reception and sports room, and contained a fridge with cold beers.

About 35 km from Gramat we crossed the Lot river and towards the end of the day enjoyed a lovely ride along the little river Bonnette near Caylus. Our relatives' house is at the top of one of the worst hills in France, but we eventually climbed up. Once there, our first Brompton holiday was more or less finished, but the Bromptons were put to good use by various people before they came home in Dahb's parents' car. On our train journey home, we kept wondering where the bikes were, but we had plenty of leisure to reflect on our first Brompton sally and began to plot other ventures. Our next trip, however, was to the Channel Islands, again for family reasons. We didn't take any long French trips for two or three years as I began studying for a degree at the ripe old age of 43 and I've already mentioned that we're not too keen on being out and about during school holidays. My degree was Geography and although it didn't teach me to read maps (my O-level teacher did a very good job there) it did include the comparative study of Britain and France, a subject I continued with for several years and for which our holidays, or research trips as we prefer to call them, became a necessity. Once a postgraduate, these trips could be taken in May or June or early autumn, so we were back to our preferred seasons.

One of Dahb's cousins lived on Guernsey so in June 1994 we invited ourselves over to stay with him and his donkey wife. Guerns are known as donkeys. Jersey people are *crapauds* or toads. All rather odd. I think we could have taken big bikes but the Bromptons probably did make it easier, especially as we didn't then have a towbar attachment on the car for a bike rack. We drove to Weymouth for the Condor ferry to St Peter Port, which no longer runs, and enjoyed a couple of days exploring Guernsey which we do like, especially St Peter Port, although the roads are rather small and busy. We especially liked the tomato museum, being keen tomatoculteurs ourselves. We also took boats to Sark and Herm, without bikes as both are small enough for walking. Herm can be got round in an hour.

We then took the Bromptons on the ferry again, to Jersey which we thought was lovely. It is bigger than Guernsey but seems much quieter, really good for cycling. I thought it a combination of Wiltshire (apart from the sea) and Normandy – lovely sandstone buildings. We pedalled along a marvellous cycle track by the beach and camped at St Aubin and did much exploring, visiting a vineyard and the underground hospital which is fascinating. It was built by the Germans using slave labour. It is hard to imagine that the Channel Islands were occupied in the war. That delightful book, *The Guernsey Literary and Potato Peel Society* by Mary Ann Shaffer brings it all to life very well, and I can also recommend Stephen R. Matthews' *The Day the Nazis Came,* which is a true story.

We had arranged to stay with Dahb's brother in Dorchester on the way back. As we rolled off the ferry, we found the whole family waiting to greet us saying things like "Dr and Mrs Birley, I presume?", which was really nice.

The next Brompton holiday, before we started the really serious stuff after my finals in 1996, was in the Forest of Dean the year before. Now if you haven't been to the Forest of Dean, you really should do so and you will probably start saying it in an odd voice as if you were trying to convey that it is an area set apart, which indeed it is. To begin with, looking at a map you realise it should really be in Wales as it's not very close to the rest of Gloucestershire. And you really should read *A Child of the Forest* by Winifred Foley, which will make you realise there is something special about it. Some friends of ours used to take part in boot sales in Gloucester and they said that some very, er, individual people would come in from The Forest, pronounced 'Ther Forairst'.

This is a reference to Ther Villairge (The Village), a silly film from 2004 which our neighbours once lured us in to watch with the promise of wine. Even the sheep are a bit strange in the Forest of Dean – I have never before or since found several of them crowded into a bus shelter, perhaps having waited days for a bus but presumably having a choice of three eventually.

We took the train from Swindon to Gloucester and stayed the night there. There are lovely things to see in Gloucester, particularly the cathedral and its close, but some of the centre is a bit grim, whether the fault of the Germans or the post-war planners or both. The docks area hadn't been done up at this stage but now it's a great place to visit and the old warehouses have been imaginatively used.

The next day we thought it was time for a little oenology, so we went to the Three Choirs Vineyard just north of Newent. Dating from 1973 the vineyard now covers 75 acres and produces award-winning wine. The name was chosen because of the Three Choirs choral festival held between the cathedral cities of Hereford, Worcester and Gloucester. We enjoyed walking round the pleasantly situated vineyard and enjoyed even more a delicious lunch-and-wine on the terrace of the restaurant. We then continued on our way, fortified against any horrors The Forest could throw at us. We arrived without mishap at a campsite near Christchurch and pitched our tent. I've no diary for this or the Channel Islands so am relying on my and Dahb's memories which often surprise us by being quite good, and if not, no one else is any the wiser.

Well, it's lovely out there in The Forest. I remember we got to Symonds Yat where there is an amazing loop in the river Wye and there we saw a peregrine, to our delight. We also met Cleopatra, a very contented Vietnamese Pot-Bellied pig who joined our List of Want Its. A 'Want It' is something one sees and wants but realises in truth that one will never have it, or perhaps don't really want it anyway. So a house, a *potager*, a field, an animal (never a human) can join the List of Want Its.

We ended by going into Wales (fortunately no passports required as we'd left them at home) and cycled into Abergavenny for the train home. On the way we stopped for an early supper at the Walnut Tree Inn and had a drink and some bruschetta, which was new to us. The owner-chef came out to chat and signed his recipe book that we had just bought, being suckers. Dahb was thrilled to have his signature. We took the book home, tried the first recipe and consigned the book to the shelf with the rest of the cookery library we never look at, though now I've thought about it again we might have another look at it unless I've forgotten all about it again by the time I next go into the kitchen, which is a very likely scenario.

1996 came round and with it my degree finals. When they were over, in late May, I did a bit of garden work and off we went the next month – destination Grenoble and thence Provence.

Chapter 3
The first of several years in Provence
(Crossing the Vercors and finally getting there)

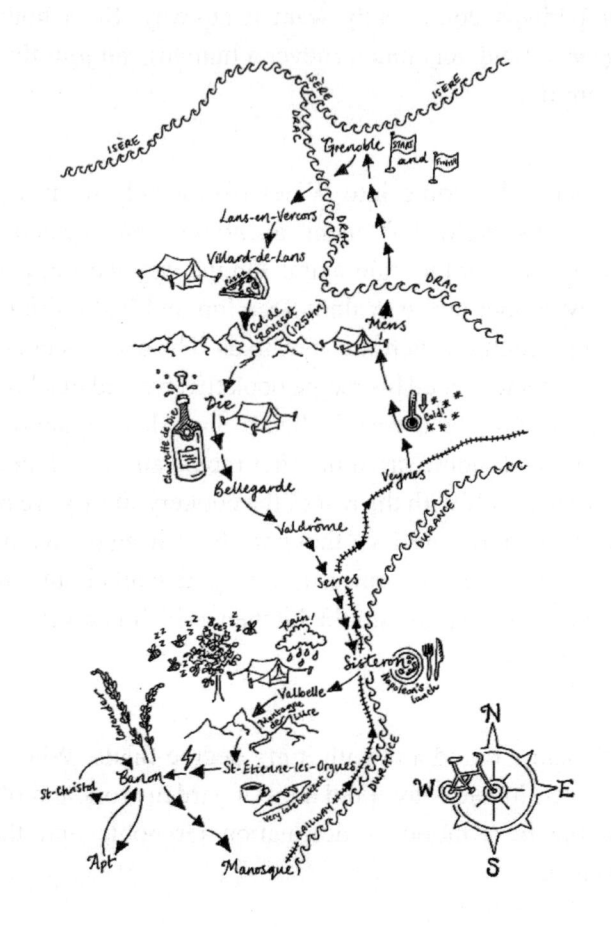

What is it about Provence? The warmth, the light, the wine, the mountains, the valleys, the wine, the lavender, the wine If only it wasn't so far away. We are ideologically opposed to flying nowadays, though have done it twice with big bikes, once to Portugal in 1983, once to Corsica in 1986, so it's the train for us, and luckily it has got a lot quicker over the years. In my youth I made a trip to the Riviera to visit a nursing friend who was working in the American hospital in Cannes. It was an overnight trip in those days, so I had booked a place in a couchette, and as I sorted out my stuff, four gentlemen walked in. They were very friendly and I quickly realised they were more interested in each other than in a poor, lorn female. The sixth occupant arrived later. As he scanned his co-couchetters I thought he looked a bit worried.

We've had five cycling holidays in Provence and are always contemplating more. It is a former province of southeast France, on the Mediterranean and the river Rhône, and forms part of the administrative region of Provence-Alpes-Côte-d'Azur which remained unchanged in the latest reorganisation. Often referred to as PACA, its six *départements* are Alpes-de-Haute-Provence, Hautes-Alpes, Alpes-Maritimes, Bouches-du-Rhône, Var and Vaucluse.

Four of our five Provençal cycling holidays have been on Bromptons. I've already mentioned the trip to Arles where we eventually hired bikes that took us to Vaucluse and the Luberon mountain. It was early May and rained heavily every other day, but the fine days were glorious and Dahb joined me in becoming addicted to Provence.

For the first Brompton trip to Provence we started in Grenoble, which is in the Rhône-Alpes region and a good 100km through the Dauphiné province to PACA, so not the most obvious way to get there. But daring crossings of borders! We decided to go via the Vercors mountains, into the hills and back again but, having gone south-west and up and over, there was no way back for about 80km. This is how routes are determined, by what's possible rather than desirable. It really does not pay to have any idea of where one *wants* to go.

We had a marvellous stay in Grenoble, which we thought very civilised. It stands at the confluence of the rivers Drac and Isère and has a reputation for economic and cultural dynamism. There are mountains all round, including the Vercors escarpments, and another time I'd like to try the panorama from the Fort de la Bastille which can be accessed by cable car. But really, panoramae were not going to be in short supply on this venture.

Leaving the town, we trudged (no other word for it) for miles to get up the Vercors. I appear not to have written a diary for this Dauphiné-Provence holiday, perhaps because I had just taken my degree finals and had had quite enough writing for the moment, handwriting being hard work for an old person of 46. But I can see in my mind's eye this eccentric English pair pushing luggage carriers disguised as bicycles up a mighty hill. No, not *my* mind's eye, but in the eyes of the French couple who lived in a house by the road and were sitting on their terrace, resting after Sunday lunch. We asked for water and they insisted on us sitting down in the shade and we all enjoyed chatting. I got the impression that it was probably the most exciting thing to have happened round there for some time.

On and on. We must have stopped for lunch as there is a photograph of me mending something — probably one of Dahb's sunhats which are generally made of patches except for the frightfully posh one he bought in Villeneuve-sur-Lot as the Bromptons transported us to a family wedding in Tarn-et-Garonne. He's always short of hats. One day I arrived home having bought three of them and found he'd done the same. Yet in no time at all the house resounded to cries of "I can't find any hats!"

After a rest in Lans-en-Vercors, where we watched tennis players demonstrate the difference between the speed of light and that of sound – we were about a quarter of a mile away from the court and it was fascinating to watch the ball hit the racquet and hear the sound follow later – we camped in Villard-de-Lans and ate at a little pizza place in the square. I wish I'd made a list of all the little places in the square where we've eaten. Villard is apparently the tourist capital of the Vercors, but it didn't look that tourist-capitally to us, perhaps because it was evening and the day trippers had gone home.

The next morning, we plodded to the top of the Col de Rousset (1254m) which was to lead us from the Vercors to the Diois region. It is well to the west so we must have decided to delay our return east for a week or so. This *col* marks the climatic limit between the northern and southern Alps, with the green landscapes of the Vercors on the north side and the arid Bassin de Die on the south.

We passed through the tunnel and began a glorious descent towards the valley of the Comane, a tributary of the Drôme. The source of the river is at about 700m, and we freewheeled mile upon mile (it looks wonderfully wiggly on the map) until Chamaloc which was at 525m and provided us with a beer. Was this our midday one at teatime? We then continued, still descending gently, to the town of Die which is at 400m. What a delight to see a sign saying it was twinned with Warkworth, an ancient seaside village in Northumberland! We found a campsite and a restaurant, and also found that we liked Die very much.

We saw signs touting 'Clairette de Die', a sweet sparkling white wine made from the Clairette and Muscat grapes. I read that a good deal of this is glugged at the transhumance celebration, when the flocks are herded up to summer pastures, probably by drunken shepherds aided, it is to be hoped, by sober dogs.

Die is in the Drôme *départeme*nt, and indeed on the river which gives the *département* its name, still in the Rhône-Alpes region so we had a way to go before we reached Provence, which all goes to show how long it can take to get there. Actually, I have no memory of whether we were trying to get anywhere in particular, but it didn't seem to matter. Along the way, at Bellegarde, we came across a hotel rather in the middle of nowhere run by some Dutch ladies, where we had a very comfortable night. When one of them showed us where the Bromptons were to sleep (in an open woodshed) I asked if there was anywhere we could lock them up. No need, she said, "It is not the season," leaving me to wonder if a Glorious Twelfth was approaching, when Brompton-hunting would begin with a fanfare of horns and cries of "View halloo, Brompton in the copse!"

Somehow or other we got to Sisteron, which lies on the Durance river where Dauphiné gives way to Provence. Its lofty setting is crowned by the citadel which, unusually, we were in time to visit. When Napoleon arrived at Sisteron having escaped from Elba, he found that the royalists had withdrawn from the town the day before, so he had time to have some lunch before setting off for Grenoble. I am glad about this as I don't like to think of anyone not having time for lunch, especially someone who had so far to go along the Route Napoléon and knew that an army marches on its stomach. The period between his return to Paris and the restoration of Louis XVIII is known as the Hundred Days.

We then cycled up a valley, or probably walked as I remember Dahb tackling a puncture when we got there, to the village of Valbelle where there was a campsite with no one else in it. There was also a restaurant with no menu, i.e., you just ate what the family were having, a system of commendable simplicity. We'd enjoyed a walk before dinner and found a lime tree absolutely thick with bees.

Overnight it rained. Oh boy, did it rain. Disaster struck – our matches were wet, and we couldn't make coffee in the morning. The restaurant was firmly shut so we packed up and started the ascent because to get right into Provence we had to cross the Montagne de Lure, an eastern continuation of Mont Ventoux described as arid and practically uninhabited. Its summit is 1826m, and the *col* wasn't much lower, and we did this without breakfast or lunch (thinking of lucky Napoleon), sustaining ourselves as we went along with remnants of bread from yesterday's lunch, some sweets and water. Well, we thought, some people are much worse off than that!

We reached the summit, where it was a bit blowy, got on our trusty steeds and began to go down, hoping that breakfast, or rather late lunch by that time, wasn't too far away. We came across an English couple pushing (I think they were pushing) bikes up towards the summit. They were on a semi-hard 'Cycling for Softies' sort of holiday, on their own bikes which had been flown out for them, with suggested routes but carrying their own luggage. They were great fun and we were chatting merrily, all four of us on the right-hand side of the road too near a bend, when a car came whizzing round, narrowly missing us. The driver looked a bit cross and was clearly saying something to us which probably had nothing to do with the continued enjoyment of our holiday.

Whether they survived the rest of their trip I don't know, but at around 4pm we reached St-Étienne-les-Orgues and finally had breakfast. I can see us sitting at an outside table in the square but can't see the beer I'm sure we consumed before getting on to the coffee stage.

If we were sitting outside it must have been warm and dry but before we finally reached Banon we went through the most horrendous storm (I am a total wimp about lightning). Eventually we were there and booked into the hotel for three nights as it was the weekend. Once in Provence, stay there! We ate, we drank, we strewed our wet clothes and tent all over the bathroom, we slept.

Banon is a very nice village, known for Banon cheese, very hard goat cheese wrapped in chestnut leaves. We made it the focus of a day trip in 2006 when we were staying in Sault. In that diary I wrote that Banon is 'nothing special but nice' which I think is doing it down, rather.

In the morning the weather was lovely, so we set off for the day *sans* luggage, which is always a treat, although by the time all the waterproofs, jerseys, maps, Green guide and bike tools were in, we didn't leave that much behind at the hotel.

We set out with a firm purpose – that of finding lunch. And so we did, we think in St-Christol. It was a good restaurant and very friendly, though not busy. One customer caught our eye, a rather rotund gentleman who was eating slowly with an expression of great contentment on his chubby face. I often think of him when I am trying not to bolt my food, a skill I learned during my nursing training (that's the skill of bolting, rather than not bolting). He turned out to be English and came and chatted with us when he had finished his meal. He was the headmaster of King David's School in Manchester and was absolutely delightful. When not dining he drove slowly along, he said (I don't think walking was his forte), and spoke of the many orchids in the road verges. We hadn't seen any but after lunch there they were, all over the place. Now every time we see orchids we think of our gastronomic acquaintance and how he opened our eyes to things other than food and wine, which is quite a feat.

Did we get to Apt? I think so. Did we do two day trips? We must have done. Did it chuck it with rain at the end of our day trip? I remember scuttling into the pizza place – yes, that one is coming back to me.

Apt is a small busy town in the Calavon valley known for its crystallised fruit and considered a good excursion centre for trips to the Luberon range. On Saturdays there is a marvellous market which we explored when we were staying in the town several years later. On the way back to Banon we passed through Simiane-la-Rotonde, considered by the Michelin guide to be one of the loveliest hilltop villages in Haute-Provence, and we were commenting to each other on some anti-nuclear poster in a window when the occupier spoke to us in English, because he was English.

It was time to leave Banon, and we did have a plan – I remember now. We had read about Terre Vivante, an ecology centre rather like the Centre for Alternative Technology in Machynlleth, and we wanted to visit it. But it is in the Trièvre, well east of the part of the Vercors we had crossed and near a village called Mens, so visiting it had to wait until the end of the holiday when we were making our way back to Grenoble.

Leaving Banon, we travelled mostly downhill to Manosque, which is in the Durance valley. If you Google Banon, you'll see a picture of the village with lavender fields in front. This is the view back as we headed for Manosque, although the lavender wasn't so well out. We didn't see a great deal of Manosque on this occasion, though it seemed pleasant enough to make us think we'd be happy to return which we did, another year. On this occasion we popped ourselves and the Bromptons on a train and travelled up the Durance and then along the river Buech to Veynes where we booked into the station hotel. Because we knew we had a mega-cycle the next day, to Mens, we asked if we could have an early breakfast. That would be no problem, said the *patronne*, as she started at 6.30am. Indeed, when we came down she was doing a roaring trade with rail travellers and we were able to get away in good time.

Something we missed in Veynes is the Ecomusée which celebrates the lives and work of the railwaymen of this important rail junction. It would have been interesting to compare it with the excellent STEAM Museum in Swindon, another railway town and near where we live.

On this holiday, we not only experienced rain but – a *Mistral* effect – a sudden drop in temperature, from 32C to 13 in one afternoon, so a café owner told us in great indignation. On the way to Mens, we passed a man looking disconsolately at his potato crop which had succumbed to frost in mid-June. We certainly kept warm on the way up but we had a long descent into Mens and I wore socks and plastic bags on my hands because I hadn't thought I would need gloves in the south of France in midsummer. Now I always pack gloves but hardly ever wear them, a few sunless days in Lorraine one year being an exception.

We arrived in Mens and pitched our tent at its campsite and soon we were cosy and happy in a restaurant, well, *the* restaurant. We took to Mens which had farms all the way up the high street. We visited Terre Vivante, which was fun, but not on the scale of our CAT. The head gardener was a young Englishwoman – nice work if you can get it, especially with the views. They were spectacular and we ate lunch outside and marvelled. Apart from lunch, the only other thing I really remember was the *compost d'un an* which we took at first to be donkey compost. We thought it was odd as we'd seen goats and sheep but no donkeys. Then we noticed the *compost d'un mois* and realise we had been admiring some one-year-old compost.

Spending one night somewhere *en route* we arrived back in

Grenoble and, staying at the campsite, enjoyed more of that city's delights. We brought back a really useful souvenir, a summer suit Dahb bought in C&A. It has been, ever since, his stalwart for summer weddings, with his Villeneuve-sur-Lot hat to complete the stylish ensemble.

Chapter 4
Some Wine Regions

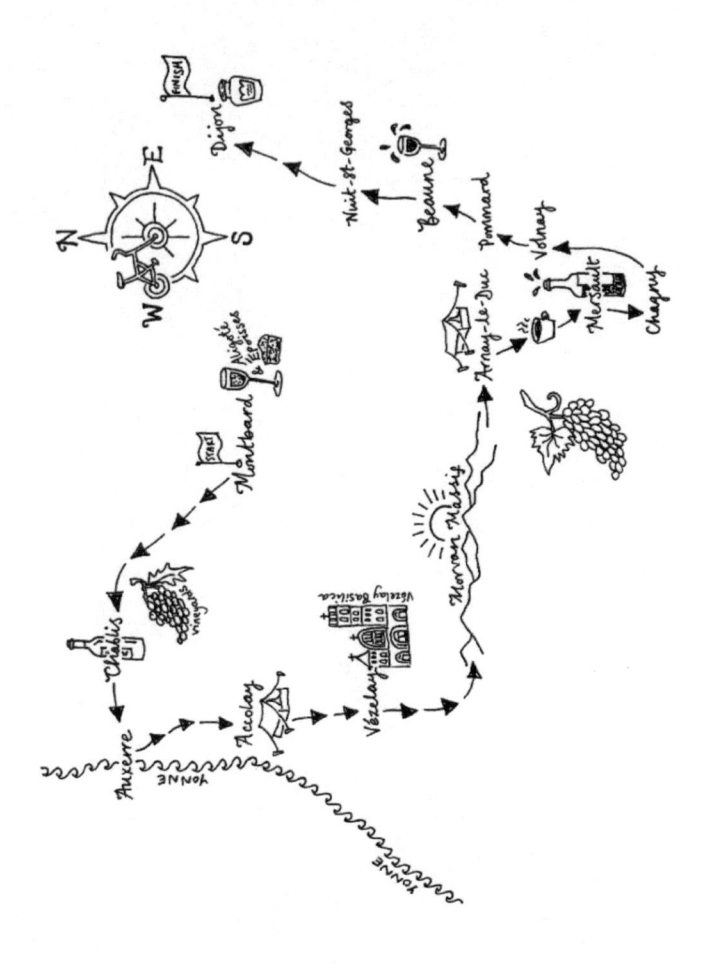

No French region is without wine. Why would we go otherwise? If it is not grown in the region, Nord-Pas-de-Calais, or Picardy, for example, there is always a wine list and plenty of French wine on it. We usually choose the most local, and sometimes it has to be champagne, which is tough. Sometimes, however, we are quite daring and choose something Provençal when we are dining diametrically opposed to it, cartographically speaking.

But some regions are more winey than others and some are more celebrated for it than others. Our Bromptons have transported us somewhat drunkenly (that's us, not the Bromptons) through Burgundy, Bordeaux, Champagne, the Jura, Languedoc, Alsace, and the Cognac region in Charentes, and of course Provence of which I write quite a lot. People often ask us if we visit the vineyards for wine-tasting, but we don't tend to on these holidays. We love to cycle through the vineyards and there are usually plenty of traffic-free roads on which to do this. Then we like to find a restaurant, which might of course be on the vineyard itself, and see how the local plonk and grub go together which is usually rather well.

Our first Burgundy trip was fairly early in the Brompton era, 1997, and it was in September, which is slightly unusual for us. We tend to go in May or June because the days are longer and they are noticeably shorter in September. I have also perceived, if camping, that there is much more dew which is a bit of a bore in a tiny tent where there isn't room to keep everything inside and even more of a bore if early morning loo trips are required. But now we poshly use hotels it's not a problem and September weather can be so lovely, and the vineyard colours are getting really interesting. We were away for just over a week on this occasion and it was a dry one except for our journey into Dijon on the last day when the rain more than made up for it. Even with taking occasional refuge in bus shelters we were absolutely sodden when we arrived at our hotel, but it was a lovely welcoming old coaching inn and our wet stuff was soon strewn all over the place, steaming and drying nicely. The rain held off long enough for a walk around beautiful Dijon and soon after that we were researching the local gastronomy, wine very much included.

The administrative region of Bourgogne has now been joined with that of Franche-Comté to form the new super region of Bourgogne-Franche-Comté. I wonder how much someone was paid to think that one up. There was an old Duchy of Burgundy and the territory is a transitional area between the flat Paris basin and the Rhône and Rhine valleys. Many people think of it as the area between Paris and Switzerland, having passed through it *en route*. The Côte d'Or is not just the name of a *département* but also that of a major wine-growing area, the edge of a slope of mountains overlooking the Saône plain. Here are found the villages giving their names to the celebrated wines of Burgundy: Gevrey-Chambertin, Nuits-St-Georges and Volnay, for example. West of the Côte is found the Morvan plateau, a fine granite *massif* with forests and farmland and wonderful villages with farmhouses next to old farm buildings large enough to take modern machinery such as combine harvesters.

All the great red Burgundy wines are made from the Pinot Noir grape which, although regarded as the aristocrat of grapes, can be difficult to grow. Its juice is colourless which is why it is used for champagne. Pinot's white corollary is the Chardonnay grape, also used for champagne as well as the great white wines of the Côte d'Or, Pouilly-Fuissé from the Mâconnais and the Chablis wines. Then there are the Beaujolais wines of southern Burgundy, which are made exclusively from the Gamay grape.

On our first day we got off the TGV at Montbard, which is in the region of Burgundy but not in the wine-growing area. The *patronne* of the Hôtel de la Gare, which I had prebooked, was sitting on the terrace with a friend, waiting for the train, and gave us a warm welcome. It was nearly 9pm so we hoofed it towards the centre where there was a fair going on and found a little restaurant of superb value – 90 francs including wine. (Let's assume 10 francs to the pound for easy calculation. After the first glass one doesn't care, anyway.)

This was the first time we drank Aligoté and we enjoyed it very much. I believe certain wine buffs are a bit disparaging about this white Burgundy but I like it and it would have had to be pure vinegar for us not to enjoy it on our first visit to the region. We were also introduced to Époisses, a tasty soft cheese made in the Côte d'Or.

We had a short walk before breakfast and in a park named after him we learnt that the Comte de Buffon, a renowned botanist and author of a very long history of nature (36 volumes), was born in Montbard in the 18th century and came back to live there, finding Paris did not agree with him. He was also a mathematician, cosmologist and encyclopaedist. How those people fitted it all in I can never quite grasp.

On the next day, Saturday, we had an appointment to keep in Chablis where we had arranged to meet friends from our village who were caravanning in France. It was only as we neared Chablis that we saw our first vineyards, passing as we did through farming and grain country that looked remarkably like Wiltshire, where we live. But there were the vineyards, and we were soon at our rendezvous point, all of us dead on time. More gastronomic delights followed. We returned to Chablis a few years later with our local wine group and stayed in a *chambre d'hôte* run by a lady who was apparently a top breeder of Shih Tzus. I'm sure they were fine creatures, but a prize should be offered for stopping them barking all night.

We had lunch in Auxerre, which was a rather short ride, crossing the river Yonne as we went into the town. The Canal de Bourgogne, which we'd walked over in Montbard, connects the Yonne and the Saône, starting at Migennes which is north of Auxerre and passing through Dijon. We camped that night at Accolay which is on the Canal d'Accolay and also the river Cure, and south-east of Auxerre. There was a loud party of British boaters in the restaurant. I think of them when I go for a meal with a group and see a couple who thought they were going to have a nice quiet evening.

Looking at the map it seems likely that we visited Vézelay the next day, staying nearby and tackling the Morvan *massif* after that. Vézelay is on the edge of the plateau and home to a celebrated basilica. It is also a starting point for the road to Compostella, and on a later visit I was asked to take a photograph of a couple just beginning their walk. I've often wondered if I took a selfie by mistake – it wouldn't have been intentional as I'm pretty clueless in that regard.

We swept downhill to the delightful Hôtel de la Poste in the hamlet of Cue and next day had a marvellous ride through the Morvan. This *massif*, lying to the west of the Côte d'Or, is composed of granites and basalts and is a northerly extension of the Massif Central. The main town is Château-Chinon, but I can't remember if we went there. I do muddle it rather with Château-Chalon in the Jura and we've definitely been to that one.

Our guidebook says the Morvan is not served by any main roads which might have contributed to our liking of it and like it we certainly did. A photograph shows us picnicking overlooking a small lake in lovely weather, and not a vineyard in sight. That night we camped at Arnay-le-Duc which we aimed for because a friend had said it was one of his favourite places. We did our best to favouritise it but I think I must have misheard him. Still, the large campsite was well equipped with showers and hot water, and although most of the restaurants were closed, we did eventually find a hotel in which to continue our gastronomic research – a very good meal was had by both.

My diary says the tent was dripping in the morning, but early sunshine dried it off. On our way to Mersault we stopped in a village for coffee and were joined by an English couple we'd met in Arnay. His drink problem was clearly even worse than ours as he was partaking of something alcoholic when our constitutions were telling us it was still caffeine time. On the way up the hill out of the village we met a man from Whitehaven, the Cumbrian town in which I was born, who was doing up a house in order to live there permanently. We passed through a village where there were a lot of exhausted dogs, according to my notes, and we eschewed the attractive-sounding camping *à la ferme* as it was quite a distance from Mersault and food. The town is pretty, but its campsite looked rather grim, so we searched for a room and found one at Hôtel des Arts where we also dined in the courtyard, with the aforementioned umbrella-toting Canadians. I hope we drank Mersault wine, which is considered to be one of the best in the world, but all I can think of is the rather old one we were offered on our later wine-tasting trip. It was disgusting.

The next morning we cycle-toured the wine villages south of Mersault, having had breakfast in Chagny, a busy but pleasant town we were to get to know rather better on a future occasion. This time we went on to Volnay (visiting it later for one of our nephew's wedding meals by which I mean for one of the wedding meals of one of our nephews) where we bought a glass of Volnay rouge, after which we went on to Pommard for lunch. All good winey names. We went on to the lovely town of Beaune where we met our Canadians again and heard that he had been ill all night after our meal together. The Beaune campsite was rather large but well run, and a 'full' notice went up soon after our arrival. We pottered off to see the magnificent Hôtel-Dieu and the interesting wine museum.

Beaune, residence of the Dukes of Burgundy until the 14th century, is a very fine town with much to see, including some splendid old houses. The ramparts are quite well-preserved, and one can walk just about all round them, a distance of about a mile. The Hôtel-Dieu, described by our Michelin as a marvel of Burgundian-Flemish art, was founded as a hospital in 1443. The Mediaeval building has survived intact and until 1971 was used as a general hospital after which it became a geriatric hospital. I would like my crumbling years to be spent somewhere like that.

Thursday night was very warm, obviously working up to the rain. We sauntered through more wine villages, and I am sorry to have to report that in Nuits-St-Georges we drank beer as it was so hot (we did the same in Châteauneuf-du-Pape). We then went on to Aloxe-Corton where we eventually persuaded a reluctant *vigneronne* to sell us one glass (each) of Corton-Charlemagne, named after the great emperor, who reintroduced white wine to the region because he ran into difficulties when drinking red, as it tended to dribble down his nice white beard. I had an uncle who had similar problems with *borscht*. After a few more wine villages we were in the outskirts of Dijon where the rain began, and we wound up our trip.

We really do like Burgundy, but the wine areas are almost too much, in contrast to the Beaujolais, where vineyards and farmland are more mixed up and the countryside therefore more interesting in our view. The Beaujolais *massif* stretches between the Loire and Rhône valleys, where the Mediterranean and Atlantic watersheds meet. It was only in 1930 that Beaujolais was recognised as part of the Burgundy wine area. Beaujolais Nouveau is well known; Fleurie, Juliénas and Villié-Morgon might also ring a bell.

**

We started a Beaujolais holiday in 2001 by staying with a nephew in Beaune, the one whose wedding I mentioned above. I see from my diary that we started the trip with a great crisis – Eurostar was late leaving. Employees of the railway company herded us onto the train in a great rush so that it didn't leave too late, rather crossly as if it were our fault.

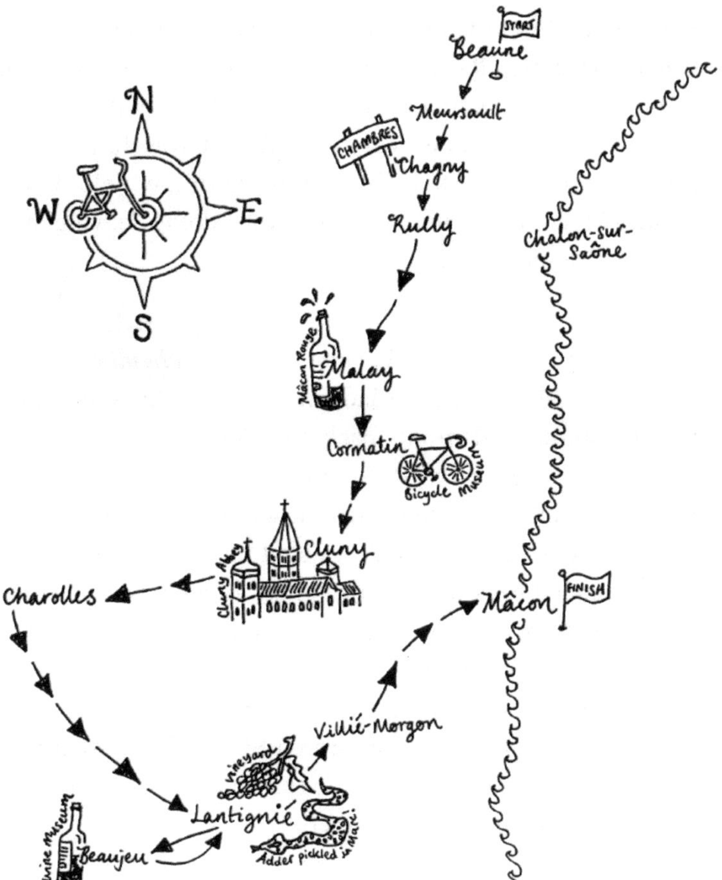

N
W
E
S
START
Beaune
Meursault
CHAMBRES
Chagny
Rully
Chalon-sur-Saône
Mâcon Rouge
Malay
Cormatin
Bicycle Museum
Cluny
Cluny Abbey
Charolles
Mâcon
FINISH
Villié-Morgon
vineyard
Lantignié
Adder pickled in Marc
Wine Museum
Beaujeu

In Beaune we slept in our nephew's flatmate's bed but without the flatmate. Our aim the next day, Saturday, was to reach Rully (south of Beaune) and we travelled again through Pommard, Volnay, Mersault and Puligny-Montrachet, a true wine route, but failed to get to Chagny by a track along the Canal du Centre - the map showed a clear way that turned out to be blocked. Eventually (8.45pm) we arrived at the Rully *Logis* (the French hotel chain) to find it was full and the *patronne* showed little inclination to be of any help. It was Pentecost weekend and what we were doing leaving it to chance, I do not know.

We found a certain Madame Bridet's *chambre d'hôte* which was also full, but Madame was friendly and helpful and recommended going back to Chagny which we did manage to access from Rully, there being a road. The first hotel was full, the second was closed and the third looked rather expensive so we made a note to try later if necessary. As we headed back up the street to try a *Logis*, we spotted an illuminated sign we had somehow missed before: 'Chambres'. We rang the bell at the gate – no response, so we rang again. A light went on upstairs and a shuffling was heard after which a man appeared at the door, wearing a dressing gown and somehow looking rather strange. He said he had a room and just stood there.

I pushed the gate which proved not to be locked and sent Dahb in with this chap who seemed to be ill or drunk or both. Dahb was shown a room and the man retired to bed again, there being no sign of anyone else. So we felt rather pleased with ourselves and went out to find food, leaving the front door unlocked as we had not been given a key. We had a meal in the excellent restaurant down the hill in the square and the *patronne* told us that our host's wife was ill in a nursing home and that he was a bit of a tippler.

About 11pm we were getting ready for bed, worn out by all the excitement, when we heard noises off and up the stairs came a man and woman carrying baggage, somewhat surprised to find us in the room they thought they had reserved. It turned out that they knew our Monsieur and Madame, so they took it all on the chin. As we hunted around for keys to another room we discovered a man staying in room 2 but there was no sign of any keys. However, when we pushed the door to room 5 we found it open, so the new arrivals went in there. All this was accomplished with much giggling, and we all had rather a good time.

At 8am the next day we could hear nothing but the sound of silence, so we left what we hoped was the right money and went, finding a café in town for breakfast. When we stayed in Chagny several years later, for the nephew's wedding, we were in a hotel on the outskirts. We went to the same restaurant for a meal but there were no longer *chambres* on offer up the hill.

If you go due south from Beaune you pass through the Mâconnais before reaching the Beaujolais mountains. On this occasion we went further west and accessed Beaujolais via

Charollais, where the Charollais cows come from. South of Beaujolais are the Monts du Lyonnais. We did later have one or two holidays where we progressed southward through the 'ais' (see Chapter 9), with Vivarais following Lyonnais. If there are any more, we will have to go there – oh, I've just noticed Chablais on the southern shore of Lake Geneva. And, oh golly, Gâtinais, Nivernais and Bourbonnais, from west Burgundy down to the northern Auvergne ...

After Chagny we cycled south to Malay, having had a room booked for us by the *Logis* at Buxy, which was full. We discovered that Hôtel La Place was not in the central Malay square but quite a way out on the main road, but we finally got there and had to be sitting at our dinner table by 7.30pm as everyone wanted to go home early. But it was a very friendly hotel and we slept like logs after half a litre of very nice Mâcon rouge.

There was a railway marked on our map heading south from Chagny. When we got nearer to it, we thought we saw cyclists high up, and when we climbed up (no signs at all) we found one of the best cycle tracks we've ever come across – three metres width of good tarmac. We deduced from the map that it was going to Cluny so we thought we would too. It was well used by other cyclists and rollerbladers too, going very fast and looking very serious. A little further down, at Cormatin, there was a cycle museum which declared itself to be unique in France. It housed a splendid collection of bicycles and associated artefacts from the earliest cycling times.

The cycle track did indeed lead to Cluny, to the old railway station in fact, and we were soon ensconced in Hôtel du Commerce, and it was still only lunchtime. We had some lunch (of course) and did the sights. Cluny is famous for its abbey which was demolished in the French Revolution, but the Order of Cluny was hugely influential in the West during the Mediaeval period. There are ruins to see though it's hard to grasp its former magnificence. Incidentally, our Michelin guide says that in the 13th and 14th centuries the monks of Cluny 'slipped gradually into a worldly, luxurious way of life' which sounds as if it might have been fun until St-Bernard came along with strong denouncings. It all went downhill from there.

On our way to Charolles the next day we saw several cyclists, including a Dutch couple going to Barcelona and carrying a folding chair. I also wrote that we saw hills, forests and leopards and am quite puzzled by that one. The next couple of days were a bit of a blur as I had a tummy bug (probably not drinking enough wine), but I did note that Dahb bought a tie with cows on it – the Charollais, of course.

I'd perked up again by the time we reached Lantignié in Beaujolais where we found a lovely *chambre d'hôte* right slap in the middle of a vineyard owned by Madame and her brother. We decided to stay two nights as one of them was Friday. On our first night we had to cycle a couple of miles to Régnié-Morgon to get some dinner (Madame would be cooking the next day) but it was excellent and well worth the ride. The next day we cycled along the valley to Beaujeu, capital of Beaujolais, where there was a wine museum and a Swiss man who said that if someone told us they were Swiss we should reply, "Never mind, you will recover."

When we got back to base we found more guests: a couple from Belgium and one from Northern France. One of the men wore a stripey T-shirt and had a magnificent moustache like the archetypal Frenchman, only I think he was Belgian. Or did he remind us of Hercule Poirot and turn out to be the Frenchman? Whatever, we were all invited to a wine-tasting and the sound of eight people all talking at once, in French, in that *cave* was truly amazing. We went back to the house for a delicious and garrulous meal and when Madame produced a huge bottle with an enormous adder in it, pickled in *marc* (the local spirit), and offered us a drink, only Dahb was brave enough to accept. I'm not too sure whether the other guests were amazed and admiring, or just amazed.

The next morning, as we were all leaving, the lady from northern France took my hand and said, in what I'm sure she thought was a good English accent (she adopted a rather high tone of voice) 'Bye-bye! Bye-bye!' and she would have said it a third time if she had not collapsed into paroxysms of laughter. After which, according to Dear Diary, we cycled in rather mizzly weather through lots of wine names, to Mâcon for a train back to Dijon and home. In a couple of years we picked up the trail and continued south, so more on this later.

Chapter 5
Languedoc

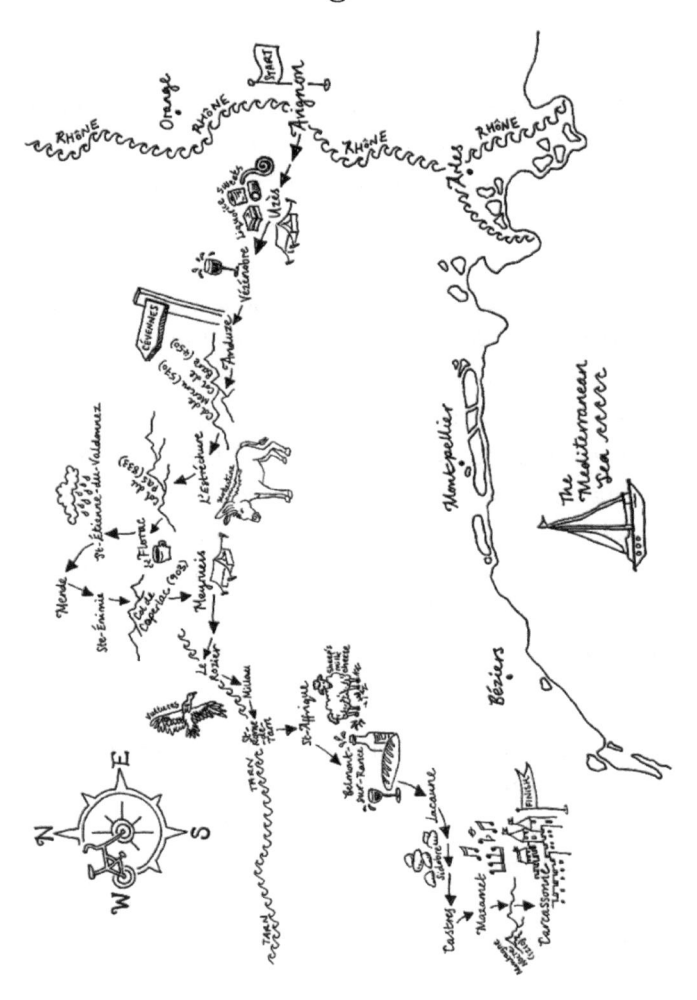

When I looked for the relevant entry in my AA/Baedeker of France, it said 'Languedoc, see under Roussillon (Languedoc-Roussillon)'. So I turned to Roussillon, fully expecting to read 'Roussillon, see under Languedoc'. But no, it merely said 'Roussillon (Languedoc-Roussillon)' and all became completely clear.

Languedoc-Roussillon is the name of the 1980s region, now joined with Midi-Pyrénées to form the new super region of Occitanie. In the old province where Occitan was spoken the word for 'yes' was '*Oc*', so here they spoke the '*langue d'Oc*', whereas up north, past the Massif Central, they spoke the '*langue d'Oïl*' which is getting on for '*Oui*'. The two parts of Languedoc-Roussillon are quite distinctive and are divided by the river Aude and the Canal du Midi, which – astonishingly – was built in the 17th century and links the Atlantic and the Mediterranean. There is the wild and woolly part of Languedoc, which includes the Cévennes, and there is Languedoc *méditerranéan*, which is self-explanatory. Roussillon is in the extreme south of France, bordering the Pyrenees and Spain. Its most important town is Perpignan and famous regional attractions include wine (Corbières) and Cathar castles.

Other well-known settlements are the coastal towns Agde and Sète, and the wine town of Béziers, scene of a horrific massacre in the Albigensian wars as Béziers was punished for backing the heretic Cathars. The basic tenet of the Cathar doctrine was the dualistic separation of good and evil. The Cathars broke away from the Catholic church in the 11th and

12th centuries, and the church referred to them as the Albigenses (after the town of Albi) and their belief as the Cathar or Albigensian heresy. The religion flourished in the Languedoc and a vicious crusade was launched against it in the 13th century.

The desire for religious independence came to the fore again in the 18th century with the Camisard uprising, Protestantism having been forbidden by the Revocation of the Edict of Nantes in 1685. Apparently, Robert Louis Stevenson chose the Cévennes area for his journey because it was almost the only part of France where Protestantism still prevailed, and he felt the Camisards were the French equivalent of the persecuted Covenanters, Scottish Presbyterians who were revolting in the 16th and 17th centuries. Yes, well, it still doesn't explain why he set off in late September and him being tubercular, too.

To the west of the aforementioned wild and woolly parts of the region are the Grands Causses, vast limestone plateau cut through by spectacular river gorges such as those of the Jonte. The wine-growing regions of Bas Languedoc are on the plains towards the coast and tourists flock to the beaches in summer (not us, though). The Pays d'Oc wines are found throughout the region, the Corbières in the Roussillon. Blanquette de Limoux, a lovely fizz we discovered not long ago, comes from near, er, Limoux in the Aude *département*.

We had two and a half weeks for our holiday in 1998 as

Dahb had taken a sabbatical from work. His medical practice had agreed to the sabbatical system and my husband, always to be heard wailing that he never had sufficient holiday, was the first to take advantage of it. In fact, he was the only one who ever did.

Having reached Provence a couple of years before by starting in Rhône-Alpes we decided this time to get to Languedoc by starting in Provence, taking the train to Avignon. A North African gentleman slept all the way from Lille, presumably aided by some substance or other. Every now and then we checked he was still alive. We heard Afrikaans being spoken – some South Africans were on their way to the Grand Prix in Monaco.

We hadn't pre-booked a hotel, which was rather living on the edge for us, but we found a delightful *chambre* in the Impasse des Abeilles – very suitable for beekeepers such as Dahb. Before dinner we explored the town and at the Palais des Papes saw a young man fall from quite a height. I am sorry to have to report that he wasn't likely to get up again.

The next day we headed west, passing through a very seedy part of Avignon. We crossed the Rhône and arrived in Languedoc, in the Gard *département*. We wanted to see the Pont du Gard; the magnificent Roman aqueduct built to supply Nîmes with water. The road part of it is closed to traffic but we were allowed across which was just as well, as we had to cross the river Gardon and Modestine does not enjoy swimming. After a lazy picnic on the other side we pedalled on, arriving at Uzès and hoping for a campsite. The municipal one was closed (too early in the season on May 23rd) but we found one just out of town, rather expensive at 88 francs. However, there was an excellent restaurant in the centre of this attractive and well-preserved Mediaeval settlement, so all was well.

The locals are known as Uzétiens, and apparently urban life in the 5th century was civilized and tolerant. The town got knocked about a bit during the various religious wars but life seems to have reverted to tolerance and civilisation. There's a long history of liquorice production in the region and Haribo still has a factory in the town. We often buy Haribo fruity sweets to keep us going as we travel, and they are sometimes the only thing between us and total starvation.

Next morning, we bought some breakfast stuff in Uzès which was bustling with life at 8am. We had a picnic breakfast just out of town and continued along lovely roads through very pretty villages. At St-Césaire-de-Gauzignan we had beer in the company of several dogs – two Yorkshire terriers, a Doberman and a two-month-old Rottweiler puppy which amused itself by eating my socks. It was an appropriately named village as my mother's Yorkie was called Caesar. He was a lovely little creature and very valiant. She later had a Rottweiler-Alsatian which was as soft as tripe.

We had lunch in Vézénobre, a Mediaeval town which

seemed to be as dead as a doornail until we suddenly found a bustling street full of artists and refreshment places. We had lunch in a *crêperie*, served by a bizarre patron called Guillaume Hugues which amused us somewhat as he wasn't unlike a friend at home called Bill Hughes. I wrote in my diary that he served us too much wine – it must have been by the bucketful to have been too much.

In the evening we found ourselves on the river Gardon in Anduze which we later heard had an amazing bamboo forest, a private botanical garden established in 1856 by a gentleman called Eugène Mazel. A charming young man welcomed us to his lovely *gîte d'étape*, a sort of rest house, often with dormitories but we had a double room, kitchen and terrace for 180 francs. He didn't mention the bamboos and they weren't at all flagged up, so we'll have to visit the Bambouseraie de Prafrance another time. There is also a Museum of the Desert in the locality which seems rather odd until one learns that it's about the history of the Huguenots and Camisards in the Cévennes. The 'Désert' period refers to the interval between the Revocation of the Edict of Nantes in 1685 and the Edict of Toleration (1787).

Although my Baedeker doesn't mention bamboos, it does call Anduze the Gateway to the Cévennes, so we were now treading in the hoofprints of the original Modestine. Actually, for a lot of the time we were travelling more or less in parallel, and we were (on the whole but most certainly not exclusively) using roads rather than tracks. Leaving Anduze we travelled up and up, and over the Col de Bare (450m) to

Lasalle, a market town where there was indeed a market at which we were able to buy a picnic. We then went over the Col de Mercou (570m) and down to l'Estréchure and a campsite where we intended to stop, but which proved to be closed until July.

A beer and an emergency replan saw us heading up a gentle valley to a huge campsite of which we were the only occupants. We reached a *Logis* restaurant in the village, Les Plantiers, just as the *patronne* was thinking that she could have the (Monday) evening off, but she served us an excellent meal and made us feel she couldn't think of anything she'd rather do than keep the restaurant open for a mere two people. Mind you, we eat enough for four. I was kept awake all night by birds – presumably nightingales. I can't say I was wildly appreciative.

Mont Aiguoal, 1565m and to our west, was now quite close. The passes were getting higher and next day we passed over the Col du Pas (833m). We went via some unmade roads (told you) and other small and pretty thoroughfares until we finally arrived in Florac, finding a room at a *gîte d'étape* in the Old Presbytery. We chatted with Madame in the garden, finding understanding over plants by using the botanical names. In the kitchen there were posters on the walls about Stevenson and Modestine and their travels; here we really converged. There was also a friendly woman from Brittany who insisted on giving us ground coffee for breakfast when she saw us get out our instant.

We were now in deepest Cévennes country and in the Lozère *département* which is the least populated in France. In the Tarn valley we found a baby viper on the road. We thought he was alive, but he refused to take our advice to move off the tarmac. Modestine and I kept a good eye out for Mummy, being ready to canter off at the first sighting. We were now plodding with considerable difficulty but cheerfully through the most magnificent scenery, much eroded and showing evidence of granite quarrying. The stone houses were gorgeous, and we took a photo of a hut Dahb wanted to take home. We came across a completely quiet hamlet, Les Bondons, then found there was a café packed with *ouvriers* (workmen) where we were able to buy a beer. We then picnicked at an official viewpoint (we always feel we have to go to these in case we've been missing something) and found it was indeed quite a panorama. Mont Lozère was a constant presence to our east at nearly 1900m.

As we continued to climb, clouds were gathering in rather ominous fashion. We passed a lovely flowery meadow with orchids and anemones and thousands of white narcissi. (I wrote in the diary that the flowers were always superb on this holiday.) In the village at the top, La Fage, we asked a resident if the incredibly sandy road went through to St-Étienne-du-Valdonnez. No trouble, he said. Well, there might not have been in dry weather, but the heavens opened and a storm began, pelting us with hail. What had been a sandy track became two rivers and further down it became a granite riverbed. We were walking our bikes and finding it hard going, but we still noted the fantastic views.

It really was difficult getting down but get down we did and rested for a while in a bus shelter. Bus shelters yield no beers, however, so we went back into the deluge and in St-Étienne-du-Valdonnez spotted a doubtful-looking building which belied its unhotelly appearance by offering us a room, hot shower, beer, dinner, wine and breakfast for 427 francs. It continued to rain and was still doing so in the morning when we had a late breakfast owing to no one being up earlier. After the most delicious home-made croissants we left the hotel at 10.30am, still in the rain, and decided to take the high road to Mende. We traipsed soggily up to 1035m, now being *above* the mist, after which the rain stopped and we had a dry run down to Mende, which claimed to be the birthplace of Pope Urban V who poped in the 15th century. Wikipedia isn't so sure about this, but it does seem that he was born in what is now the Lozère *département*. And he didn't have far to go to work in those days as it was the time of the great schism and there was a papal branch in Avignon.

We booked into a hotel and after lunch did The Walk round Mende which is very pretty. Near the river Lot we found a *météo* office sporting a forecast for a drier tomorrow. Drier it was and we set off to explore the Grands Causses, climbing up from Mende (712m) to 1000m and finding ourselves on the Causse de Sauveterre. Passing over the plateau we saw drystone houses still roofed with limestone slabs before descending again to Ste-Énimie, on the Tarn. After beer and shopping we were starting another long climb up out of the Tarn gorge when we heard the most appalling squeaking sound which turned out to be coming from the brakes of a French cyclist coming down towards us.

After 2 hours going up (this is why we need good shoes) we reached the Col de Coperlac, at about 1000m, and we were then able to cycle quite a long way on the Causse de Méjean, the least populated of the *Causses*. It was certainly very quiet, and the few villages were lovely. There were vultures circling above us and Dahb told me to keep moving in case they thought I was dead. Griffon vultures, recently reintroduced into the Massif Central, are up to four feet long and with a wingspan of nine feet they are quite a sight to see.

We descended to Meyrueis (at about 700m) on a lovely evening with magnificent views of the Gorges de la Jonte, a tributary of the Tarn. We found an excellent campsite and an splendid meal in the village, our drenching trog to St-Étienne quite forgotten. The restaurant hung over the river, and we talked to some Israelis who had been to the Cannes film festival.

It was wet again the next morning, but we were able to pack up in a sort of pavilion and the weather started to clear so that, after coffee and shopping in Meyrueis, we were dry for the easy climb up to the Grotte de Dargilan. This consists of amazing limestone caverns discovered in 1880 by a fox, a shepherd and a speleologist. The shepherd was chasing the fox which disappeared through a crack in the rocks. Later it was 'officially' discovered by Martel, the speleologist, and opened to the public.

It being a Saturday we expected a crowd, but our party consisted of ourselves, three other Brits and the guide. It was a fascinating tour but as I was acting as interpreter I wonder what impression my countrymen went away with. Afterwards we picnicked on a terrace with a cat enjoying some of our yoghurt (weird cat) and cycled down a tarred but deserted road to reach the Jonte again, seeing more vultures as we went. As we neared Le Rozier, which is where the Jonte flows into the Tarn, we passed some coaches parked to let the occupants see the vultures. Some of them (the occupants, not the vultures) were a bit yobby and sniggered at us and our cycles but we sniggered rather more as we left them; we had seen lots of vultures but there wasn't a feather to be seen near this grockle hole. 'Grockle', you may or may not know, is a rather derogatory term for 'tourist'. All grockles are tourists but not all tourists are grockles. We do not consider ourselves to be grockelly tourists, though others might.

Now it was Saturday, and Pentecost, so we weren't doing very well as we hadn't booked anywhere. We think we got the last room in the Le Rozier hotel, other people (in cars) being sent away roomless. We could have camped but the campsite looked somewhat soggy and it was starting to rain again. We had dinner in a very nice *crêperie* and retired to bed reflecting on our good luck.

Sunday was wet to start with, but we spent time eating a marvellous breakfast and it was the sort of hotel you could lounge about in, so we sat and read a bit. Then it started to clear, so off we set. We found a lovely road to Millau which is a large but pleasant town. After a walk round we had beer and 'gweges' at a café by a roundabout where it was very amusing to watch people going by. I daresay we would also have had a good view of the famous viaduct, but it hadn't yet been built. Designed by Sir Norman Foster, the viaduct – the tallest bridge in the world – spans the Tarn valley and was opened in 2004. The other thing about Millau is that it is the home of José Bové, the environmental activist.

Important note: gweges are pronounced 'gwayghees'. We lived in Malawi for a couple of years and on the drive from the new to the old capital (Lilongwe to Blantyre) we would stop at the Everest café, outside which was a sign indicating it was possible to buy and consume 'sandgweges'.

It was feeling quite summery as we left Millau and we saw herons and buzzards, the latter less scary than vultures although we have read of a buzzard in Devon that attacked helmeted cyclists. We cruised down the Tarn on a quietish road which surprised us as we thought the Tarn would be somewhat touristy over a holiday weekend. There was nothing much happening on this stretch, however, and we found a very rural campsite at Comprégnac, run by a man who had married a Burkino Fasan who had decided to stay in Burkino Faso. Dahb frolicked in the river, but I decided to have a shower. Alas, it was the campsite of the *douche froide*!

There was an appalling system of electric heating which our man didn't switch on until anyone came and anyway took a good 24 hours to heat up to tepid. There was also a dearth of beer, but we drank (quite a lot of) a palatable Spanish white wine and he cooked us something to go with it. Apparently we were the first campers of the season, and he clearly was not expecting anyone despite it being a bank holiday weekend. A little cat seemed pleased to see us and joined us camping.

June! Still not as summery as it should be, says my diary, but I regretted having to eat lunch indoors in St-Affrique, so it must have been nice weather. Dahb pointed out that we weren't exactly short of fresh air. Discussing a suitable regional wine, our waitress informed us we had strayed into the Midi-Pyrénées region. We were now near Roquefort-sur-Soulzon where the famous sheep's milk cheese is made. Only cheeses aged in the local natural caves, where the necessary mould is found in the soil, can bear the AOC label (*Appellation d'Origine Contrôlée*). Every now and then a lorry would go by, bleating, the *brebis* (ewes) presumably being taken down for milking. Another requirement for AOC is that the milk should be from the Lacaune breed of sheep.

En route to Belmont-sur-Rance (still in Midi-Pyrénées, *mon Dieu*!) a farmer stopped his van to talk to us and we responded enthusiastically but couldn't understand a word he said. Arriving at Belmont we thought everyone had fled the plague, but we pushed open the door of an *auberge* which had all we needed within. The *patronne* was very friendly and so were the locals who insisted on plying us with drinks. One was the *boulanger* who was on his way to work. We then had a rather drunken shower and wobbled down again for a meal that included wine which of course we had to drink. Madame showed us how to get out in the morning as she was a late riser. The Bromptons were accommodated in an enormous sort of ballroom, possibly secretly dancing in the night when they were sure everyone was asleep.

At this point the diary runs out, or my inclination to write it. We had already been away nine days which is our usual holiday length, so I must have gone on strike unless there is a hidden notebook on the shelves, which is quite possible. So, what follows is from memory but some events are easily recalled. After Belmont we stayed in Lacaune having visited a peat bog with duckboards on the way. As we walked along the street in Lacaune, a man hailed us and said he had just seen us on the Sidobre, where he ran the visitor centre. This was strange and rather creepy as we hadn't yet been up there. Do ghosts go before?

It's not surprising that this concerned the Sidobre as it is a rather odd place. It is a granite plateau delimited by the river Agout which flows west to join the Garonne near Montauban. There is much evidence of quarrying and there are also some strange rock formations including huge round boulders balanced on top of each other that one longs to prod.

It was on the Sidobre that we had our only two bad dog

encounters in France. Normally we'll hear barkings and growlings, but the dogs are generally penned in or chained up and there is no danger. As we went along a tiny road we came across a young boy cycling around accompanied by a large Alsatian. There wasn't much room to get through and the dog became rather protective. The boy was quite old enough to understand the situation, but he just gawped at us and did nothing to restrain the dog despite our entreaties. We eventually got past and perhaps the dog had an angelic temperament, so the boy thought we were making a fuss about nothing, but said dog was doing a good impression of something very fierce.

Another time we were following a not very convincing track-cum-footpath which we thought should go through as there was a sign saying there were 'poneys' for hire. As we approached what was presumably the 'poney' home, a Doberman came snarling out from the farm and came to a halt, just, as it reached us. We kept going on the track, keeping away from the farm, and it didn't come any closer, but I must say I was terrified and heartily relieved when we lost sight of the dog, as I thought it would easily outdo Modestine's best gallop. I wonder what happened to the 'poneys' – perhaps it had eaten them.

Somehow or other we got to Mazamet, which the guidebook suggested was a bit industrial so we decided we didn't want to stay there. Or perhaps there was nowhere –at one place which had no rooms, the *patron* kindly phoned a country *Logis* about four kilometres out of town and secured us a booking. By now Dahb had a puncture so we walked up, and it *was* up, and he mended it at the hotel. It was a lovely place although a big noisy dining party meant we were a bit neglected. Dahb made the mistake of eating *cassoulet* and couldn't sleep all night. We were told later that it needs a long digestion time and is better eaten at midday, presumably followed by a siesta.

On returning to Mazamet in the morning we found it was rather nice, with sounds of piped Mozart. People used to live above the valley in Hautpoul, but Simon de Montfort in the 13th century and then the 16th century Wars of Religion did for it. The river in the valley – providing pure water for washing wool and power for machinery – enabled the textile industry to expand so the local folk thought they'd come down and founded a new town they called Mazamet.

We followed a sort of cradle-of-the-Industrial-Revolution valley and went up and up, up and up, over the Montagne Noire, a mountain range which forms the south-west tip of the Massif Central. At the highest point, the Pic de Nore, it is 1210m. The top is the boundary between the Aveyron and Aude *départements* and on our road we reached 730m. At the top, just before we started the long descent, I saw that Modestine had bitten through her back brake cable. Dahb gallantly swapped bikes as I do not like to go down hills with only a front brake. It was absolute marvellous, down and down and down with superb views of the Lastours castles, Cathar strongholds that managed to resist Simon de Montfort for quite a long time. Eventually we found ourselves on the plain and a lovely campsite with exceptionally friendly owners. We picnicked on the site's terrace with organic wine grown a field away. We decided to stay two nights as we were only about three miles from Carcassonne.

The fortified town of Carcassonne, now the *chef-lieu* of Aude, was the largest fortress in Europe and was brilliantly restored in the 19th century. It is an amazing sight to see, and I wouldn't have missed it for the world, but it is very touristy and some aspects are rather tacky. All the restaurants were heaving but we found a snack bar in a lovely shady garden and wondered, still wonder, why there was hardly anyone else there. We rather liked the newer part of Carcassonne, the Ville Basse.

We finished our holiday with a night in Montpellier, having taken the train from Carcassonne. Montpellier used to be the regional capital, but the much larger Toulouse heads up the new super region. I've been there a few times and it's one of my favourite towns, but I was a bit taken aback this time to be met by armed soldiers and police cluttering up the station and forecourt. The mystery was soon solved – it was the European Cup. Dahb thinks France won that year.

We reached home on June 6th and found a jungle where there used to be garden. It took us one day just to cut it back so that we could see what was going on, and I definitely saw an elephant at one stage …

Chapter 6
Franche-Comté (Jura)

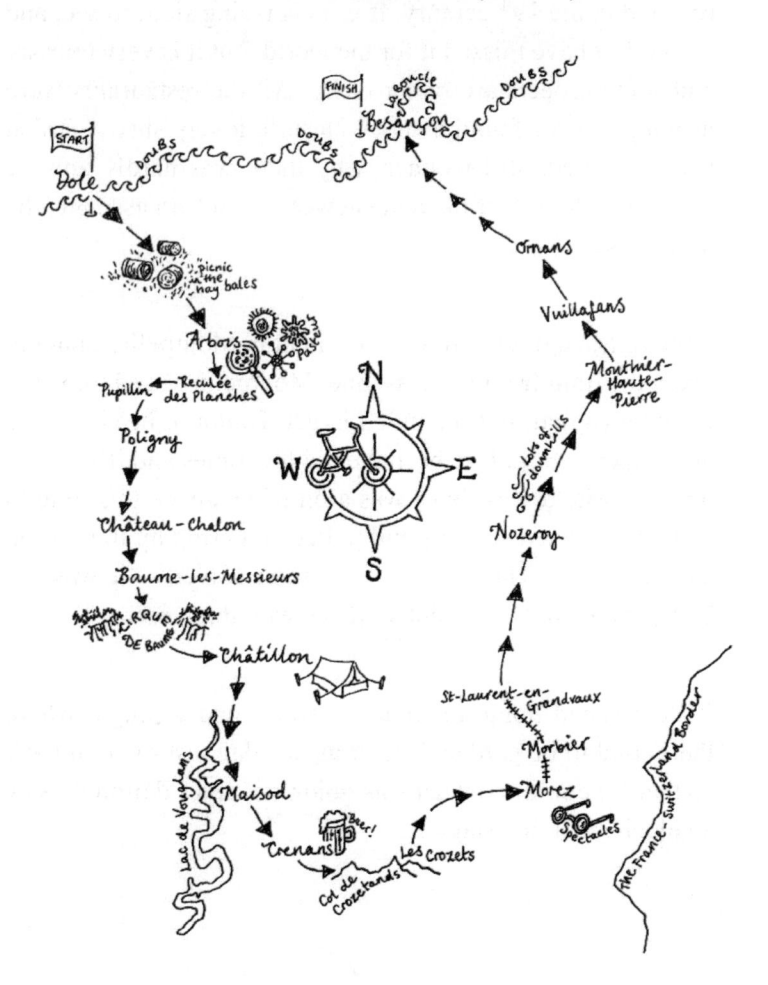

It wasn't that the Jura was somewhere we'd always wanted to visit. A sentence about it, found in some book or other, just about sums up our previous knowledge of the area:

'Jura, an eastern French wine region, is located between Burgundy and Switzerland.'

However, after our trip to Burgundy we felt, we should continue to head east.

It is also an area we nearly didn't get to, and I do wonder if I would ever have gone again if I hadn't done so the first time (I have returned on several occasions). We don't usually let anything stand in the way of our French holidays but there were various pressures, and it was only on the morning of departure that we felt safe to leave home with our trusty Bromptons, and to brave buying a Eurostar ticket at Waterloo itself, which thankfully did work.

Historically Franche-Comté was a free province of Burgundy (the 'free county') that was conquered by Louis XIV. Even the name 'Jura' means at least two things here – one being the *département* of that name (Franche-Comté is made up of four of them), and the other the mountain range covering most of Franche-Comté and which gave its name (without being asked) to the *département* in the reorganisation of French territory during the Revolution. The geologic period, the Jurassic, is named after the Jura mountains. The Jura of the Inner Hebrides appears to derive its name from the Old Norse for 'deer' so we can forget that for now.

The Jura range, which runs for 250 kilometres from Rhine to Rhône, is 61km at its widest point and, if only 1717 metres at its highest, has a most striking relief, the limestone Jura plateau dropping down in steps from Pontarlier near the Swiss border to the regional capital Besançon. We were fortunate also to drop down to Besançon, so at some stage we must have climbed up. My abiding memory, though, is of wonderful mountain pastures gained with little physical effort.

The Jurassic, or Secondary Era, was named after these mountains owing to the vast amounts of sedimentary rock laid down in the Jura at the time. They were still under ocean water then but in the Tertiary era the Alpine folding movement was so successful in thrusting up the land and forcing back the water that the region is now about 400 kilometres from the nearest sea.

The last Ice Age brought glaciers whose retreat left features such as the Jurassic lakes and the *reculées*, blind valleys ending at the foot of a cliff. With gorges, river valleys, waterfalls, caves and forests thrown in, the area is a geographer's dream. It should be a dream to anyone who loves fabulous scenery, pretty towns and villages, friendly people, and an accent (or lack of it) far less impenetrable than those to be found in the deep south of this magnificent country.

I have talked of where Franche-Comté is, and how it is when one gets there, but what do they *do* there? One thing they do is forestry. There are a lot of forests – deciduous up to about 800 metres, then evergreen forests, above which spruce forest is found (from about 1000 metres), alternating with wooded upland pastures.

They also do time. Even before Swiss clockmakers sought refuge there in 1793, their political ideas being too advanced for their Calvinist home country, Besançon had been a centre for clock and watchmaking. The resident makers were distinctly unamused by the influx and mildly suggested hanging as a remedy. The French government of the day, however (the Convention), was more welcoming to the refugees.

One's greatest impression of Franche-Comté is of a bucolic and sub-alpine calm, so it comes as something of a surprise to find the region is home to major centres of car and train-making but there they are, with Peugeot long established at Montbéliard and TGVs at Belfort. St-Claude is the capital of pipe-making and spectacles have long been manufactured at Morez, which is also the centre for Morbier cheese.

Cheese is what they make a lot of and when one sees the glorious flower-rich pastures that nourish the lovely red and white Montbéliard cows, surprise is far away. The *fruitières*, cooperative cheese dairies, are the basis of the production of the famous Comté Gruyère, with Morbier (containing ash),

Bleu de Haut-Jura and Vacherin being other examples of Franche-Comté cheeses.

Then there are the Jura wines. A Jura government official told me once that they summarise the *département*'s economy as *vignes et vaches*, vines and cows, but how many of us here are familiar with this alcoholic regional product? Naturally we did our best to familiarise ourselves with the appellations (Arbois, Pupillin, Château-Chalon and Étoile), the grapes themselves (the indigenous Savagnin, Trousseau and Poulsard, Pinot Noir and the ever present but ever varied Chardonnay), and the different wine types – *vin jaune*, *vin de paille*, whites, reds, pinks, and *Crémant*, a sparkling wine 'invented' at the same time as champagne and using exactly the same method. It is, however, somewhat cheaper and available in Britain at a supermarket that shall remain nameless owing to my dislike of supermarkets. (It is called Aldi.)

Vin jaune is indeed yellow, being deliberately oxidised to achieve the colour and a somewhat distinctive flavour which doesn't go with everything. However, as a good vintage can last a century, there is plenty of time to discover something it does go with (such as the Comté cheese). It is also rare and expensive. *Vin de paille* is made from grapes which are 'hanged' for three months, which seems unnecessarily vindictive. As the name suggests, the ripe grapes are dried on a bed of straw for two months before pressing (having become creased, presumably).

There is also the *macvin*, the Jura dessert wine for which the grapes are blended with *eau-de-vie* and which can be 16-20% proof. Usually served chilled as an aperitif, it is also used in *cuisine* (not just 'cooking', please note), which surely explains the menu item I once saw offering (in English, to be helpful) a dish 'cooked with regional spirit'. This conjured up visions of local folk in native costume, stirring the dish with great gusto and with a glass of hooch as cook's nip.

For me, a particularly attractive aspect of the Jura wine region is its lack of the monocultural look (as opposed to Burgundy, where there can be nothing but vines to see for miles). But for such a small area and considering that the wine-growing region is interspersed with other forms of agriculture, the *vignes* part of the economy seems to produce quite a variety of products. These are not easily available in Britain, with the above-mentioned exception, but a quick internet search reveals a host of wine growers who are eager to deliver to your door, and there is a stockist in Welshpool, which is handy for some.

I suppose we chose to start at Dole because it was just over the border from Burgundy, between which and Switzerland lies Franche-Comté, as mentioned earlier. We also found there was a train there from Dijon, and we knew (from the Burgundy trip) where Dijon was. But that was about the limit to what we knew about Dole. It now ranks as one of my favourite French towns, and also has my sympathy for the punishment meted out by Louis XIV for daring to resist his attempted conquest – he took away its regional capital status and gave it to Besançon.

Spotting Hôtel Moderne just by the station, we established ourselves and went to do the town. After returning several times in later years, I dubbed our temporary residence the 'Hôtel-not-so-Moderne', but this is a term of pure affection as it was, and I hope still is, cheap and clean and served wonderful coffee because it was made in the bar machine (many hotels dish up disgusting stuff). There were also some very eccentrically furnished rooms. High on my list of favourites is the one where the bath was set tight into the walls and I had to step into it from behind, which is surprisingly difficult (but how many people have had the opportunity to discover this?). However, my highest accolade is reserved for the room where *en suite* really meant what it said – the bath stood in splendid isolation in the large space between the bed and window. It might be that Hôtel Moderne now lives up to its name, but I do hope not, and any future trip to the Jura clearly must begin with an inspection.

We enjoyed dinner at a crêperie by the tanners' canal, wearing and feeling a little like anoraks as we *had* to wear them, so determined were we to be outside. At least it was *dry* – the last fortnight at home seemed to have consisted of nothing but rain and slugs. Next door was the house where Louis Pasteur was born. It was closed for Sunday evening, and also closed the next morning because it was Monday, but I visited it on a later trip, and I do recommend it. The evening concluded with a short stroll in the *son et lumière* of Dole, thankfully without the *son*.

The next morning, I explored Dole on my own, then read more about it on the terrace of the station café as I waited for Dahb to return from Dijon, whither he had had to repair to fetch the 'toy bag' we had left on the train. The station master had been able to telephone and ascertain the whereabouts of the said bag, but apparently it is forbidden for bags to travel unaccompanied on French railways, unlike bicycle tyres on our Great Western Railway, so there was nothing for it but to go and get it. A 'toy bag', by the way, is one of those tough PVC shopping bags one doesn't seem to be able to buy nowadays. Being capacious and waterproof, it is ideal for carrying books, maps, picnics, etc and into it are put all the toys needed for playing on the rail journey.

Eventually we set forth with our trusty steeds, just in time to buy lunch from a shop before it shut for the same purpose. Picnicking in a hayfield not far from Dole we were entertained by a display of *Mirages*, suggesting that the French air force remains open on Mondays if not much else does. I mentioned this sometime later to an acquaintance and he said that a French friend of his always looks up and sighs '*Voilà où vont mes impôts*' (that's where my taxes go).

Soon we were in great distress – no beer. At last we found a roadside pizzeria and drank a cool beer on the terrace (the joy of having to seek shade) at 4pm, a disgracefully late hour for a lunchtime beer and slightly early for an evening one. Also on the terrace was a charming little 'folk museum' with items including a small threshing machine; only our tiny carrying capacity prevented my fine upstanding citizen of a husband from stealing it. Four years later, on my way to a research interview with someone in the village, I sat down wearily to lunch at a café, having lost myself temporarily in a forest and found myself again by the sun (rather cleverly, I thought, as I'm not a natural navigator) and there was the threshing machine. I had absolutely no idea that the village I had been seeking was the same one. Nor was I in any better position to steal the thresher, as I was on foot and carrying only a small rucksack.

Arriving at Arbois we found a room in Hôtel de la Poste. I wrote in my diary that it was 'somewhat characterful', but the Freudian slip I made when typing up that diary probably describes it better – I wrote 'Hole de la Poste'. But we are clearly of hobbit stock as holes suit us well, especially if cheap. And as it poured during the night I was very happy not to be camping, one of the main drawbacks of which is that the loo is not *en suite* (certainly not in the Hôtel Moderne sense) and even in the Hole de la Poste the passage to the bathroom was dry.

The memory of the area being an ocean seems to be strong still, as we ate a delicious seafood meal in *Breton's* restaurant, though surely not by a 'bug church' as my typed-up diary suggests.

Arbois is where Pasteur spent his youth after being born in Dole (unlikely to be before). Needless to say, the Maison de

Pasteur was closed on Tuesdays. A word here about Louis Pasteur (1822-1895). That wonderful man not only produced vaccines to cure rabies and anthrax, did invaluable work for the silk industry through his study of silkworm illnesses, and revolutionised the field of medicine through his theories in microbiology resulting in what we take for granted today – antisepsis, sterilisation, immunisation, etc. He also discovered what we now call the 'pasteurisation' process that prevents wine, beer and vinegar from going off, a service to man- and woman- kind that alone should earn his place on the highest possible pedestal. *And* he went south to sort out the phylloxera that was ravaging the vineyards.

The wine museum was also closed but had an outside section in the form of a vineyard, so we inspected the various grape varieties before breakfasting at Snack Café le Centre, the Hole de la Poste being yet another closed institution on Tuesdays, though fortunately we were allowed out once Monday night had finished.

After breakfast we went up the Reculée des Planches, a blind valley near Arbois which is a typical feature of the Jura. The valley has high-sided cliffs, having been gouged out of the limestone by erosion, and ends in a rocky steep-sided amphitheatre. After cycling up and down the reculée we felt quite exhausted, so had a leisurely lunch back in Arbois before proceeding to Poligny for dinner and bed in the *Logis* hotel, the campings being closed for refurbishment. Insult was added to injury by having to pay a 15-franc garage fee for the Bromptons!

The day's journey had taken us through the village of Pupillin, which gives its name to one of the wine appellations. It was on this day that I felt very struck with how much more pleasant a wine region is when mixed up with other things, rather than an area like Burgundy where one can get a bit sick of the sight of vineyards sometimes, though oddly enough it doesn't put us off the product. We felt rather the same the next day when visiting Château-Chalon which was quite unfair, as it is truly a lovely place in the most pretty setting. Our opinion must have been coloured by the disruption to our daily routine, there being nothing but wine and restaurants available. It was beer time. Fortunately, tragedy was averted by finding a roadside hotel that served beer, and we could proceed to our picnic and the next stop, Baume-les-Messieurs. This was originally Baume-les-Moines, a monastery for aristocratic monks. The ladies' version was founded as Baume-les-Nonnes, now Baume-les-Dames and many miles away in the Doubs valley. Both institutions changed their names to reflect their sense of their high breeding but got their come-uppance in the Revolution.

This is a truly chocolate-box place, a real honeypot for coachloads of tourists, but the abbey and its setting in another reculée (Cirque de Baume) are well worth seeing, and we got a wonderful bird's eye view as we plodded personfully up the road leading out of the valley in which the abbey lies. The road led to one of the best campings we've ever had, in the village of Châtillon. Dahb got 100% for choosing a camping spot overlooking a bend on the Ain River, and the day came to a perfect close at the only restaurant in the village which was nonetheless excellent and sported a terrace with magnificent views.

We had now arrived in the *Région des Lacs*. What happens in Lake Districts is – rain. I know, I was born and brought up in one.

The next day, Thursday, dawned fine enough. We had breakfast at Chez Yvonne, on yet another bend in the river, chatting for some time in French to a fellow breakfaster before we discovered we were all English. He had a ponytail and a Landrover, was a flower photographer, and had once sailed through the French canals, something Dahb would like to do.

When the wetness began it rained steadily for a few hours, but we had our waterproofs and found a restaurant for lunch where a parasol on a shady terrace doubled as an umbrella. We visited the Cascades du Hérisson, the Hérisson being a river rising in a lake south of the waterfalls. We waved at the photographer as he passed in his Landrover, and at the end of our soggy tour the Bromptons sheltered in the cavern of Châtillon's only restaurant whilst we enjoyed another excellent meal with rainbow and misty panorama. To be fair, it could have been wetter and doubtless often is. The diary says 'Rain ceased! Skies cleared! Chatted to four Dutch geomorphologists. Tent. Bed.'

As we were to leave the Région des Lacs the next morning,

the mist gave way to sun. The morning's chat was to a retired but very young-at-heart-and-body Dutch couple who were cycling from their native land to Stes-Maries-de-la-Mer in the Camargue, an amazing coincidence as it is another town in which we had lunch on a shady terrace under a parasol doubling as an umbrella. The Dutch were on beautiful new but old-fashioned bicycles, and made a very elegant picture as they travelled along. We came across them again later in the day and shared cherries on a village green – bought cherries, I hasten to add, not stolen.

We enjoyed a picnic lunch in peace and quiet by Lake Maisod – the road was blocked to cars and doesn't the name sound funny in English? We used a concrete table at a picnic site in dappled sun overlooking this artificial but beautiful lake. The *auberge* in Crenans had just shut for lunch but we wanted only a beer – the very pleasant *patronne* had lived in Croydon, which might well share parts of the alphabet with the French village but surely little else.

Up and over the Col de Crozetands, a lovely route with wonderful meadows and still few cars, then at 940 metres or so we succumbed to a night in the comfortable Hôtel Les Routiers which was open in spite of a sign a few miles back saying so. (We often find 'open' means 'closed'.) It was hard to imagine the snow that enabled it to offer Nordic skiing, though we have seen it on photographs taken by French friends who have a house nearby.

An exciting time was had by all four of us the next day as we cycled along a road parallel to and not far from the Swiss border. Nearby was Pontarlier: people who travel from Pontarlier to Switzerland for work, and those who travel in the other direction, presumably waving to each other on the way, are known locally as *frontarliers*, which I like. The Pontarlier museum houses a fascinating display about absinthe, which was prohibited in 1905, an act that must have had a bad effect on the local employment provided by Pernod. Also nearby is the scenically situated Château de Joux, where the unfortunate Haitian rebel Toussaint Louverture was imprisoned in 1802, dying a couple of months later.

We visited Morez, of the spectacle-making, and thought how necessary spectacles would be to see up the incredibly long street. We took a train for a while to help us up a hill (I think that was the reason), and then cycled to Nozeroy. We nearly didn't stay there, and certainly didn't stay in the village a few kilometres before where the hotel was closed on Saturdays. But the *patron* had said we were not to worry as there were plenty of places in Nozeroy. It wasn't quite the case, however; the campings were shut, and so was the hotel.

We should have known better about the promised hotels, after our experience in Sagres, Portugal, where the very helpful, smart, articulate (in excellent English) lady in the tourist office assured us that there were plenty of B&Bs in Carrapeitra, fifteen miles up the coast. Carrapeitra, however, appeared to be a collection of hovels. I don't wish to sound judgemental – it's just that clearly none of them were offering B&B and their occupants looked rather surprised to see us. Henry the Navigator had a palace in Sagres, by the way, and with the view of nothing but sea, it is little wonder that he felt the need for exploration. When I read that he himself had never actually left Portugal, it somehow explained why the Portuguese maps we were using were so useless – they had never been properly tested.

There was nothing hovellish about Nozeroy, and the accommodation crisis was solved by a kind restaurant owner who telephoned all the way round the corner to a lady who had a *chambre d'hôte* but didn't want anyone to know about it. We rewarded the restaurant by eating and drinking almost everything they offered.

It was now downhill almost all the way to Besançon, apart from the occasional hill going up. Our swoop down the Loue valley was sensational, if a little drizzly, and reminded me of pictures of the Three Gorges or of Vietnam, with the dramatic limestone formations jutting out of the deep river valley. The source of the Loue was discovered in 1901 when it was noticed that the water tasted of absinthe. The day before, there had been an industrial accident at Pontarlier, and the Pernod poured into the river Doubs like manna from heaven. An experiment with green dye proved that the Loue was a resurgent spring of the Doubs.

After a night in a *gîte d'étape* halfway down, fortunately

with no-one else there as it happened to be Monday, we stopped at Ornans for coffee. Ornans is famous for the reflections of the houses in the water, and for the artist Courbet, who produced many paintings of his lovely river.

My first sight of Besançon, a city I later came to know well and to love, was from a statue of the Virgin Mary overlooking the *boucle* – the loop in the river Doubs into which much of the old town is tucked. Standing out in 3-D (which it is, of course) was Vauban's magnificent citadel, built to defend Louis XIV's newly acquired territory and to stop the natives from being bumptious and getting ideas of regaining their independence.

After lugging our Bromptons up a steep flight of stairs in the picturesque Hôtel du Levant, we headed for the citadel, which beat us to it by closing for the evening just as we approached. The way up there is worth the walk in itself, however, and one can see a fair amount of the moat and outer walls even after closing time. After negotiating a steep flight of steps down to a square where beer was provided, we wandered further through the interesting streets, finding a pleasant small restaurant where we chatted in French for some time to the *patronne* before discovering she was not only English but came from the English Lake District. She and her French chef-husband failed to make a go of it in Besançon, I discovered later, and went to open another restaurant in Poitiers, where presumably people have bigger appetites.

I think the next day was Tuesday, and therefore time to go home. We climbed up to the station, which is well above the river, and took an early train, presumably arriving home with few hitches as nothing is recorded to the contrary.

If I could write a whole book on the Jura, the same would almost be true of Besançon. It is a fascinating place, and until relatively recently was prevented from spreading too far by the constraints of the river. Someone told me that the good burghers of Besançon tried to keep out the Nazis by destroying the bridges. The invading army simply flung some new ones over the water, and the citadel bears testimony to the invaders' unwelcome presence.

Chapter 7
Var (Provence actually)

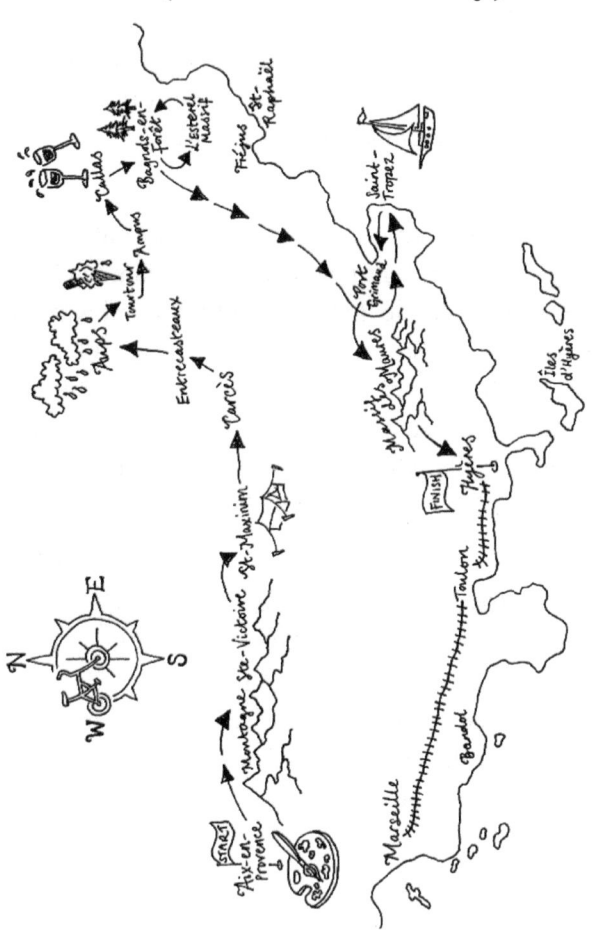

One year we not only stayed in the one region, but we also stayed in the one *département*, Var. It is part of the Provence-Alpes-Côte d'Azur region or PACA, which remained unchanged in the 2016 reshuffle. The *département* takes its name from the river Var which flowed along its eastern boundary. That is, it still flows but the boundary was moved in 1860 when Nice and its hinterland returned to France having belonged to the Italian House of Savoy since 1814. Toulon, the *chef-lieu,* is the main port of the French navy, and Var is also known for its Mediterranean resorts, some fine Mediaeval architecture and for its wines.

I'm not sure what our overall plan was but it did include visiting St-Tropez, not just because it is famous but because someone had told me that the country around was pleasantly rural and quiet. So on Saturday 6th May 2000, five days before Dahb's fiftieth birthday, we travelled on the earliest train to Paddington (5.30am), then caught the 8.27am Eurostar to Lille where we bought beer and gweges for the trip. The 12.17 from Lille landed us at Marseille at 5.45pm.

At Charles-de-Gaulle-Roissy, the airport stop, a vast number of people carrying vast amounts of luggage swarmed onto the train. A German woman who lived in Grenoble and who had lived in Australia explained to us in English that there was a strike by Air France because of the 35-hour week, which they all wanted but for the same money. I do love the French.

We changed at Marseilles for Aix-en-Provence, arriving just before 7pm which is dangerously close to refreshment time. We cycled to our pre-booked Hôtel des Arts which was very small but central, clean and *en suite*. We douched, had a beer aperitif and then dinner round the corner and were in bed by 11pm, worn out by the stresses of travelling. We had to block out the streetlight by jamming a t-shirt in the window.

The next day was Sunday, which often follows Saturday, and the weather was a bit dodgy so we decided to stay another night and 'do' Aix which is a fine town. Its origins go back to Roman times and after a period of damaging Saracen raids, all was prosperous during the Middle Ages when it was the capital of the County of Provence. A centre of Provençal literature, the university was founded in 1409. Towards the end of the century Aix came under the French crown and its architectural heritage owes much to the building activity that took place in the 17th and 18th centuries.

We breakfasted in a square, then visited the tourist office. It was now pouring, but cleared again and we explored the old part of Aix. We then went to a Jean Moulin exhibition which was fascinating. I hadn't realised that this leader of the French resistance was quite an artist and dealt in and exhibited pictures. When given paper by his torturer, Klaus Barbie, so that he could write the names of other Resistance workers, he drew caricatures of his captors instead. What a man.

We continued on our walk. The cathedral and cloisters were closed, presumably because it was Sunday, so we dove back into the streets and apparently had lunch with buskers (I must say the diary is a bit pithy for this holiday). We then walked out to the Oppidum d'Entremont, a sort of Old Sarum on the north side of the city, having a quick squint at Cézanne's studio *en route,* the painter having been born and died in the town. Once back in the centre we naturally looked for beer, Dahb ordering a pint of beer or rather 50cl, to the great amusement of all in the bar. No signs of disapproval, though, (see Chapter 9) especially when he explained we'd had a long and dusty walk. We went Spanish for dinner.

Having breakfasted at the hotel next morning, we headed east, a dramatic ride along the southern side of the Montagne Ste-Victoire, a limestone ridge extending over 18km and 1011m at its highest point. Cézanne could see it from his house in Aix and just couldn't stop painting it. We had a hot wind in our faces but were able to refresh ourselves at one of two bars in Pourrières, reaching St-Maximin in good time. Going in, the traffic was hideous owing to a fair *and* it being May 8th, Victory in Europe day. The campsite was 3km out of town but quite satisfactory and at least it wasn't raining.

We set up and douched, then cycled back to the town which was quite lovely and fairly new (mostly 17th to 18th century). There were some marvellous 14th century arcades in what had previously been a Jewish ghetto. There was a huge basilica and monastery, a fine Hôtel de Ville and we found good food in a restaurant with a terrace. The chef's wife spoke English

– it turned out that her parents were running the Institut Français in Edinburgh where I went in 1969 on a course from school. Her father looked rather like Picasso and kept saying '*Oo là là*' which we thought was thrilling. How was I to know I would meet his daughter 31 years later on a cycling holiday in France with a man I hadn't yet met and on a bicycle that hadn't yet been invented?

Having said we stayed in one *département* all holiday, Aix is in Bouches-du-Rhône and we crossed the border just before St-Maximin. But we were now firmly ensconced in Var. The next morning, we struck camp over coffee, loaded up the steeds and zipped back into St-Maximin for breakfast in the square. We took the usual small roads and tracks and picnicked early as rain was threatening. It held off, but arriving early at Carcès we decided against camping and booked in at Hôtel Chez Nous which was a lovely old building and marvellous value. The *patron* was a garrulous chap but looked after us well. There was a Swedish woman on an art holiday but otherwise it was fairly quiet, and we had excellent food in an enormous restaurant. There was a violent storm in the night and Dahb slept through it all. When we revisited Carcès in 2014 there was no sign of our hotel, merely a snack bar in its place.

The sky was blue the next day until we set off, when it clouded over but was still pleasant. We passed through Entrecasteaux, seeing the château and visiting the village which was very quaint. Picnicking somewhere, we climbed up to Aups on a busier road than the map indicated. We got there just as the rain started and had to (really had to as the hotels were shut during the day) take shelter in a café with beer. By then it was fair chucking it. I eventually sallied forth with brolly (Yay! Using the brolly!) and booked into the *Logis* Provençal. It was a good hotel but the receptionist was a bit unsympathetic and wouldn't give the Bromptons a bed, ruling that they could stay on the terrace (we took them up to our room anyway when she wasn't looking).

The evening cleared and we discovered it to be a pleasant town. It being Dahb's birthday the next day, he rang his parents in order to remind his mother of the torment she had suffered bringing him into the world fifty years earlier with self in background yelling 'It wasn't worth it!'

At last, the next day was the birthday of Dahb (11th May and, btw, also the 50th of Jeremy Paxman whom Dahb didn't ring but only because he didn't have the number) and I gave him his exciting presents: a wobbly frog card, a frog pencil and a frog-green nailbrush. A bit of a theme there? We had breakfast in the square as we so often seem to do, then climbed up and out of Aups, finding a superb road which might have been dead flat or slightly downhill, a wonderful route to the pretty village of Tourtour. As we freewheeled along, we saw what looked like a new château with a plantation, La Tourenne. Eating an ice-cream in Tourtour, we realised what was wrong with it, apart from all the tourists – it was too clean. That's the village, not the ice-cream.

On to Ampus to find a birthday lunch – the square seemed dead except for a restaurant which was crammed but we were directed to a *Logis* with purple shutters (*volets violets*). We had a very good lunch with some rosé, in the company of a Yorkie-like puppy which was enjoying a meal of a piece of wood. In good time we arrived in Callas, a village we fell in love with as we did with its Hôtel de France and all who sailed in her. We have talked of going back and another visit to that hotel is a must. But it could be disappointing, and they could have joined the trend of making vinaigrette with Domestos as in Bourg-Argental (Chapter 9).

Nowadays people are more used to Bromptons but in 2000 we had yet to see any in France and we still haven't met anyone else holidaying in the way we do. (Several people have suggested we're not quite sane.) Once upon a time people used to laugh and almost throw stones but we would quell them with a glare – or two, one each – and point out that it was all because of their lousy railway system. That usually brought instant sympathy and understanding. There are more folders around now and probably most people think we have a car somewhere and are just pottering around on day trips. As we plodded up a hill in some region or other, a Tour-de-France-type cyclist once asked me why I had so much luggage. When I told him it was for two weeks, he was suitably chastened.

Back to Callas; a couple of young lads begged to try out our bikes and of course we let them, feeling slightly worried at the thought of them cycling off into the distance and never being seen again. But their interest was a real one and they even offered to buy them.

The hotel really was a hoot. Like Carcès it was wonderful value, and delightfully ramshackle with naughty pics on the corridor wall. There was a 'shady terrace with dog and yoof' – I quote from my diary. I've also written 'Delicious mean solo at hotel' by which I presumably meant 'meal'. Perhaps what I meant to say was could there be a more perfect way of spending one's (the other one's) 50th birthday? On a cycling holiday in Provence, in what is still probably our favourite hotel in a lovely village, a quiet probably candle-lit dinner for two (I might be waxing lyrical about the candles), cooked and washed up by someone else with the Bromptons nearby as that night they slept in the hotel restaurant as befits their station.

After dinner we phoned Dahb's sister Jo from the square so that she could congratulate him on his coming of age. The 'yoof' were rather noisy until the small hours but, hey, it was summer.

If Dahb's birthday was on a Thursday that year, the next day must have been a Friday. Our dodgy TV gave us a reasonable *météo* so we breakfasted with confidence on the terrace, and then bought a picnic lunch from the very nice shop opposite. It really was a village with everything. If we return, we will certainly book in advance in order to avoid disappointment owing to the aforementioned habit of the

French of discovering our nice hotels and making them less secret than they were when we first found them.

I didn't write much in my diary which suggests we didn't take many long stops, but we do remember that it was a perfect holiday, undulating but not overly mountainous, and the weather was just right all the time except when it rained in Aups. After another lovely day cycling we arrived at a very good small campsite in Bagnols-en-Forêt. There was a French camper van with three people in it, otherwise there was nobody. A French lady joined me for a swim in a still-covered swimming pool – mid-May is early in the south of France, holiday wise, or at least it was in 2000. We then went for drinks on one side of the main street and dinner on the other side in the Hôtel le Commerce (which we earmarked for a future trip). We ate in the conservatory with a wonderful view and our pizzas were cooked on the fire with long shovels. The waitress was delightful and said '*Oop là*' every time she brought us anything.

We decided to stay two nights and had a wonderful day Bromptoning without luggage in the Esterel *massif*, the hills behind the Riviera. We did over 80km which is quite a lot for our little donkeys, and we collapsed with gratitude in the hotel restaurant and probably consumed more pizza.

On Sunday we went to St-Tropez, feeling rather posh. We found a campsite about 5km out of the town, more or less on a beach and very quiet. We then cycled in (were these the first Bromptons to visit St-Tropez?) and bought beers at a café facing the harbour. We were hugely entertained by the smooth people on their grand yachts – it was like something out of James Bond. Our waiter was perfectly polite but became positively friendly when he found I could speak French and had bothered to find out something about the town and St-Tropez himself. (It's not difficult, it being all in the Michelin guide.) St-T was a Christian centurion beheaded by order of the Emperor Nero. He was placed in a boat with a cockerel and a dog who were meant to devour his remains but didn't. (Legend doesn't relate whether the dog devoured the bird.) The boat is supposed to have reached land where St-Tropez is now situated.

The setting of the town is fabulous, and we enjoyed walking along the harbour walls. As dinner time approached, we headed into the back streets and found a lovely restaurant with really friendly people. I was being plagued by mosquitoes at the time (Dahb is too ripe for them) and the *patron* sympathised and said this was just the time the water warmed up and they came out of the sea, obviously seeking to feed on succulent Englishwomen.

We pedalled back to the campsite and bed. The next day we went back through St-Tropez to get to Port Grimaud which is a modern (1960s) imitation of a Mediterranean fishing village but is in fact a complex of luxury housing, marina and beach. Reading about it beforehand made us wonder if we would find it rather twee (and expensive) but it is really attractive, and we found a perfectly ordinary and reasonably priced bar, so Port G went up in our estimation and stayed there.

We then headed inland again, though the non-port bit of Grimaud and into the Massif des Maures. The Maures are described by Michelin as a range of geologically old crystalline mountains covered with fine forests, with shady valleys and wild ravines. We stayed the night in a small place called Collobrières, where there was a very pleasant *Logis*.

Passing time before we could decently have our evening drink (we must have been really early), we walked in the hills above the village where there were cork oaks and where Dahb was entranced by a group of wild boarlets. I thought they were entrancing too but carried that with me as I put distance between me and them and their doubtless irate mother who might be reappearing any minute, with tusks. I could have done with Modestine, at least to put between me and said irate and tusky mum.

The next day we continued westward through the Maures Massif and booked into a hotel in Hyères which is just east of Toulon and apparently the most southerly and the oldest of the Riviera resorts. I can't see that Hyères plage can be much fun as the map shows an airport just behind it, but the old town is attractive. The Îles d'Hyères, which would be part of the Maures if they were still attached, lie just south of the town and I must say I'd like to pop over one day, especially to the Île de Porquerolles as I remember reading a Maigret story where *he* popped over in pursuit of a criminal. Our green guide says it is best toured by bicycle – I can't remember whether Maigret did that.

We caught an early train next morning to Marseilles where we had a wait of a couple of hours for our TGV, so we took it in turns to bomb down to the old port and have a dekko. It was no penance for the one who waited and looked after the bikes – the view from the station café terrace is quite something.

Time to go home. I've said this was a perfect holiday – the weather, the terrain and the wine – but I haven't mentioned the parasol or umbrella pine. This is a typically Mediterranean species and is easily recognised due to the shape which gives it its name. It would have to have a distinctive shape for us to recognise it, but it does and we did, and we saw lots of them and they have forged a lasting image of Var in our minds.

Chapter 8
Mordagne via Auvergne

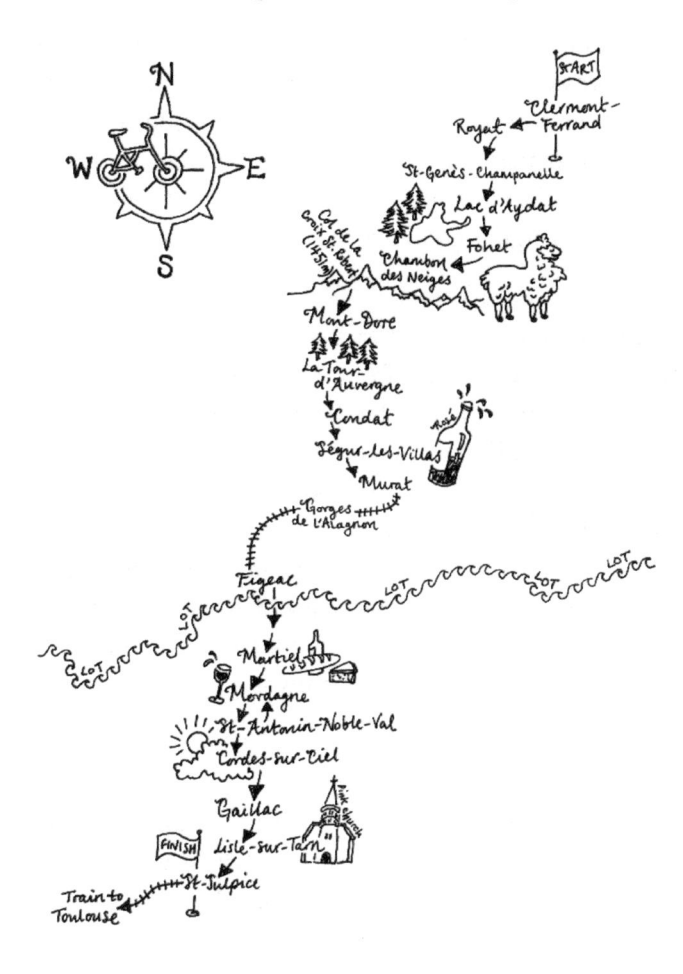

We felt it was time to visit the Auvergne again after our near-abortive attempt on big bikes in 1990. On that trip, we got there almost as it was time to set off again for the return journey, as we had to cycle the bits where trains would not carry bikes. But we still managed to get quite a taste of the region and looked forward to another holiday there.

We had been invited again to join family in Mordagne (see First Forays, Chapter 2) and planned to start in Clermont-Ferrand and traverse the region as it's on the way to Mordagne if that's the way you go. We went in September and after a dismal August in the area, we got mega Brownie points for bringing good weather.

Wednesday 4th September 2002 and it was one of those early starts, the 5.35am from Swindon to Paddington. We loved this train as it was the boat train from Fishguard and there were usually sleepy but cheery Irish people on board. We then took the 8.53am Eurostar to Paris and the RER to Gare de Lyon where we no doubt had beers or even lunch. The RER (*Réseau Express Régional* or Regional Express Network) is a rapid transit system and is faster than the Métro with fewer stops. We don't really like travelling on it with all our clobber as it tends to be crowded but it's a quick and efficient way of crossing Paris.

After the RER it was the TER (*Transport Express Régional*) to Clermont-Ferrand which was the regional capital until 2016 when Auvergne joined forces with Rhône-

Alpes. On arrival there was no need to unfold the Bromptons as the Hôtel St-André I had booked from home was just by the station. We dumped everything and hurried into the main drag. It's a fine town, with black buildings constructed of volcanic rock. There were good views, as there had been from the train, of the Puy de Dôme, an ancient former volcano standing high at 1465m. Amazing to think that until 1751, when the volcanic origin of the Puy and its fellows in the Dômes mountain range was recognised, they were believed to have been part of enormous Roman fortifications.

We had a drink at the interestingly named La Chardonnay near the cathedral, returning there later for a dinner of avocado pâté, *aligot* and sausage, and an Auvergne rosé, the first we'd ever had. Eating on the terrace with the cathedral and the Puy de Dôme as scenery – lovely. *Aligot*, not to be confused with the wine Aligoté but often consumed with it, is a creamy mashed potato with cheese. So, we ate bangers and mash but with a difference.

We slept like logs for eight or nine hours (it's the rosé) but woke to rain and a not very brilliant *météo*. We whiled our time away on breakfast and a visit to Turismu for some hotel guides, after which, according to Dear Diary, we 'met God Save the Queen chap and lots of too-brown retirees'. We found an internet café as I needed to check emails because of a forthcoming academic research trip – closed.

We had a coffee somewhere and then moved on to another

café, sitting outside but under cover as it was still raining. A Clermont resident started talking to us, wanting to practise his English. We wish they wouldn't, as we want to practise our French. But he was very pleasant, and we enjoyed a friendly argument as to which was the better, the French word for 'comfortable' or the English. I favoured the French, but he was adamant that the accolade went to the English and stood there for some time repeating the word, bouncing off the 'm' and fuffing the 'f' in what I do admit was a somewhat onomatopoeic sort of way if somewhat un-English.

The weather began to clear, and we set off for Royat, a spa town to the west of Clermont, lunching in the old part by a fortified church. Aiming for St-Genès, we went via the Charade motorsport racing circuit, using the old Michelin route which is now banned for motors and no wonder. We took the easy way, the *pente douce*, and thank heaven for that. Goodness knows what the tough route would be like – I can't imagine how anyone could drive along the track we were taking. It ended as a footpath, but we eventually found a road and made our way to Lac d'Aydat, clearly very touristy but quiet now after the *rentrée* (back-to-school time).

Lac d'Aydat lies in a pleasant, wooded setting at an altitude of 825m and was formed by a lava flow damming the river Veyre. We found a room at Hôtel des Cygnes, by the lake, and went out for some more cycling and in search of a beer, I expect. Nothing much was happening in the village of Aydat, but we found a *Logis* a bit further on which supplied us with bottled beer. A nice route through some woods took us back to our hotel and we finished the day with an excellent meal in a restaurant by the lake, 'watching silly duck with bread'. I'm dashed if I can remember what said silly duck was doing with the bread. Some of our fellow diners were non-French-speaking English and Dutch – unusual in the case of the Dutch.

At breakfast the next day we met a couple of the non-French-speaking English who were walking a grand circuit from the town of Mont-Dore. They were with a company which carried their luggage, a jolly good idea for walking holidays. We also discussed the merits of walking boots vs walking sandals. They were wearing the latter and waxed lyrical about them, which interested me as my old, very comfortable, boots were on their way out and I was finding it quite difficult to find satisfactory new ones. After a few false starts I found the answer in the RSPB magazine and an advertisement for Fife Country boots. I make no apology for this little bit of marketing (no profit to me) as they are inexpensive and absolutely brill.

Off we set. We saw a llama near Fohet and had beer and a gwege by the road, near Beaune-le-Froid, which it was rather (cold). There was also a Saulzet-le-Froid so someone was trying to make a point. As we were doing a bit of climbing we met a cycling Frenchman who said we were taking the suicide route to Mont-Dore. Oh good, we thought, we must be on the right road. On and up, to a ski station, Chambon-des-Neiges, and finally to Col de la Croix St-Robert at 1451m. We then swooped down to Mont-Dore, hands frozen and me regretting bring woolly gloves as they made it so difficult to grip.

Mont-Dore was *very* grockly and most lunches were *terminés,* but we did find a teashop with quiches and crêpes and gradually warmed up a bit. We also bought some nice fruity bonbons which gave me the idea of making my own from our soft fruit but, needless to say, I never did.

We consulted our hotel guide and I telephoned for a room in La Tour-d'Auvergne, after which we cycled through lots of woods and arrived at about 7pm. It is a pretty town and was also fairly dead. There were at least four hotels and only ours was in the regional guide. The others, including a *Logis,* looked rather unlikely, but one of them served us a pre-dinner beer in the bar. Our own hotel was pleasant although the *patron* was a bit dour. Dinner was served rather early and there were big hints to move out of the dining room before 10pm.

We now had the choice of cycling via the Dordogne or taking the mountain route and, as the *météo* was good, we chose the latter. It was very rural, and just before we went down a very bendy road to Condat there was a wonderful viewpoint. Condat was somewhat one-horse, but we found the lovely Auberge de Trois Rivières for lunch, sitting outside in *hot* sun by a badly traffic-calmed street.

We climbed up again, to Ségur-les-Villas along a lovely 'alternative' route which was quite busy. We tried what turned out to be an annexe to the main hotel and were told the real one was two kilometres away. It was more like four but at least it was downhill. Dahb had a slow puncture so needed to stop occasionally to pump up the tyre. When we got to the large *Logis*, we were greeted as if we were expected. We hadn't booked and I wonder why, as it was a Saturday. Perhaps it was yet another hotel that wasn't in our regional guide. The mystery was solved with the arrival of a gaggle of *motoists* and the patron realised we had only *vélos*. Luckily there was still room for us and Dahb was able to mend his puncture before dinner, which was apparently a bit native (I have no idea what I meant by that) but accompanied by a tasty Châteauguy rosé.

Now look here, dear reader. The word *motoist* is Brompton-speak for motorbike because in France they call these *motos*. It is not a typographical error for 'motorist'. There might well be typos in this book but that ain't one of them.

The *motoists* were up early for a Sunday, already breakfasting by 8am. As we munched our croissants a coachful of French persons joined us for coffee so the dining room was quite chaotic. After talking to a French couple who lived in Fontainebleau, we were on our way by 9am.

It was a lovely morning but beginning to cloud over. Continuing south we had an easy climb up to a *col*, then down to Murat, a gorgeous Mediaeval town. Dahb took half of a two-shot panorama of the rooftops, then ran out of film. But we bought a new film and saw some cats at a first-floor window (wild living). As we had decided to let the train take some of the strain, we found the station and bought tickets to Figeac. The 11.55am took us along the Gorges of the Alagnon with the Plomb de Cantal in view. It's 1855m so quite something to see. Altogether a great ride.

Arriving at Figeac just before two, we found and booked into Hôtel des Bains, by the river. Then we did the Michelin walking tour of the town but couldn't find any lunch. We had an ice-cream followed by a bit of quiche. We saw the Mediaeval bridge and the ramparts, and there were cats galore, one clearly very special with his own mousehole. We went back to the hotel for a drink and met some English people who warned us that there was only one restaurant open, and it was likely to close early. We headed that way pretty darned smartish and had a good meal on the terrace, served by a rather sulky girl.

We were up with the lark (well, a slightly late lark) and breakfasted and set off by 8.30am. There had been a storm with a lot of rain in the night and it was still a bit mizzly. We were a little way out of Figeac when my back tyre, which had been bulging since the beginning of the holiday, finally gave way. Luckily there was an open garage opposite a house and we asked the lady of the house, who was putting out the bins, if we could shelter there whilst mending the puncture. She was only too happy to oblige and was a very charming and friendly person, and a rather unusual one. We supposed she was a Thalidomide victim as her arms were extremely short and I can't quite remember if she had anything in the way of hands. Anyway, she was getting on with life in a most cheery fashion and I was rather touched by the concern of the postman when he called. He wanted to be sure we weren't causing trouble, but she explained our problem and she assured him that we were *gentils* which was very sweet of her and I'm so glad for her sake that we were.

By the time we were on our way again (it took Dahb an hour and a half to change the tyre and refix the gears) the weather had cleared and remained brilliant all day. For a while we followed the Célé which is a lovely river, then went up and over to the Lot. We went along the left bank, then up the valley of the Flancon, passing through places that looked promising on the map but had nothing in the way of food or drink. We were getting decidedly peckish. It was marvellous ridge cycling and eventually we found Martiel, which looked nothing much but had a very nice shop which was open at 2pm – the last thing we expected to find. We bought beers and a picnic and ate royally on the village green.

On we went, up and over, and in Comusson, which was towered over by a huge château, we met a Yorkshire terrier standing in the middle of the road. We chatted to him in English for a while, which I am sure helped to alleviate any homesickness. We then went up and along to Espinas, where our niece was married in 2007 (on that occasion we cycled there from Bordeaux). The last lap saw us reach Mordagne by 6.30pm, so we had a quick shower and then dived into drinks for which it was getting dangerously late.

During drinks, for which we were joined by some neighbours, the telephone rang and Dahb's brother-in-law learned that his 80-year-old father was to have an emergency quadruple bypass the next day, the other son (a medic) having noticed that he was a bit breathless when hauling in the lobster pots. As all his arteries were found to be blocked, it wasn't surprising he was having some difficulty.

The next day was lovely and the views from the balcony gorgeous. Dahb and I went out for the day, leaving the others to work, poor things. We cycled to St-Antonin-Noble-Val which is a lovely well-preserved Mediaeval town. I believe the (then) recent film *Charlotte Gray* was partly made there. It is situated in the gorges of the Aveyron river where it is joined by the Bonnette and is overlooked by magnificent limestone cliffs. It is also, as so many settlements are, on a route to Santiago de Compostela.

We poddled around, had beers and food, and found a shady bench by the river and read our books. We returned via the Bonnette which we were pleased to see again, having first met this lovely little river in 1993, and climbed back up to Mordagne (climbing is the only way to get there) for the usual round of shower, drinks and dinner. We swapped bedrooms so that Dahb's sister and her husband could sleep in the house where the telephone was, and we went over the garden to the *pigeonnier*. The operation was to start at 6pm English time. By the way, the *pigeonnier* had been converted into a bedroom so we didn't have to share it with our avian friends, or is that 'fiends'.

In the morning, we heard that mother had telephoned at 1.30am and that all had gone well. Indeed, he lived to the age of 99. We left after breakfast to cycle to Cordes-sur-Ciel, about 20km south-east of Mordagne. Just before the halfway point, in a village called Varen, we found a lovely restaurant but when we poked our noses in it seemed rather posh, which we were distinctly not. We apologised for our attire, explaining we were cycling, and the *patronne* assured that it was not a problem in the country. Goodness knows what they think of us in the towns. Lunch included a nice bottle of dry white Gaillac.

We continued up as we always seem to do, along and over, and at last reached a point from which there was a fine view of Cordes. It really is an extraordinary place, houses clustered up a hill seemingly trying to reach the sky. It is generally thought to be the first of the *bastides* of south-west France and received its charter in 1222. *Bastides* are fortified 'new towns', new that is in Mediaeval times, in south-west France, England and Wales. They mostly date from the reign of our Edward I when Gascony and Guyenne belonged to the English. Some of the first were built to replace villages destroyed in the 13th century Albigensian Crusade. Often the castle was the starting point, and this can be seen in Conwy in north Wales, which I once had fun exploring when I was having a little break at Llandudno. (The next day was very misty so I missed walking on the Great Orme and seeing the goats. Remember the goats coming into town during the first coronavirus lockdown?) Now Conwy I can see as a *bastide,* but I didn't have Cowbridge down as one. And apparently Wallingford, which isn't too far from me, and has a brilliant fabric shop so I'll go and have a peek before long.

Back to Cordes; as recently as 1993 the town's name changed from simple Cordes to Cordes-sur-Ciel to indicate its height above the clouds that gather in the river valley (it is 1050m at its highest). It can be very touristy but mainly with day visitors and on our arrival, we found it fairly quiet. When we reached it, we saw that the street through the Porte des Ormeaux went straight up (very up). We went to the top and found a hotel overlooking the market hall, very pleasant and we thought very reasonable for such a grockly place. We had a beer and did the tour – we particularly liked the houses and gardens on the slopes. The restaurants were all closing, and we just caught one near the hotel. The service was appalling but the meal wasn't bad and we had a fragrant rosé by the name of Greddé. After a little more pottering, the rosé was beginning to kick in so we retired to bed.

We were up to see the sunrise which shows how much later it is at that time of year. We breakfasted on the terrace of the hotel with a friendly West Highland Terrier, then cycled down the town 'tail' to a big busy square which was fun. We bought a picnic, and cycled down a valley, then slowly up again with lovely views back to Cordes. We passed over the Gaillac plateau, finding an excellent picnic site (Dahb is very fussy about picnic places but good at finding them) by a wood near a very quiet road. We reached Gaillac town at 5pm and found it very busy – presumably due to schools coming out and rush hour. There were loads of coaches. We found Turismu and a Midi-Pyrénées hotel guide, and the Turismu chap very kindly rang round. The hotels were very busy, he said, but he booked us in at Hôtel de Paris, just out of the old town. It was marvellous, a very friendly *patron*, 20 euros for the room, no frills but all mod cons except breakfast, which isn't a problem in a town. Some German cyclists turned up, having flown their bikes from Frankfurt to Montpellier – the cheapest way. One of them told us, in the forthright way some Germans have, that it was impossible to explore the Auvergne on our Bromptons. Too late, chum.

We walked round Gaillac and rather took to it. There is nothing twee but much intriguing old stuff. It lies on the north bank of the Tarn and there is much pink brick as in Albi and Toulouse. We went to walk over a bridge and found it was a viaduct over another road. We found a nice pizzeria in Place Libé and just by way of a change, had a bottle of wine – a Gaillac perlé by the name of Gaysson, I think.

Friday 13th! We breakfasted in Place Libé and as there was a market going on, there was lots to watch and lots of yummy stuff on offer. Yes, Gaillac was a very good place. We left it on a quiet route, finding some back roads on the left bank of the Tarn towards Toulouse. It was sunny and hot and there was a lot of interesting stuff to see to do with the river (Gaillac had been surrounded by rather flat monoculture).

On Dahb's brother-in-law's recommendation we visited Lisle-sur-Tarn, which was lovely. Lunch was eaten in an enormous square after we had done the tour. There was a huge pink church with a pretty garden and lots of incredible Mediaeval buildings. We met an Englishman who had retired there. He told us that property prices were rising, and that London had had extremely heavy rain on Monday. We didn't need to know any of this, but Monday was the day we arrived in Mordagne in glorious weather, so we allowed ourselves to feel smug.

We went on for 15km or so to St-Sulpice and boarded a very crowded train for Toulouse. On arrival, Dahb went off hotel hunting and found one for 43 euros bang opposite the station, so we went in and installed selves. The receptionist was very friendly and said the hotels were always busy owing to the aerospace industry so we counted our blessings and dove into the city, having first gone back to the station to get TER tickets to Paris. We had to cross the Canal du Midi to get from the station to the hotel, which we thought was cool as it's such a major waterway and I can never get over the fact that it was built in the 17th century.

Toulouse is one of France's big cities with a conurbation population of nearly half a million. It is the capital of the new Occitanie region, and the Garonne river runs through the centre. It is known as La Ville Rose owing to the terracotta bricks of many of its buildings. We reached Place du Capitole (the name of the huge old Hôtel de Ville) which is a pedestrianised two-and-a-half-acre square. We then went down to the Garonne and the Quai de la Daurade, an old and lovely area.

After a drink in Rue Metz, watching fascinating people, we wandered off to the Cathedral (huge and pink) which with the *préfecture* is in a gorgeous quiet area – it was all very elegant. Dining in a quiet square we noted the restaurants were not busy which seemed odd on a Friday evening. Perhaps the aerospace industry works late.

Our train was at 7.27am, but we were up in time for breakfast at the station (we hadn't slept much owing to traffic). We travelled in a compartment with no one else in it until Brive when a pleasant young Frenchman joined us. At Limoges an English girl got on; she had moved to France three months ago with her partner who was a builder. He was gradually getting work (with Brits) but they needed cash, so she was going back for a month to earn some. She had been given half an hour to connect between Gare d'Austerlitz and Gare du Nord, which didn't sound long enough to us, then about four and a half hours before her flight from Charles de Gaulle airport, which is about 25km north-east of Paris. The flight was costing £5 – I know it would have cost her a lot more just to jump on Eurostar at Gare du Nord, but it would have been a lot easier.

The train arrived at Gare d'Austerlitz at 1.35pm which is most definitely lunchtime, but even after that was sorted, we still had plenty of time. We went along cycle tracks along the quays towards Quai de Bercy which I don't think we found but we saw that the track led to Vincennes, 7km or so to the east. We then took some big roads to Gare du Nord, most of which were horrible except where they were closed to motorised traffic owing to some sort of parade coming up. I wonder if I could swing it that big roads were closed every time I'm forced to cycle through Paris.

Our Eurostar left at 6.16pm and coming out of the tunnel at 7pm local time it was cloudy and therefore quite dark. The 8.45pm from Paddington was on a go slow and arrived at 10pm (normally an hour). We treated ourselves to a taxi to get home and arrived there to find a very neglected cat – that at least was the feline opinion – and no hot water as the solar switch had been turned off. We were sure it wasn't either of us, so it must have been either an itinerant switcher-offer of solar switches or our neighbour who mistook it for the immersion. Humph!

Chapter 9
The Ais

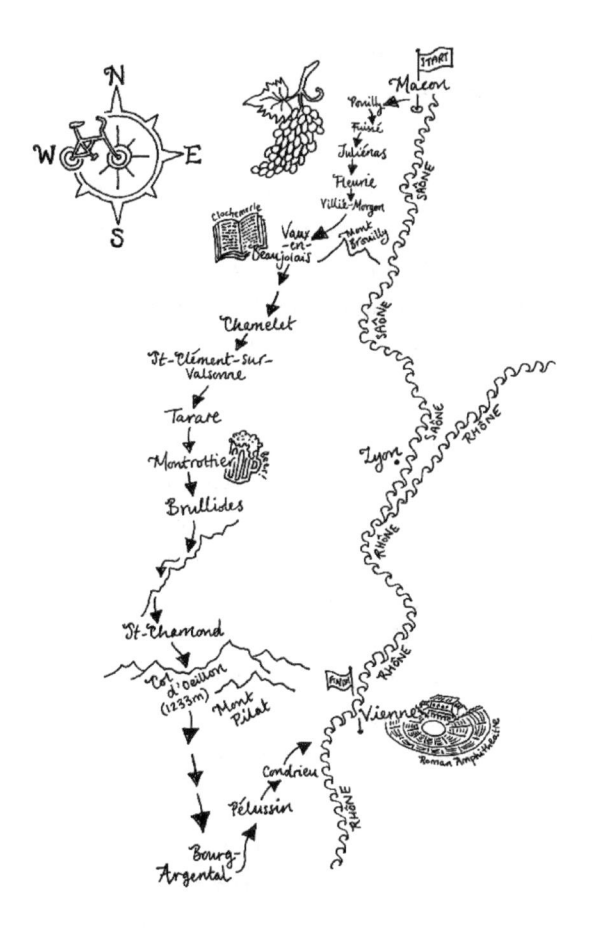

We enjoyed a couple of holidays following the 'Ais', not a river or a range of hills but a sort of fantasy region I made up consisting of (in southwards order) Charollais, Mâconnais, Beaujolais, Lyonnais and Vivarais. Chapter 4 has already described Beaujolais and Charollais and a bit of Mâconnais. Beaujolais and Mâconnais are known for their wines, Charollais for its cows. Sadly, no lions in Lyonnais, which is the region round the great city of Lyon, and Vivarais, which covers the Ardèche *département*, is named after the town of Viviers on the Rhône.

On the 10th of May 2003, we set out for Mâcon, somewhat early in the year for which there presumably was a good reason. We also had only a week. We hadn't finished with Beaujolais so our intention was to head south and see how far we could get before it was time to go home on the 17th.

I had booked a hotel and, having left Swindon at 6.30am and changed at Lille and Lyon, we arrived in Mâcon soon after 4pm. The Hôtel Concorde was very pleasant and friendly, our room being round the back looking onto a little garden. We walked round Mâcon noting how many roses there were for the time of year. Another thing about Mâcon is the southern-type tiles – it is thought by many to be the first southern town. We crossed the river to St-Laurent-sur-Saône for a delicious meal accompanied by wine from 'just up the road' though I can't for the life of me remember the name.

Sunday 11th May dawned, and it was Dahb's birthday, so we would be looking for somewhere lunchey at lunchtime. We headed south south-west, cycling through Pouilly and

Fuissé (put those together and you have one of my favourite wines). Soon we were in Beaujolais and arrived at the wine village of Juliénas at beer time. We were now, just, in Rhône-Alpes, the historical province and wine-producing region of Beaujolais covering part of the Rhône *département* and part of Saône-et-Loire which is in Burgundy.

We were approached by an elderly local who insisted on buying us another drink and who talked volubly in a heavy accent. He drove off after two Pernods with a great crashing of gears. We went on to Fleurie where the wines are apparently fine and light and should be drunk young. I'm sure we did that with our lunch which we ate outside in the sun. Here we heard the only English voices of the week but saw no British cars, so we presumed they had hired a French one. They didn't look as if they had come by bicycle.

We continued via Villié-Morgon (pickled adder country and there was a corner of the road with some tree fluff which we recognised immediately) and round Mont Brouilly (wine from its slopes is Côte de Brouilly) and other places to Vaux-en-Beaujolais. This had been the plan and I had telephoned earlier to secure digs in the Auberge de Clochemerle for this is the village on which the famous tale by Gabriel Chevalier was based. Dahb rang his parents, having to lean out of our bedroom window at a precarious angle to get a signal. How modern, to use a mobile. This was his 53rd birthday and way back in 2000, telephoning from Aups, he had to use a telephone box!

After dinner we did the tour and found the, or a, *pissotière* made famous by Chevalier, in the square by the church. Dahb made use of it, but he might as well have used the middle of the square for all the fuss it would have caused – the place was as dead as a doornail.

We had a short walk before breakfast and noticed the Bromptons had disappeared, but they were soon found tucked up nice and warm in the garage. After a fine climb, some of it by footpath, we came down to Chamelet where we found a café and ordered beer and *croque monsieur*. As we were waiting, Dahb cleared his throat and announced in a well-projected tone quite unlike his usual mumble, '*J'ai pissé à Clochemerle!*'. There was a stunned silence from the few people by the bar, then a mannishly dressed woman saw the light and cried '*Ah, il a pissé à Clochemerle!*', hardly enlightening the others much until she explained that he must be talking about Vaux-en-Beaujolais. As the others made '*Ah! Mais oui! Bien sûr!*' noises, she came over and said she was a journalist from the local *La Patriote Beaujolais* and were those our bicycles outside? She took a picture of us and the Bromptons and made lots of notes, taking our address and promising to send the article which would have the dazzling headline '*Ils ont pissé à Clochemerle!*' (It was very kind to include me, but I made no claim to have used the *pissotière*.) We felt dizzy with fame and eagerly awaited the article, but we heard nothing from her and felt deeply betrayed.

After lunch and all this excitement, we climbed up to 650m and had a long walk through a lovely valley which was a nice rest for Modestine as she only had to carry my luggage. There was a field carpeted with dandelion clocks and broom recolonising where trees had been felled. We went down alongside a stream, not in it for once, then found a back road to St-Clément-sous-Valsonne. I had telephone-booked the *Logis* which was just as well as it looked extremely closed and we might have felt we should go on otherwise. The restaurant was indeed closed to non-residents. We walked around – another doornail-dead place. But it was very sunny, so we sat happily on the hotel terrace with beers and books. Two Germans and a Frenchman joined us – they were drinking champers. We chatted, then it was time for dinner, which was very good. There were also two German women staying and two single men – a veritable throng.

It was a bit rainy next morning as we climbed over to Tarare which wasn't very attractive, but had the wherewithal for a picnic. It lies on the delightfully named Turdine river. We ate lunch in a sheltered lane, serenaded by frogs in a nearby pond. Above Montrottier I phoned ahead to book a hotel in Brullioles. We were now in the Monts du Lyonnais so celebrated with a beer in Montrottier, which sounds as if our Alsatian-Rotty ought to have come from there, and arrived at Brullioles to find a funeral party finishing at our hotel. It was a very nice place, and we had a huge room with loo nearby.

The weather was getting better and better so we pottered around until 7pm dinner which was excellent – no menu, just what you were given. We had finished by 8.15pm and were sent upstairs, though with a carafe of wine so we were quite content to sit and read for the rest of the evening. Holidays ought to be a time to catch up with reading but we don't find we read much. During the day we're on the move, consulting maps and guidebooks or writing the dratted diary. At bedtime we'll read a page or two and then – zonk.

We bought the next day's lunch in the village and then set off. We achieved a lunchtime beer and then apparently had lunch with ants. We had earlier seen ants crossing the road and then saw they had gone ten feet up a sweet chestnut tree.

We cycled along a marvellous ridge and the weather was now glorious. There were hen harriers, male and female, quartering a field – always a lovely sight. We went up hill and down dale, and over a final *col* and down to St-Chamond. This is quite a big town but there was very little going on. However, we found a hotel which looked seedy but was quite all right, found a beer with some difficulty and a restaurant, Le Chalet, with a little more ease. We were now in Loire, having crossed the *département* border a little earlier.

The next day, Thursday, it was a little tricky getting out of town, but the weather was fabulous. We got up quite high, the Col d'Oeillon being about the highest one could get to by road at 1233m. We were in the Mont Pilat regional park, and Pilat itself is 1432m so we weren't far off. We arrived at the *col* about 4pm having walked a fair way, lots of cyclists rushing past. There were views to the snowy Alps and a can of beer available at a little café. We went down and down and soon after 6pm arrived at Bourg-Argental where we secured a room in a very pleasant hotel. My diary says I had a hot bath so I think it must have been a little chilly. My mind's eye does see me wearing an anorak at the top and the wind was a bit northerly.

Bourg is a very pleasant little town, originally fortified. We found a bar and tried to get one large beer and one small but were met with disapproving glances and served with one small and one *very* small. Back at the hotel we had an excellent dinner with a bottle of Baumes de Venise. B&B, dinner and wine cost 91 euros (compare Vaux 129). Not a trace of Domestos, and why would there be, you might ask. Read on …

The next day we bought some strawberries and ate them overlooking a fruit farm. They were not very good at all, but we were able to look forward to our own starting soon. It was a beautiful day with a warm southerly wind, much better than the north-westerly we had been grappling with. We came to Pélussin, an interesting old town with ancient *halles* (covered market halls) and narrow steep streets. There were roses again – too cold for them in other places we'd passed through. We had a beer in the square then saw signs to a restaurant in Chuyer. We sat outside for lunch but had to hold down the tablemats and the croutons, even the chairs, the wind having got up as soon as we sat down. But it was an excellent lunch.

We were aiming for Vienne, and we didn't pass through anywhere much but there was lots of downhill, Vienne being on the Rhône. Quite near the town and just before a footbridge Dahb got a puncture which luckily he didn't need to mend until we'd got home. We walked into Vienne and found a room in Hôtel de la Poste which was very nice and very central. Starting at the station to check trains, we foot-toured Vienne and found a particularly fine grocer/greengrocer where we bought our favourite salad oil – walnut. The town is a great place for Roman remains with the largest Roman theatre outside Rome. We had our beer by the Temple of Augustus and Livia and there was a very Mediterranean feel to it all, with outside cafés, all pleasant and friendly and not a Brit to be heard or seen. The French 'yoof' were very much in evidence outside our hotel, however, so it was a rather noisy night. But apart from that, it was a great holiday with no hitches although it's a shame I didn't know a *friture* would be whitebait.

We had lunch at the Irish pub in Lille on the way home, and arrived at Swindon after 5pm, going straight from the station to a wedding party. What a stressful existence.

**

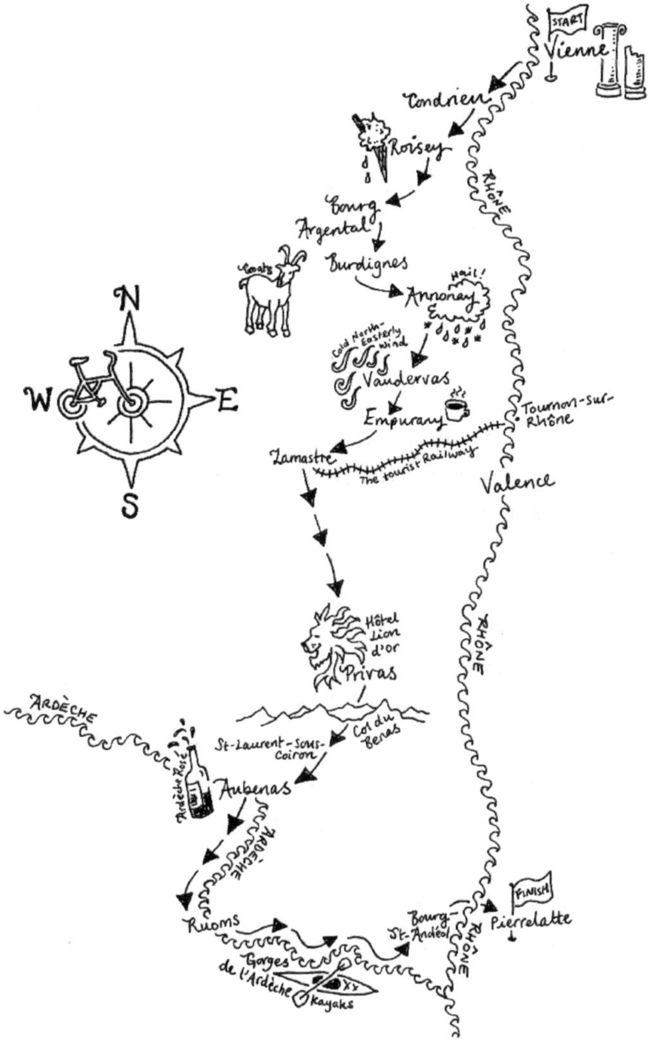

START
Vienne
Condrieu
Roisey
RHÔNE
Bourg Argental
Burdignes
Goats
N
W
E
S
Annonay
Hail!
Cold North-Easterly wind
Vaudervas
Empurany
Tournon-sur-Rhône
Lamastre
The tourist Railway
Valence
Hôtel Lion d'or
Privas
RHÔNE
ARDÈCHE
Col du Benas
St-Laurent-sous-Coiron
Ardèche Rosé
Aubenas
ARDÈCHE
Ruoms
Gorges de l'Ardèche
Kayaks
Xx
Bourg-St-Andéol
RHÔNE
FINISH
Pierrelatte

It was a couple years before we returned to Vienne in order to continue our journey through the Ais. Again we set off in mid-May, though after Dahb's birthday this time, and again we stayed at Hôtel de la Poste. And again it was a noisy night, but we were very comfortable and Dahb at least slept well. We had had a drink at the same café by the Temple of Augustus and Livia but had dinner at a Maître Kanter where we were given a free aperitif on account of the hotel we were in.

Before breakfast the next morning we walked up to the Belvedere of Mont Pipet, a 19th century chapel on the site of a Roman fort. There were fine views, but rolling mist was coming down the Gère valley. Before leaving we bought our picnic at the market and were pleased to find some radishes. Quite often there are none, which suggests I might not be the only one who finds them difficult to grow. We tried a cycle track by the Rhône, but it soon ran out and we crossed to a small suburban road with a lot of fine villas. It was a bit busy getting through an industrial zone but then we were on a small road between the river and the railway. There were swans and lots of fishermen. We passed a marina and then reached Condrieu by a 19th-century suspension bridge which had been destroyed by the Germans and subsequently rebuilt. Apparently the largest market of the region is held here, and the port was once known for its sailors – not sure what they got up to but sailors will be sailors.

We had beer at Condrieu with a curly-headed dog, then found a little road out, picnicking on a bench before a short cut up a bridleway to a panorama. We revisited Pélussin and crossed the valley by a pedestrian bridge on which cyclists were tolerated at 'feeble speed'. In a village called Roizey we bought a magnificent blackcurrant ice-cream made in Switzerland by Mövenpick and I now keep my eyes peeled for it. We went through St-Julien-Molin-Molette which we remembered as we had bought stamps there in 2003. We then took a different route to Bourg-Argental, extremely steep but shortish and magnificent. The weather had been beautiful all day. I think we were now well into the Vivarais.

We found the hotel we'd stayed in before. I had booked it from home though with a little difficulty. When I dialled the number I got through to a private house, but the very friendly lady occupant explained that France had changed all its telephone numbers and she very kindly looked up and gave me the number I wanted. So, with that one fell swoop all the guides we had collected over the years were rendered somewhat useless.

In the hotel, the same Madame welcomed us, remembering us and our bicycles. We were given a very nice room in the same annexe as before but, alas, all did not go so well from there …

We showered and changed, intending to have a drink on the terrace, but it was very full so we went in search of the bar we'd used two years earlier, forgetting the rather Puritan approach to alcohol. Dahb asked for a demi-litre and the *patron* nearly fell over in shock. He eventually got it, and a whole 25cl for me (I don't think I'd been allowed that much in 2003). We explained that drinking pints was the English way, but he insisted it was not normal. I think when the French suggest one is not normal they don't mean to be as rude as it sounds. A young French friend told me he thought my cooking was not normal, but I was relieved to find he was paying me a compliment. He was staying with a landlady in Radstock (as if that explains everything) and all she seemed to cook was burgers and chips. He was also tickled to see me digging up some potatoes and we agreed it was going to be a real *menu du terroir*.

Back to the hotel for dinner, just us and a French couple. I ordered *crudités* and the dressing tasted of something very dubious. Dahb tried it and agreed so I pointed it out to Madame. She took it away, explaining that her husband, the chef, would have used *vinaigre de la maison*, implying I was too pathetic to appreciate it. She said that as I didn't like it (who would have?) she would make me a nice salad with an oil and lemon dressing. It was fresh lemon all right but I'm not sure she put in the oil, and we couldn't help suspecting it was deliberate and I was being punished for rejecting her husband's special vinegar (special, indeed). The rest of the meal was good, but the fun had rather gone out of the evening. I didn't sleep much which was probably due to food poisoning. It rained heavily all night, but I suppose we couldn't blame them for that.

Breakfast was good and we got some new hotel guides from

Turismu. We climbed up and up, with the weather clearing until we got to the hamlet of Burdignes. There were goats on the way and very contented cows in lush pasture which had a sub-alpine look (the village is at about 900m). As we neared the building we saw the words *Ferme-Auberge* and Dahb said 'Oh, look, it's closed' which is our little joke and usually true. But this *auberge* was open and doing a roaring trade inside. Several generations of family farmed there and ran the restaurant, a chambre d'hôte, gîte, campings and farm shop – all very enterprising, and we took two and a half hours over a delicious lunch with a nice white Jonquières from the Languedoc which isn't very far away.

But a visit to the loo was interesting. As I entered a whiff assailed me, redolent of the *vinaigrette* at Bourg-Argental. In a loo it was fine, and it seemed to be coming from a bottle of Domestos or something similar. So did someone get their bottles mixed up?

The *patronne*, when after chatting she found we loved *la France profonde* (the wild and woolly bits of France) and hated our fellow countrypersons, on holiday anyway, said they didn't get many English there but she and her husband had gone on holiday to the Lot which was like an English colony. The *patron* of a restaurant they went to was amazed to find they were French as they didn't get many of those round there. (In our neighbourhood we say, "Not from round 'ere, are you?" to anyone who isn't local, i.e. lives round the corner.)

It was fine outside, but chilly (we'd dined inside as it was a bit draughty) so we donned anoraks and made our way down to Annonay through hillsides of burnt trees — I think someone told us they had had fires in a heatwave. It was quite a busy road into town, but we found a semi-pedestrianised square with Hôtel du Midi where we got a marvellous and cheap room at the back for 38 euros, with loo and douche. We pottered around this rather seedy but interesting town. Annonay is in the Ardèche *département* and it was from here that the Montgolfier brothers made their first balloon flight in 1783, and Séguin was also born here in 1786. He improved the steam boiler so much George Stephenson used it for his Rocket.

We made it to Café du Midi just as the heavens opened with torrential hail. We sat under the canopy which was dripping a bit and a large wet dog came along. We were worried he was going to shake all over us, but he passed us and shook all over a Frenchman whose friends nearly died with laughter as they said he was the only one amongst them who didn't like dogs. Animals do have wonderful instincts.

After thirty minutes of torrent, we moved off to find food in the only restaurant open (it was Monday) but it was excellent and we also enjoyed a Côte du Rhône 'Blason' – quite a pale red which is fine when it's supposed to be summer.

The next morning, we were away quite early having

shopped for food and stamps, presumably in order to send postcards. We are getting lazier and lazier about writing cards, but we do keep a few people on our list and thus the lucky things hear from us twice a year, the other time being Christmas (also a dwindling list). We passed through a village with the most foul loos, a *Mirage* screaming overhead and a flock of goats crammed into one corner of a field. Flock is what I wrote but surely goats come in herds? We had beer in a bar by a bridge where there was a strange *patron* and loos in a cavern. Goodness me, my diaries are full of the most fascinating detail.

Through a village named Vandervas, where there was a cat by an *auberge* that really was closed, we found shelter in a meadow for our picnic. This wasn't shelter from the beating sun, by the way, but from a chilly north-easterly wind which luckily was behind us as we cycled. We reached the lovely village of Empurany via a small road and had some coffee on the terrace of a bar/tabac. There was a cat on the till and another in a box by the fridge, presumably ready to pounce when the fridge was opened. Though really it didn't look in pouncing mode.

Then we took a fabulous mountain route with the sun coming out again after a cloudy afternoon, down to La Roue which was in the most lovely valley, lush and well-tilled … though I wrote in my diary that there was a slag heap, which seems odd. There was a 'natural' man gardening (what on earth did I mean by that?) and masses of chained dogs shrieking, though they all seemed quite friendly – an amazing place.

As we neared Lamastre, where we intended to stay, we could see the *ligne touristique*, the tourist railway we intended to go on the next day. The descent into Lamastre was steep and it seemed bigger than expected (population 2,700 according to our guide) but it was busy in a nice sort of way. I had telephoned from our picnic spot to book a room at *Logis* Les Négociants, and the room was huge. One look at it and we booked a second night. There was no one else around but the patronne was very friendly, as were her dog and cat.

We had a little wander round and a drink in the square (how many squares have we had drinks in?) then went back to our hotel for a very good meal and a Crozes-Hermitage. We dined in a slightly chilly conservatory with a cat looking at me with its eyes closed and making the occasional attempt to get on my lap. We were told that it was cold for the time of year and they had had snow earlier, which is unusual. We retired to bed and were probably asleep by 10.30pm after quite a cycley day. We reckoned we'd done 53km which isn't bad, as the terrain had been by no means flat.

Modestine and her pal had the next day off as we took the train to Tournon-sur-Rhône. We left without breakfast as we had to be at the station at 7.45am. The instructions in our leaflet were to arrive half an hour early but there was no one around. There was a train or rather a one-car autorail (sometimes steam, but that didn't fit in with our times) and eventually a man appeared through a 'no unauthorised persons' door and sold us two return tickets at 20 euros each.

The 'train' was from the 1930s, ran on a one-metre gauge, had desperately hard seats and didn't look in the least bit safe. It was a sort of Bluebell line kept open by devoted obsessives and three of them sat in the front whilst we were behind in solitary freezing splendour as we rattled down the absolutely fabulous valley of the Doux. I think someone else got on a bit further down which would have made it less solitary but no less freezing. We arrived around 9am and we hoped we could find some warmth – there was now a howling *Mistral*. We found a lovely warm *salon de thé* and had two coffees and two croissants each and read the paper. We soon felt much better!

We visited Turismu and got a town map and some wine information. Being a Wednesday, the museum was closed. We liked the town – quite old with narrow streets and a river frontage (not all towns claiming to be on a river are actually on it). We explored the ramparts and climbed up and up (nice not to be pushing the Bromptons for a change but it was a good path) to the Belvedere de la Chapelle where there was a *table d'orientation* and the most magnificent views. The flowers were lovely, too.

Now we were thoroughly orientated, we went back and explored a little more, then crossed the river by a footbridge to Tain-l'Hermitage, a very winey name. I've written here 'see Enfield' so perhaps he had adventures in Tain. I no longer have the book or it's at the bottom of a heap. It would be fun to see if our routes and opinions coincided at all.

Well, it was all very pleasant and calm on the left bank but there didn't seem to be much in the way of edibles, so we crossed the Rhône again and found a marvellous café with a conservatory which soon got too hot which made a nice change. We ordered one glass of Viognier and one of Chardonnay. We enjoyed them but couldn't tell the difference – that should make all the wine buffs drop to the ground.

We did some shopping after lunch, and according to my diary we bought a map (fair enough) and some windows (distinctly bizarre). After a little more wandering – such a nice place to wander in – we caught the 6.15pm train which was packed. Apart from us and a Dutch couple, everyone was French. The conductor talked non-stop to the French all the way to Lamastre. The views were just as good going that way and we arrived back in time to change and potter a bit (what a pottery day) before dinner in a café in town where we ordered some Viognier to confirm we couldn't tell it from Chardonnay. We also taught the waitress that the Brits have vinegar on their *frites*.

An English couple came in for coffee. We chatted and found they were from Banbury and were travelling in such a large motorhome they weren't allowed into the Duchy of

Luxembourg. They spent five months of the year in their house in the Alps and had a son in the Aveyron *département*. They were very pleasant but their coming from Banbury sounds a tad academic as they didn't seem to be there much.

Interesting diary entry for the next day, Thursday 19th May: 'Pd in hotel with dogs and small boy. ***write up*** Hôtel Lion d'Or in guidebook.'

So presumably somewhere there is a diary not typed up, or I didn't write much and need to look at the map and see if it brings back any memories. Anyway, the said Hôtel Lion d'Or is in Privas, which has a very Protestant history. In the 16th and 17th century religious wars, the town was conceded to the Protestants by Henri IV under the Edict of Nantes in 1598. In 1629 the Royal Army took it back again, with much massacring of the residents. A few years later there was a reconciliation twixt Royalty and townsfolk (the few that were un-massacred) whose loyalty was regained by the offer of a bridge over the river, and Privas was gradually rebuilt. Goodness me.

We climbed a hill to get into the town and as I turned my head to the right, the very picture from the guidebook came into view – the Lion d'Or through an arch and up a street. The picture proved to be a real hotel, open and with a very friendly lady in charge. We were soon installed and went walking, taking in a viewpoint. We had an excellent dinner on the terrace of a pizzeria and thought that Privas was very pleasant indeed and quite relaxed despite its warring history.

Getting out of town the next day was quite tricky. We crossed the Louis XIII bridge which led us to an industrial estate. The road we took out wasn't the one we were aiming for but it turned out very well. We did a lot of upping, passing a closed *auberge* at the top, then cycled along a plateau with stunning views of the Vercors, and past the site of a proposed wind farm to which there was obviously a lot of opposition. We could see one turbine in the distance, and saw a male hen harrier. At the Col du Benas we headed for Freysennet but there was no beer, no nothing. We went on down and heard the most amazing birdsong in the valley, not seeing the birds of course which is our usual way.

We went down a superb limestone gorge from which was coming the whiff of fennel, to another dead-looking place. There was a restaurant, however, and we had beer on its leafy terrace. There was a French coach party inside and they were all singing along to some sort of musician and having a jolly time. The driver was outside catching up on his fags ration.

There was a bit of up after beer as there usually is, then we went along and down. We needed shade (joy) and found it by the road, with views of St-Laurent-sous-Coiron which has black basalt houses perched on the hill. Two rather odd-looking men approached with three dogs, one of which – a large black thing – roared up to us. It was frightening at first, but it soon became clear that it was composed of marshmallow.

St-Laurent and another black village, Mirabel, are visible for miles, looking very dramatic against the skyline. We continued to go down, seeing some lovely red-backed birds from above. We thought at first they were kestrels, but they were probably too small. We now had magnificent views over the Aubenas plateau. Three lady walkers spoke to us in Dutch. People often do that because apparently, we not only look Dutch, we sound it. Especially when there are two of us speaking double you-know-what.

In Aubenas, which is perched above the Ardèche river, we found a Turismu which was shut, but there was a town map so we made our way to Place de l'Hôtel-de-Ville where we expected to find Hôtel Les Négociants – which we did (same name as in Lamastre). It was open and there was a room – a lovely one up a Mediaeval staircase. It was an amazing place, but as soon as we had showered we were out and drinking beer (who needs water?) in the square. We then pottered around without a map – very daring. There seemed to be a dearth of eating houses – had Protestantism gone too far? Then we turned a corner and found a square packed with restaurants. We had *crêpes* and some delicious Ardèche rosé, watched from a balcony by two cats and a Yorkie. At the next table four French girls giggled and smoked all the time.

We were now heading for the Ardèche gorge. On Saturday we stayed at a rather odd hotel at Ruoms, which lies on the left bank. There was no one else there, strange for a weekend. We had beer in the square and must have had dinner somewhere, otherwise the lack of it would be indelibly etched on my mind.

We set off early to get ahead of Sunday tourists, finding breakfast at a very nice campsite *en route*. Our ride down the Ardèche was wonderful, though a lot of it was up owing to it being a *corniche* road. We had superb views of canoeists far below. There was a sort of local Tour de France going on, so we hung around a bit to let them all get past. At the top they just *hurtled* down, most alarmingly.

We saw some British cars, the first all week. It was nearing lunchtime, but I suggested keeping going as it was likely that the tourists would stop for lunch and so the road would be quieter. This proved to be a good wheeze though I wouldn't have been popular if the restaurant we found just before St-Martin had shut. I think they were closed, really, but the family was eating on the terrace, and they tossed us the odd crumb so all was well. More than the odd crumb, of course – it was a delicious lunch.

The Ardèche isn't a particularly long river, rising not far from the source of the Loire but, my golly, it packs some punch. Michelin says it ranks among the most impressive sites of natural beauty in the south of France, which I think is fair 'nuff, though I'd be tempted to scrub out the 'south' bit. The river joins the Rhône at Pont-Saint-Esprit but we hove off northish after lunch and reached Bourg-St-Andéol which was an odd sort of place. But there was a very nice *Logis* with *vinaigre de la maison* which was distinctly superior to that of the other Bourg.

Monday 23rd May was our last day. We cycled two or three miles over the plain to Pierrelatte, which had a station. We liked the look of it and wished we'd found it the night before. Taking a local train to Lyon, we had some time to wait. There were no luggage trolleys, all having been stolen we were told. We took it in turns to wander about. I needed some bits and bobs, presents for the neighbours and that sort of thing, and had to use the most ghastly, huge Carrefour supermarket in which there was perfectly good stuff. Our neighbours look after not only however many cats we have at the time (nowadays usually only one but there were three at one point) but plants in three glasshouses. So they do deserve a little something.

When Dahb was on his walkabout I was half reading a paper I'd found and half chatting to a lady sharing my bench. She looked around furtively, then leaned over and said in a warning sort of voice, did I realise I was reading a Communist newspaper. The tone she adopted would have suited a warning against the hardest of porn mags. I thanked her very much and said that I didn't think it would do me much harm. At last, a train to Lille arrived and we were on the way to London, Swindon, and home, doubtless to a whingeing feline and a lot to do in the garden.

Chapter 10
Alsace, the contested region

Hundreds of millions of years ago an upheaval of the earth's crust pushed up the bedrock of the Vosges mountains and what is now the *massif* of the Black Forest. Later the area in the middle sank to form the Rhine valley – the Alsatian plain. In geology this is known as 'horst and graben' (eyrie and trench, i.e., high bits and the low bit between).

Until the reorganisation in January 2016 and although not the smallest in population, Alsace was geographically the smallest administrative region; it has now joined Champagne-Ardennes and Lorraine to form Grand Est. The economic and cultural capital as well as the largest city of Alsace is wonderful Strasbourg, the seat of many international organisations. It remains the capital of the new region.

For more than 300 years, from the Thirty Years' War to World War II, the political status of Alsace has been heavily contested between France and various German states in many wars and diplomatic conferences. In the Thirty Years' War (1618-48), one of the longest and most destructive conflicts in history (it was about religion, of course), Alsace was particularly badly affected, becoming a battleground with armies tramping to and fro. An example of damage done in this long war is found in the great Mediaeval castle of Haut Koenigsburg which was besieged by Protestant Swedish forces. After a 52-day siege they burned and looted it and it remained unused until the end of the 19th century when the local council cunningly (so that he could pay for it) offered it to Kaiser Bill who did it up as a bijou residence, only to see it return to the French in 1918 after he'd spent all that money on it. We met some Swedes on electric bikes and suggested they keep quiet about their origins.

The Thirty Years' War came to an end with the Treaty of Westphalia which awarded Alsace to France, confirmed in 1678 by the Treaty of Nijmegen. At the end of the Franco-Prussian War (1870-71), Alsace and part of Lorraine, including Metz but not Nancy or Verdun, fell into German hands. In 1918 these areas rejoined France but suffered more years of occupation in the Second World War, finally returning to France at the end of the war – at least one hopes it's final. In 1949 the Council of Europe was established in Strasbourg, and in 1993 it was confirmed as the seat of the European Parliament.

When not at war, trade with Germany and Switzerland has been important, that great waterway the Rhine contributing to regional prosperity. Many crops are grown on the fertile plain, but the long strip along the foot of the Vosges is used almost exclusively for grapes which make up about half of overall crop production in the region – the seven grape varieties of Alsace (though it does seem to depend on who's counting).

On Saturday 5th June 2004, we left home at 7.40am after the most hectic week and made a note never again to go away when both sets of helpful neighbours were away. I gave detailed garden instructions and Beatrice, the next-door mutt, to other friends in the village and we pedalled furiously to reach Swindon station in 35 minutes, catching the 8.20am to

Paddington.

We arrived at Waterloo as the previous train was also checking in, causing bedlam, but when it had gone peace reigned. We had coffee then caught the 11.40am to Paris, walking round to have a beer opposite the Gare de l'Est. We then realised the station clock was slow, so only just caught the train to Nancy.

We were changing trains at Nancy so took a loaded luggage trolley to a café opposite the station and had dinner, in a bit of a rush. We then caught a little train to St-Dié-des-Vosges which is in the Lorraine region, and a fellow passenger told us all about the area including the fact that St-Dié was the *marraine* (godmother) of America. It turned out that the name 'America' was conjured up by 16th century St-Dié sages to name the land discovered by Amerigo Vespucci.

Dumping our stuff in the prebooked Hôtel des Vosges and discovering that the man I had spoken to on the telephone was a very nice woman with a smoker's voice, we walked round the town to look at the *son et lumière*, recommended by our friend from the train. It was just *lumière*, as it usually is, which suits us fine. Sights to see included the Tour de la Liberté which was erected in Paris for the bicentenary of the Revolution and transferred to St-Dié afterwards. It was white and modern and apparently the view from the top was splendid, though we didn't go up. Poor old St-Dié has been partly destroyed by fire four times, the last being at the end of the Second World War. Let's hope the Tour de la Liberté helps to make up for it.

The next morning, we had a daylight walk round the cathedral and cloisters and admired the fine modern traffic-free square. Then we set off to cross the Vosges into Alsace. Before starting the climb, we cycled along the valley and by Saulcy-sur-Meurthe found a First War German cemetery which was beautiful. After some tricky navigation through the forest and Mandray village, Dahb triumphed and brought us out at a *col* of 1007 metres, then we went slightly down to Col des Bagenelles at 903m. There were grockles and *motos* everywhere, but it was a whizz down to Le Bonhomme and beer. We were now in Alsace. We were also in the Ballons des Vosges Regional Nature Park, and I think we stayed in it for most of the trip. It was designated in 1989 and is one of the largest and most populated French regional parks. Apparently there are lynx, but of course *we* didn't see any.

Then great excitement. Coming towards us was an elderly gentleman in blue overalls, pushing a Brompton along a perfectly flat piece of pavement. We learned during our long fan club chat that he'd had to go to Paris to buy it and had had several modifications effected. For some reason I think he came from Toulouse, and I don't remember him having any luggage.

We then took another forest road, a very steep one with wonderful views to the Rhine and the Black Forest. After getting a bit lost we made it to Orbey where there were supposed to be two or three campings, but they all seemed to be out of the village and it felt a bit chilly at 600m, so we weedily opted for a nice warm *Logis*. After an excellent meal with Sylvaner and Muscat, we crashed out quite early.

A word about the wines of Alsace, which we tested assiduously on every possible occasion. The vineyards are concentrated in a narrow strip, roughly north to south, on the lower eastern slopes of the Vosges, with the Rhine to the east. It is said to be the sunniest region in France, and Colmar is the driest city. The seven grape varieties are Riesling, Gewürztraminer, Sylvaner, Pinots Blanc and Gris (or Tokay Pinot Gris as it's known), Muscat and the only red, Pinot Noir. As I say, accounts do seem to differ as to the number of varieties but seven are quite enough, or too many, for us to remember. Edelzwicker often pops up – not a variety but a blend.

Orbey is in the valley of the Weiss river, and we enjoyed a pre-breakfast wander through the village and a park with massive trees and an icehouse. We were joined at breakfast by a group of cyclists from Pau, a very pleasant bunch of middle-aged and retired folk. We bought our picnic from a lady whose accent was Alsatian, we suppose, and who spoke to us in German, as people often did. We like to think they looked pleased when they discovered we were English and also that they are getting economic revenge from all the German tourists for the times this contested region has been absorbed into Germany.

We were still very much in the Vosges and aimed to reach the valley of the Fecht. We climbed up to Les Trois-Épis, a tourist resort where the Virgin Mary appeared in 1491 holding three ears of corn (*épis*) as a sign of divine mercy. We managed to get some campings and hotel information from Turismu and enjoyed fabulous views to the east. We went downhill a bit for beer, then down again to Niedermorschwir, a chocolate box village in the valley.

As we came down the east side of the mountains, we were very struck by the dramatic change in climate and vegetation. On the west there were mountain ash and beech, the sort of stuff we might find at home. On the east side the acacia looked wonderful in full bloom and there were great groves of chestnuts.

We were now in wine country and cycled on through the vineyards, finding shade under a cherry tree just before Turckheim for our picnic. Here we saw our first storks–one was flying just above us. For many centuries white storks have been a yearly presence in Alsace during the warmer months and are a great feature of Alsatian folklore. With father and mother jointly raising their fledglings, they return to the same nest for their entire lives, after a winter migration of up to 15,000km, sometimes as far away as South Africa though some do stay over winter nowadays. Owing to industrialisation in the 1960s they were nearly wiped out – in Alsace down to fewer than ten mating pairs by the mid-70s. Thanks to huge conservation efforts the stork has made a comeback and there are now roughly 600 mating pairs living in Alsace.

One of the main reasons for so much mortality was electrocution by power lines crossing the storks' migratory route. It is simple enough to fix electric poles to prevent this, but progress has been painfully slow and there is continued loss by electrocution. Towns and villages erect platforms on which the storks can build their nests and there is a wonderful drawing by Hansi of a smug-looking stork clearly having just arrived back in the village, judging by the delight and amazement of the residents. Storks really do look smug and perhaps the occasional woolly head peeping out of the nests is a reason. They can also be seen in fields chomping away (if a stork can chomp) on newly cut grass. If you see a stork carrying a baby – and I have to say we have yet to see this, even after an evening testing the seven grape varieties – it has picked it up from the underground lake where the souls of the dead have been reincarnated as babies.

About Hansi: he was a native of Colmar, less well-known as Jean-Jacques Waltz, and was a caricaturist and watercolour artist. During the German occupation between 1870 and 1914 he kept alive the traditional image of Alsace with his drawings that ridiculed the Germans but portrayed the natives as good-natured and likeable in their regional costume.

We explored Turckheim, finding it to be a lovely place and

its Porte de Brand was dubbed the gateway to the Munster valley which was exactly where we wanted to go. We bought some postcards and headed up the vale of Munster, or the Fecht valley, by road I think, not finding the cycle track until later. The Fecht river joins the Ill at Illhausern, north of Colmar. At a village called Wihr-au-Val we found a lovely campings, Au Moulin, where there was one other tent whose occupants were out when we arrived but whose car declared them to be Dutch. There were loos, hot showers, a field with a stream – perfect. After setting up camp we went off to hunt for drink and food, possibly a problem on Monday evening. But we found the cycle track to Munster and at the next village, Gunsbach, we found a campsite with a bar, and had beer in the evening sun.

Then we continued to Munster, the track dumping us on the main road via an industrial estate, seemingly not being a wholly completed track. Munster was quite a big and busy place, though more peaceful in the back streets. It derives its name from a 7th century monastery built by Irish monks, and is famous for its cheese of the same name. We found Auberge de l'Alsacienne behind the church and had a nice meal on the pavement. That is what I wrote but I distinctly remember a table and chairs. We chose a Tokay Pinot Gris but it wasn't terribly interesting. Next to us, touring on a 1100cc motorcycle, were two jolly Flemish persons – very jolly indeed.

We heard a clacking noise and looking up, saw storks on the church roof. Storks don't really speak but announce their presence by a loud clattering of their bills. The Flems said the building behind had lots of nests, so we went to look afterwards, and it did, with plenty on the church as well. Feeling we'd had a good stork experience that day we zoomed back to the campings down a minor road which was closed for roadworks at the Munster end and therefore quiet. It was still just light as we crawled into bed at 10.30pm.

The next morning dawned fabulous. A tree was shading the tent but once Dahb had hunted down some croissants we moved breakfast operations nearer the stream where it was sunny. Fortunately, the stream hadn't moved any nearer the tent in the night, which can happen. We once camped by some boulders in Yugoslavia and in the morning found we were by, but luckily not in, a sizeable watercourse, snowmelt having apparently occurred overnight. This Alsatian stream behaved itself impeccably and flowed where it was meant to.

There was no campsite management in view, so we departed without paying though it was quite obvious we were intending to stay another night. We headed off up the Krebsbach valley, stopping at Soultzbach-les-Bains to buy our picnic. Soultzbach is a spa and is described as a Mediaeval city. It's certainly not a large one but there are a lot of timber-framed houses looking very pretty with flowers everywhere.

The road went up to Wasserbourg, then up and up and, fortunately, to Auberge Ried for beer and a whole bottle of fizzy water. There were lots of French walkers and, luckily for us, they went indoors for lunch so we could grab their shady table. We were about to get up and continue on our way when I discovered a collie was lying on my foot, one of two nice dogs belonging to the house (the *patron* was also jolly though his accent was quite a problem). The collie adopted us and snuggled up to me in a craven sort of way when told off for attacking a visiting Labrador. There was also a cow wandering around – it was a great place and there was a lovely view of Le Hohneck (1362m).

Le Hohneck is one of the most famous and one of the highest summits of the Vosges mountains and is the highest point of the ridge which, before the First World War, marked the border between France and Germany. In clear weather the summits of the Alps are visible, but we didn't see them because a) we didn't climb to the top and b) if we had done, you can guarantee that a bank of cloud would immediately appear out of nowhere and spoil the view. And the guidebook says, 'Beware of freezing winds near the summit', so we might have died. No vultures here, though, to swoop in on our cadavers, but I wonder about storks? Anyway, we were on the wrong side of the valley.

We did yet more climbing, then had lunch on (yes, *on*) a shady footpath near another *auberge*, some pony trekkers using the first perfect picnic spot. There was a fine view back to Wasserbourg which has 9th century origins and a 13th century castle. There was still no way but up, so up we went, past a third *auberge* and round the Petit Ballon (1272m) on an open flat road in searing heat in the middle of the afternoon – typical. We had gone up from 321m to 1160m, and having done that it was now time to go down.

We whizzed down to Sondernach where the altitude is about 500-600m in the centre. We didn't stop as we were on a mission to find ice-cream, which we found further down in Metzeral, back in the Fecht valley. The clouds had been building up and it started to rain, but by an incredible miracle we were sitting on a bar's covered terrace. It was still very hot. We looked for the station, knowing it was the end of the line from Colmar, but there appeared to be none, although there was a train. We found a cycle track back to Munster via Muhlbach which is the birthplace of the German publisher Johann Carolus, founder of the earliest known newspaper in 1605. The train passed us which was very exciting.

We found a nice way into Munster this time, and got a regional timetable at the station. We parked the cycles in the square, under the eye of the storks, and flopped into a bar for a beer. Exploring Munster, we found a stork enclosure and a lady feeding the birds helped by a cat, the storks flying in and out like geese.

Hunting for food we found, well hidden, Caveau Marcaires behind Turismu. It was a very friendly place and we enjoyed a good meal on the terrace, jugs of iced water interspersed with a lovely Ingersheim Riesling. There were amusing dogs to watch, and a paper with the *météo* which said it was going to be hot. Back at the camp we managed to pay and to book in for another night.

A rarity occurred – I slept well, in a tent. Dahb went on a croissant hunt the next morning; the *boulanger* in Gunsbach was closed on Wednesday so he came back to the one in Wihr, which was not terribly good, but otherwise we enjoyed our breakfast by the stream, and I noted that it was pretty damn hot by 8.45am. Time to head for the hills.

We started on the same route via Soultzbach, stopping this time to take a proper look at it. Forking left up the road, we climbed gently and coolly through the Forêt Reculée de Soultzmatt reaching a mere 720m before descending again to Osenbach. Going down to the village we had a great view of the highest mountain in Alsace, le Grand Ballon (1424m) so gave it a 'done, tick'. There were pretty tall pink scented flowers – stocks, perhaps?

Arriving in Soultzmatt, we followed signs to a bar and cycled straight onto the terrace which was in a stable. We drank beer and a bottle of *Liesbeth*, the local mineral water (there was a posh spa being done up). It was really icy and tasted good.

Then we found Restaurant 'Better' which, though declaring it was closed, served us a cold platter and a chilled Pfaffenheim Riesling. We took our time, sitting on the cool terrace opposite a very smart-looking Mairie. Some boys were having water fights by the fountain. We foolishly omitted to fill up our water bottles.

Whereas most sensible animals would find shade, we went on even though it was piping hot – the *météo* had suggested 34 degrees and it certainly felt like it. Passing through Westhalten we took back roads northwards to Pfaffenheim where if there was nothing else there was a lovely fountain for face splashing, but the *eau* was '*non potable*'. Another fountain had a tap which was broken. We went on to Gueberschwihr where again there was little sign of life, but Dahb got our bottles filled at a pharmacy, which was a relief.

We were now more or less on the plain, though having reached it naturally we went up again a bit, on to Voegtlinshoffen and Husseren-les-Châteaux which at 380m is the highest point of the Alsatian vineyards. The 'les Châteaux' refers to the three belonging to Eguisheim which is the starting point for the Route des Cinq Châteaux–how confusing can you get? At last, we were in the wine village of Eguisheim and there we found 'Le Café' run by an Australian-educated German. We drank two bottles of Perrier and a jug of water on a cool terrace, the time now being 7pm. We had a look at Eguisheim which is very pretty, if touristy, not that there were many tourists around at that time.

We went back by the cycle track having had some difficulty in finding it (typical of cycle tracks). We had our eyes peeled for beer spots and eventually found a rather dismal looking hotel by the main road, in or just out of Wintzenheim. But the terrace was shady and cool and there was beer, so that was fine. Then it was cycle track back to Wihr–firstly by a main road and then the proper track though the woods above the road and the railway. There were rollerbladers all over the place. We reached the *auberge* by the station just as it closed, so whizzed up to the Pizzeria by the crossroads.

It was 9.10pm and the room was empty, but the waitress set to with a will, and we were soon munching *tarte flambée* and drinking Edelswicker, the blend of wines that the waitress said she used for cooking. We felt it was important to try it and it was all right, not very exciting. She had the right idea. Dahb finished with a strawberry melba with extremely nice strawberries – I know because I nicked some. The restaurant was supposed to be open until midnight, but the waitress was firmly shutting up as we left – not that that detracted from the warm welcome she had given us.

Well, it had been quite a day. We sauntered back to the campsite, of which we were now the only occupants, and very nobly stayed awake long enough to have showers.

It was time to leave the Fecht valley and our lovely campsite. We didn't know it at the time, but it was to be our last Brompton camping trip and with the site and the weather, we certainly went out on a high note. Dahb went to Soultzbach on a quest for better croissants, which they weren't much. But in the sun with a coffee, well, it wasn't all bad.

We left nothing but flattened grass and took the lovely cycle track back to Wintzenheim and thence to Turckheim. On the way in, we talked to a lady with a lovely garden and an interesting plant that turned out to be a camouflaged cat. After coffee, shopping, and a wander round Turckheim we went on to Ingersheim, whence the Riesling we had drunk with our second Munster dinner. In Ammerschwir we had a beer on the terrace of a hotel sporting a notice saying there was no service on the terrace, and in Kientzheim we had a 'shady picnic with Germans' which sounds like something out of a spy novel. From the wooden benches we sat on we could see the road up to Riquewihr; it seemed to be a hidden valley as cars kept disappearing.

We could just see the Nécropole Nationale on the hill where German soldiers were buried facing the Fatherland. Dahb and I are booked into our local woodland burial site, and I would like to be buried facing Liddington Hill. I thought I'd better mention this to the world as Dahb might forget, not that I'm going first. I always say that the one who does the cooking controls the cyanide.

In Riquewihr we eventually found the campings, but it was a bit out of town and rather big and busy with camper vans. It had also been getting cloudier and closer and we wondered if rain was coming, so we tried to find a bed. A nice looking *chambre d'hôte* on the way back to Riquewihr was run by a grumpy woman who said it was two nights minimum and we felt glad she'd had to flog out of her vineyard to say it. We cursed her quietly and said, "May all your beds be empty ones."

We didn't want to stay that far out anyway, we agreed sulkily, so went back into the centre and after a bit of a search we found Hôtel St-Nicolas where I think we got the last room. The *patron* or receptionist or whatever was somewhat chubby and a bit of a 'character'. Luckily, our room being on the third floor, the Bromptons were offered a stall in the garage.

Out on the town – it was very touristy though calming down towards evening, but it was extremely pretty. Well, all those Alsatian towns and villages are. A highlight of the tour was seeing a plot of Grand Cru Schoenberg in the north of the town though I don't think we ever drank any. We found a friendly enough *brasserie* but had some problems with the waiter at first. He wouldn't let me swap the main course on the all-in menu even though I would have ended up paying more. OK, rules of the house, but then he brought a warm bottle of Grand Cru Muscat which took a long time to cool on ice. No ready cold ones, apparently. But the other waiter was fine, and the food was good.

Two people came to sit near us on the terrace; they were English and were expecting four more. They were driving from Maidenhead to Umbria in three cars and had stayed in Bruges the night before. They'd come through the most foul rain on the way to Alsace. Now a storm was brewing with thunder and lightning starting, so we scampered back to the hotel and made it just as the rain began. The storm was right overhead and there was a short power cut, a Frenchwoman complaining at *us* about it. We met a nice Francophone Belgian with his wife and daughter who was nervy about storms. It went on and on but still felt very hot in our room. Suddenly we could smell smoke – was the hotel on fire? No, it was an English girl in the house opposite, leaning out over the very narrow street with a ciggy.

It was still raining early next morning but beginning to dry out. We found a market setting up, including 'Tracey's' van which we thought was fun as Tracey is the name of the stallholder selling wonderful vegetables at the farmers' market we run in our village. Taking a cycle track we got to Hunawihr where there was a 'perched' church with a double graveyard; Catholics are buried inside the graveyard, Protestants without. The church has been shared since about the 16th century. There were lovely views and a Parc des Cigognes (storks), *sans cigognes*. We went on to Ribeauvillé which is larger than Riquewihr, but still very attractive. It is also one of the few places with a really French name.

Parking in the square by the Mairie we walked through the old gateway, did the Old Town, and went back through the gate for a beer in an un-touristy bar in Rue des Juifs, probably the one where we had a meal thirteen years later. We collected the bikes and went down to the New Town, finding a nice restaurant with a terrace on which we could shelter from the rain. Dahb had *choucroute* though I don't know why as I thought he already knew he didn't like it. I had cheese, potato, and sausage in pastry. We had aperitifs: one Muscat, one Crémant, then 50cl of Gewürztraminer. That was one hell of a lunch and somewhat heavier than we normally have but I don't remember any ill effects.

The weather was improving nicely so we went through the vineyards and up the Bergenbach valley to Thannenkirch. The climb was gentle, cool, and pretty, up to 580m from 220. The village had a 'welcome' sign and an *eau potable* spring. We felt good being in the hills again so thought we would stay the night but the hotels there were a bit smart-ish, not our type, so we changed our mind as it was only 5pm. We went on up and up to the shoulder of the road just under Haut Koenigsburg, Kaiser Bill's bijou castlette, which was very dramatic being perched at 720m. We didn't go right up, thinking it would be closed at that hour, so enjoyed an easy ride down to St-Hippolyte, yet another wine village and another one with a French name.

We found a rambling *Logis* and after securing a room, went exploring. We found some *potagers* (allotments) up by the old ramparts, one of which was obsessively tidy. After beer in a bar near the church, which we failed to find thirteen years later when in dire need, we explored a bit more, then went to the hotel dining room to find it absolutely jam-packed with Germans, some of whom were walking or cycling, some of whom were clearly not. The noise was deafening but we very much enjoyed the meal and looked suitably appreciative when the *patronne* told us that a Pinot Noir on the wine list was made by the father (Herbert Bléger) of the current Miss France. Naturally we plumped for that one and it was a good choice, being light and fruity. We heard some French voices amidst the Teutonic tumult and, do you know, some of those Germans sat up late, disobeying the rule to be quiet at 10pm!

The next day (Saturday 12th June) was the last full one of our holiday, which was rather sad. But there are so many nice things at home (felines, greenhouses, and garden, and plenty of wine) and we know we can always come again (which we did a mere thirteen years later), so we cheerfully checked out and started to make our way back to Nancy. It was pleasant and fresh, and we went to visit the *potagers* again hoping to find Monsieur Obsessif but no luck.

We cycled along vineyard tracks, weaving in and out of the villages, on a footpath in the case of Orschwiller. Through Kintzheim again where there was a château with an eagle park, an ape mountain (Montagne des Singes) and a stork park. Eventually we found a good cycle track into Scherwiller but failed to find the back way to Séléstat. However, there was a good cycle lane on the road, so we found it easy to get into the town. They made good use of wide pavements with cycle tracks painted on them.

Parking the bikes, we found a nice bar for beer, and I was very much struck by the high standard of its loo which, according to my diary, had something to do with 'Willy Wurm'. We wandered around, finding some Vauban ramparts, and liked it very much. Nothing fancy, just a nice place and a proper town. We did some shopping including a Hansi tin tray we still use. We also, very unusually for us, brought some wine but for a special reason. Our wine group was to have a session on holiday wines, so we bought a half bottle of Riesling and a half of Pinot Noir which we wrapped up very carefully in our clothes – the ones we were carrying rather than those we were wearing, and I say this advisedly because our normal method of carrying wine is wrapped in our tummies. We later gave up our membership of that wine group, mainly because of my inability to learn much about the subject, apart from the practical side.

We then caught a train to Strasbourg and another for Nancy. We didn't have time to stop in Strasbourg on this occasion, but had been before and were to spend some time there again. It is such a lovely city. The Ibis by the Nancy station was doing a special deal for the weekend, so we booked in there and headed for the centre.

We had visited Nancy the September before and it is a very fine place, on the river Meurthe and not far from the Moselle. The former capital of the dukes of Lorraine, it was taken into the French kingdom in 1766. The central square, Place Stanislas, is a World Heritage Site and the École de Nancy was very influential in the Art Nouveau movement.

We had a beer in Place Stanislas where there was a streaker running round the fountain. I do think he should have dived in. We then pottered around the Old Town and in the Grand'Rue found an exceptionally nice restaurant (Le Romarin) with delicious home-cooked food. Because it was organic, we chose the Cuvée Maison rouge, a Vaucluse wine. It was a bit rough but went well with Potée Lorraine which was a sort of hot pot with carrot, beans, cabbage, and potatoes.

The station area was obviously where the local males went at night to make a lot of noise, but never mind. We got an early train and were home by mid-afternoon. While we were away Ronald Reagan died, there was a G8 summit, the D-day leaders had a meeting 60 years after the original event and Chirac didn't go to Reagan's funeral. There were English local elections, the full results yet to come, and Red Ken won a second term as London mayor with a green deputy and therefore a green programme. Goodness me, what a lot had been going on.

Chapter 11
Provence again: circuit from Valence

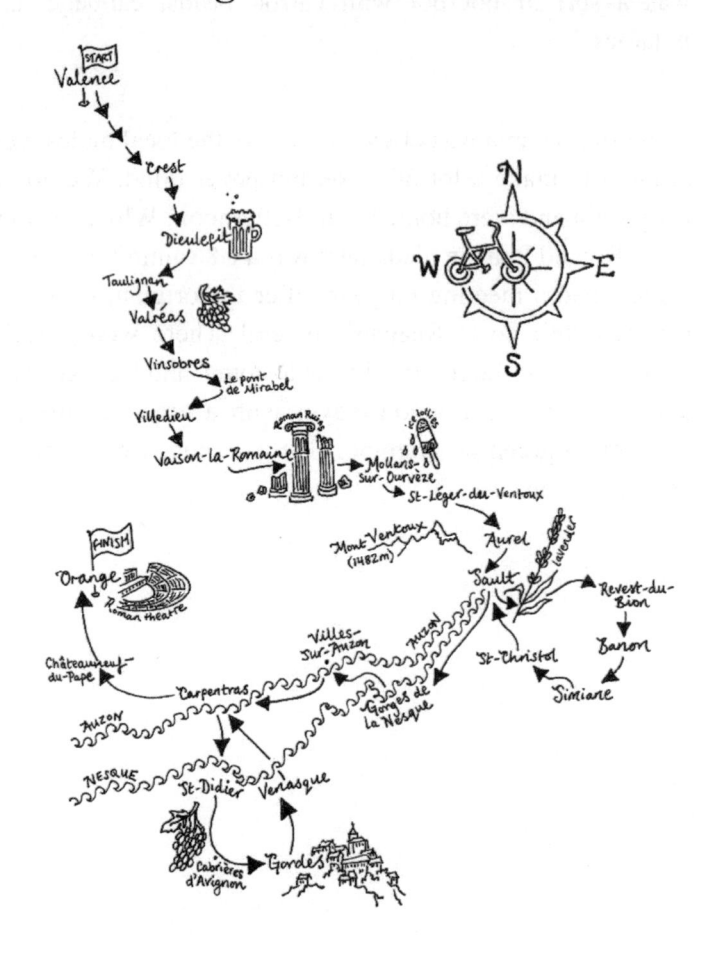

Once again, on a Saturday in 2006, we left home in mid-May. Our neighbour Martin kindly drove us to the station and we caught an earlier train than planned, leaving plenty of time at Waterloo for coffee and buns. We chatted about bicycles to an Australian couple. They had a daughter in Paris and were planning to keep bikes there for 'doing' France.

Our train to Lille arrived at 3.25pm French time, so we quickly made up our beer deficit at the Irish pub before boarding the TGV for Valence. It was difficult to make out the train's route and we thought perhaps it was a special new TGV line. We think we made out Beaujolais and Lyonnais as we approached Lyon, after which the line went well east of the Rhône and the scenery was very pretty. We arrived just before 8pm to find the Vercors staring us in the face making us suspect we weren't at the town centre station.

We had no idea how far we were from town and when I asked a heavily accented employee of the railway company I thought he said three kilometres, then realised he had said thirteen. Oops, a bit far to cycle at that time of the evening so we bought tickets for Valence *ville* having established a train was going there. We couldn't find the platform, then realised the train was a bus so rushed out to the station forecourt insofar as we could rush with all our clobber. The bus was about to leave but the driver waved at us cheerily as we bunged said clobber into the hold and clambered onto the bus, panting somewhat.

The TGV station is north-east of the town, and after driving through the suburbs we were deposited at the central bus station which is next to the central railway station which is next to the hotel I had booked before leaving home. Finding that Valence had an out-of-town TGV station did us no harm on this occasion, unlike the near catastrophe at Besançon a few years later. There the TGV station had only recently been built and we thought our train left from town. Again, it was 13km to the new station so we leapt in a taxi and just made it by a whisker.

Hôtel de Lyon was fine but a bit cramped. Although the room was a reasonable size the *en suite* was so small we had to put our feet in the shower when sitting on the loo. This sort of thing is all right as long as one person isn't using the shower while the other person sits. But it was very quiet, facing onto a back court.

The night was still young, meaning we had yet to find beer and grub, so after a quick shower (being careful to avoid soaking each other) and a change, we went out to explorificate. At the end of our hotel street, we found the Champs de Mars and had beers in the sun in this enormous space, looking over a park to the other side of the Rhône.

Valence is in the Drôme *département* and therefore in the former Rhône-Alpes region. It is ancient and Gaulish and owes its development to being on the Rhône river, not far from where it is joined by the Isère and the Drôme. Rabelais studied at the university in the 16th century and Napoleon Bonaparte lived here as a young military cadet, learning how to conquer the world at the School of Artillery.

We wandered around the old lanes below the cathedral and going up some steps found Place de Pierres where there were plenty of restaurants. We chose one where we could sit out, but along came *un déluge* so we had to dash inside. Having dashed, however, we had excellent salads and *crêpes* washed down with a satisfying *pichet* of rosé. After dinner we walked through more streets as the rain had stopped – it was all very pleasant if nothing out of the ordinary.

We got up quite late and went for an amble before breakfast. We had left one of our large-scale maps behind and hunted in vain for another. Eventually we settled for a decent Michelin which gave a good overview. We breakfasted in a gloomy dining room, the only ones there. The weather was fine as we headed south-east along lovely small roads. We stopped for a beer at a village which shall be nameless because I can't remember what it was called, where there was a *vide grenier* (sort of car boot sale). It was all very jolly and Dahb bought a little glass we used during all the holiday, feeling quite posh.

There weren't many restaurants around and when we found one at another nameless village it looked distinctly closed. Dahb tried the door which opened to reveal two men eating but he was told that lunch had *terminé*. As we were preparing to carry on, the *patron* came out and said he could make us a couscous. Well, that was absolutely fine by us especially as it was accompanied by a red Spanish plonk and followed by gâteau. The bill came to a lordly 20 euros. We all chatted, though the *patron* sounded hoarse, as if he had a tracheotomy. Apart from that, it was all good fun.

We continued in a south-easterly direction and eventually came out near the hospital overlooking Crest, which is on the Drôme river. From the bridge there was a wonderful view to the Vercors. Down and down we went to the town, and up the main street where we found a *Logis* which was closed on Sundays. There was apparently another *Logis* but it seemed well out of town and we also failed to find Auberge du Square. We did find Hôtel Kleber, but it was also shut. We then spotted a sign to Hôtel du Pont, which was over the bridge, and found it to be a very friendly hotel with lots of people drinking outside.

We joined them asap having secured a room for 24 euros and 6 euros each for breakfast. After drinks we pottered around the town and went up to the *donjon* (castle keep), which was just closing, and through some very pretty streets. Most restaurants were closed but we found one called the Donjon and had very good salads on the terrace. There seemed to be a wedding going on with lots of young French having drinks on the terrace and smoking hugely.

Heading more south than south-east, we had a big climb the next morning and were still not at the top when we stopped for a picnic by the side of the road. In Dieulefit we had a post-lunch beer on a café terrace in a long main street. A notice said it was open from 10am-12pm and from 12pm-8pm. We went along the valley of the Lez to Taulignan which was a very attractive Mediaeval town. Then over the plain we got to Valréas, a 60km day.

We wanted to visit Valréas because for some years we have bought wine from Vinceremos, who supply organic wines and beers. The Valréas is one of our favourites. We found it very pleasant in the old town and after playing Hunt the Turismu for a while we found it outside the walls, closed on Mondays. So we had a drink in Place Hôtel de Ville and went up to the church at the top of town. Back at our hotel we had a very good dinner with another excellent organic wine, Domaine des Treilles. On the way in we'd passed a sign to that vineyard, so it was good to be drinking really local stuff. We had hoped to find our Domaine de la Garrelière but we'd probably got home before remembering that was a Touraine and the Valréas we used to buy was Grande Bellane.

On Tuesday we woke to a deluge that hadn't been forecast but by the time we left, not very early, the sky was clear. We got some guides from Turismu (goodness me, open on Tuesday mornings) and I bought a Mary Higgins Clark in French to replace the two books I'd brought with me, neither of which I liked. I tried leaving them at the hotel but was foiled by an assiduous chamber maid. I'm afraid I had to bin them as I was unlikely to find a charity shop anywhere and I really can't expect Modestine to carry three books.

We left Valréas through the suburbs and had an easy cycle to Vinsobres. I can't remember having a drink there, but we must have done, with such a name. Dahb photographed a Basil-like cat sleeping in a hole in a wall. Basil was the next-door cat when we first arrived at our house and was an absolutely lovely creature. We met him sleeping in our greenhouse and when we heard cannabis had been grown there we felt that explained his contentment. Basil was a ladies' cat but got used to Dahb and would lie stretched on his chest, dribbling copiously and occasionally sucking the wool of his sweater.

After Vinsobres we picnicked on the way down to the river, overlooking the water before the Pont-de-Mirabel. In Villedieu we did a little circuit in the village, finding a map on the way out. We then had a beer at a bistro where there were several cyclists and three people eating. The woman just picked at her food and we were worried she wasn't going to finish her *frites*, meaning we were worried we weren't going to get them. But she gave her meat to the fat man of the party and finished the *frites* herself.

Along we went to Vaison-la-Romaine, which is in Vaucluse and therefore Provence (there is a reason for calling this chapter 'Provence'). We had ices in Place Montfort and noticed a parked tandem. We met its American lady owners as we were all securing rooms in Hôtel Burrhus (Burrhus was Nero's tutor). It was a very nice hotel with a choice of three rooms. I'm not sure we made the best choice as our room overlooked a side street and at 6.30am they started digging it up. Still, 6.30am in May is no great shakes.

The evening of our arrival saw us walking up to the old town, which was extremely quiet and offered no beer. We enjoyed the lovely old streets, though. Back in the exciting beery new town we learned that the river Ouvèze had flooded in September 1992 leaving 37 dead and the industrial zone ruined.

Because they were closed we walked round the outside of the cathedral and the Vestiges Villasse where there were incredible amounts of Roman ruins. It was time for beer, so we went back to a café in the square and enjoyed drinking in soft comfortable chairs. We had dinner at a nearby restaurant, sitting outside as were half a dozen Americans. The tandemists arrived but went inside.

We looked at some more Roman ruins before breakfast in the Quartier de Puymin where the amphitheatre had just been restored. Leaving just after 9am we turned left upriver just before the Roman bridge. The tandemists were going to tackle Mont Ventoux and I felt rather wistful as I saw them on the opposite side of the river, but somehow we didn't think of doing it ourselves, not yet anyway.

Still, if we didn't go up the mighty mount on that occasion, we did 50km of quite hard work getting to Sault. We stopped at Mollans-sur-Ourvèze for ice lollies on a lovely café terrace in a very nice village. Unfortunately, the lollies were Coca-Cola flavoured and absolutely disgusting. We then set off along a doubtful-looking road and were put right by a 'face' who sent us up an unmade track which eventually joined a tarred road at the head of a gorge. A face, by the way, is an old person, a resident of an area, and frequently depicted on postcards as the 'face of Andalucia' or wherever.

We gradually went down to St-Léger-du-Ventoux where there was a potable fountain at which we were soon joined by several other cyclists. At Savoillan we spotted picnic tables with a view of another village and were spotted in our turn by a Siamese cat. We went on and on, mainly up but sometimes losing height in a dip, and in considerable heat eventually reached Aurel at nearly 800m where there was a *Logis* with a terrace and beers. Then it was down and down until we turned off to a more minor road. There were bushes with silk-like cobwebs – we could see little worms. The road went too far down so we had to go up again to reach Sault at 725m (this kept happening).

Sault seemed to be a nice little town. We could see Hôtel de Louvre straight ahead, but it was shut. However, we found an excellent room at Hôtel le Signoret and booked for two nights. We walked round the really lovely old streets, finding a cat asleep by the *Mairie*. Beer was found on a terrace by the Promenade from which there was a marvellous view of Mont Ventoux. I read that Sault was the world lavender capital and made a note to visit in lavender time. After a bit more pottering, we had dinner on the terrace of our hotel. There were two Dutch persons, two French and the waiter from our beer café, and there were more inside. No sign of our

American women.

On Thursday we had breakfast at the hotel, contemplating a circular route for the day and writing up the diary. In cloudy weather we set off *up* out of town, reaching Ferrassières where the café was closed until June. We had beer at Revast-du-Bion in the company of a child with a water pistol. He didn't squirt it at us and was therefore still living when we left. We then went on to Banon, our aim being to revisit the little town we first saw ten years earlier. We had a big swoop down into it, and lunched at Hôtel de Voyageurs, where we had stayed the first time, a month later but in much colder weather. There was a hotel cat begging – she was rather pretty and so quite successful.

We left Banon by the road we had taken to Apt in the *Mistral* all those years ago. It was downhill so we must have been frozen then. We went on to Simiane where we had met a resident Englishman, climbed up further then took a flattish road to St-Christol. We then walked for about three km to 1001m, meaning we had a long way to drop to Sault. We'd hoped to zoom straight into town but as before, the road took us below so we had to plod up again and the heavens opened before the top, so we had to tog up. But we were in the rain for only a couple of minutes and were back in our room by 7pm, for a quick shower then out for drinks and dinner. Strange that we never tire of this routine …

Friday dawned clear and fresh. There was an English cyclist

at breakfast. He was doing the Mer-Montagne route and had taken the cycle bus from Sheffield to Calais, cycling through Sunday night and sleeping for about three hours, and so on. He was quite elderly and said his saddle gave him grief. Cycling along the Rhône was not very nice – a main road? Honestly, and some people call *us* mad.

Our aim for the day was to travel down the Nesque gorges, then visit Gordes or Roussillon. We started by going down from Sault, through La Loge. Then up to Monieux, then up and up, which we didn't expect but I suppose you have to go up to get down a gorge. It was easy enough cycling, though. Near the top we stopped to chat to a German couple who were camping at Roussillon and doing day cycle trips. They had driven to France because it was so difficult to take the bikes by train. We met them again at the Belvedere at the head of the gorge.

Then we put on jerseys to go down as it was quite chilly, the wind against us especially in the tunnels. It was about 15km down to Villes-sur-Auzon and the scenery was truly astonishing – I do love limestone gorges and this one is particularly spectacular. We had beer at Villes which seemed a nice place, as we were to rediscover several years later. There was a German or a Dutchman trying to hitch a lift with the most enormous rucksack. We went on through vineyards, finding a perfect picnic spot under a tree. It was breezy, though – our crisps kept blowing away. We could still see Ventoux and had radishes *and* cherries. What a day!

Continuing in the Venasque direction we passed along lovely small vineyard routes. We decided to head for Carpentras and stay for two nights, perhaps having a day trip to Gordes. *Mein Führer* excelled himself in his map reading, finding tiny roads by an old church and culminating in a carved-out road, hewn from a high rocky embankment, which led us to town. Carpentras was a bit busy on the outskirts and we had the usual hunt for a Turismu. When we did find it, we were told that the SNCF shop at the former station would be shut as it was 5.30pm and it wouldn't be open until 10am. We went there anyway to find it was open until 7pm and would reopen at 8am. Good old Turismu.

We found some timetables and decided to visit Orange on Sunday and get a train to Valence for the night as our departure time from there was 8.30am. Thus informed, we aimed for and found (after being held up in a narrow street by an ancient Labrador who couldn't quite lift himself up to let a car pass) Hôtel La Malaga in Place Something or Other. It was a very nice modest establishment, with an excellent room. We wandered about and had beer in Place Charles de Gaulle by the cathedral – all very attractive. There seemed to be a bit of a dearth of restaurants, however, but by sheer persistence we found something suitable. It was a pretty good meal apart from the waitress frequently getting my order wrong. She brought out squid instead of asparagus which takes some confusing. Then she said there was no more asparagus. I said I didn't think it was much of a substitute, so she brought out Salade Carpentricienne which was all veggie but very tasty. The chef came out later for a chat. I think he was Algerian or North African anyway. There did seem to be a lot of Maghreb-type restaurants, which is not surprising as it's not far to Africa.

Saturday 20th May and our Farmers' Market would be in progress at home. Hooray, a day off running it! We dawdled over breakfast then pottered around gathering up picnic stuff. We met a wonderful puppy called Whisky who was desperate to meet new friends, so we had quite a chat with him and the lady on the other end of the lead. Picnicked up, we left town to the south-south-west via fields of monocultured melons in polytunnels. We saw fields of young vines, their stalks painted red. Pleasant small roads got us to St-Didier where we went through an arch to see the church and château – an attractive-looking place with bustling cafés. Further on we came across two huge *bories*, ancient stone-built tunnels used for shelter of all sorts. It was good drystone country in general – Dahb is quite an expert waller and is therefore a good judge.

We climbed up further then swooped down via Saumane which was pleasant but lacking in life. There was a lovely restaurant which was closed on Saturdays. Down and down and then on the flat to Fontaine-de-Vaucluse. This was incredibly trippery, coaches and caravans crammed into a car park on the edge of the village. But it was exciting to be there because the 14th century poet and humanist Petrarch liked it, and the resurgent spring is the source of the river Sorgue, the most powerful emergent spring in the world. Coo.

We found a pleasant and fairly quiet bar by the river and had beer on the terrace. Then we went up the street with all the grockle shops and bought four singing cicadas as presents for the folks back home. We had to wrap them carefully to avoid setting them off sounding like a bomb ticking. Just out of town, halfway up a steep hill, we found a shady bench opposite some blocks of flats and stopped for a picnic. Then we carried on up as we so often do, via a Belvedere looking over Lagnes, went through Cabrières-d'Avignon and reached a main road with lots of cars which we slogged up, but at least there was a cycle lane. Then we found a bit of the old road designated as cycle track, before joining the main road again. At the top we had a wonderful view of Gordes, which is a real built-into-the-rock town with smart-looking homes. We also had a great view of Roussillon in the distance.

Then we went round and right into Gordes which proved to be another tourist honey trap. We had very expensive drinks in the square but enjoyed the refreshment and the fun. We remembered climbing up a very steep road to this square in 1991 when we were camping at Bonnieux. We went back down the road to the Venasque turn, then went up and up again. At the top we overlooked another lovely limestone gorge, and as we went down we overlooked a fabulous abbey with wonderful *potagers* and lavender and vines. This Abbaie de Séanques has been settled since the 12th century.

Then of course we had to climb up again, on and on and on with not another mad cyclist in sight. At the real top we donned jerseys, then anoraks as there were some spots of rain. We swept down a superb and quite steep gorge towards Venasque, which is bypassed. We decided, however, to make the effort and climb up to get some beer. It was a bit of a slog and there were no bars, just rather snooty hotels. One café said (despite a notice saying it was open all day so do come in and have a drink) that it was the hour of *restauration*, and we couldn't just have a drink. Humph – more curses on our part along the lines of "May all your tables be empty ones".

So, we turned our backs on Venasque and swooped down again, then had a very quick cycle back to Carpentras and into the town centre by 7.30pm despite getting lost in the little streets. Our hotel restaurant was closing but we got a beer, then changed and went dinner hunting. We had hoped to eat in the cathedral square but there was a party at the restaurant. Instead, we found Bar de L'Univers where we had excellent salad and omelette on a covered terrace. In spite of a bottle of refreshing white Ventoux we found our way back with no complications.

Sunday 21st May and time to start the journey home. We had breakfast at 7.30am having done most of our packing. The morning was a bit cloudy but gradually cleared to a lovely day. We headed west to Châteauneuf-du-Pape via Monteux and Bedarrides which was a very attractive place. So was Châteauneuf, not too touristy and with wine *caves* everywhere, of course. We climbed up to the château whence there were fine views, hills all around and Avignon's Palais des Papes shining against the Alpilles. We were fascinated by all the vineyards in this area; the soil was not so much stony as bouldery, rather like coming across vineyards on a rocky beach.

Well, it was hot and thirsty making, so instead of a glass of something red and fruity we had beers in the square, watching *jeunes hommes* ducking *jeunes femmes* in the fountain to the accompaniment of much shrieking and giggling.

It was 10km further to Orange and we found a very easy route in, and suddenly there was the Roman theatre which is huge. We had lunch on a shady pavement, opposite the theatre, this time with a bottle of the local tipple which we didn't think a lot of although it improved as we drank it with the food. I was given Salade Niçoise instead of du Marché which would have been *crudités* – why can't they get my salads right in this region? But it was good as was the rest of the meal. A riotous party came out of the interior of the restaurant and piled onto the little tourist train which we felt was liable to collapse, some of the group being rather large, if French.

We left the cycles to have a rest and pottered into the town and up to the Roman Arc de Triomphe. After coffee near the Hôtel de Ville we climbed to the park behind the theatre where we got a good and free view of it. We took an early evening train to Valence and secured a room at Hôtel des Négoçiants which was next to Hôtel de Lyon and much better. We aimed for a drink at the same bar, but it was closed and we found another nearby. Then we aimed for dinner in the same square, but all those restaurants were closed. We went to the square by the cathedral where we found the only open restaurant in Valence, or so it appeared. We had a very nice Viognier which was just as well because the service was extremely slow and then the waitress brought the wrong order and we had to wait ages more. There was a fine long-tailed, short-legged dog wandering around, apparently on his own.

The next morning, we got the 7.17am train to the TGV station where we had breakfast. We were in London by 1.30pm so must have been home in time for tea, no doubt closely followed by drinks.

Camping near Gramat, the Lot

Modestine meets Modestine

I checked my tent and found a man in it

Gordes, Provence

Taking a rest – note we're not on a road

The Thiepval memorial, the Somme

Our last and lovely 'campings', Alsace 2004

La Rochelle

St Claude, Jura, is a centre for pipe-making

Picnic lunch in Provence (not a drop of wine...)

Dahb conquers another Col. The bike is fully laden!

Made it to Ventoux Summit!

Chapter 12
In the Footsteps of War

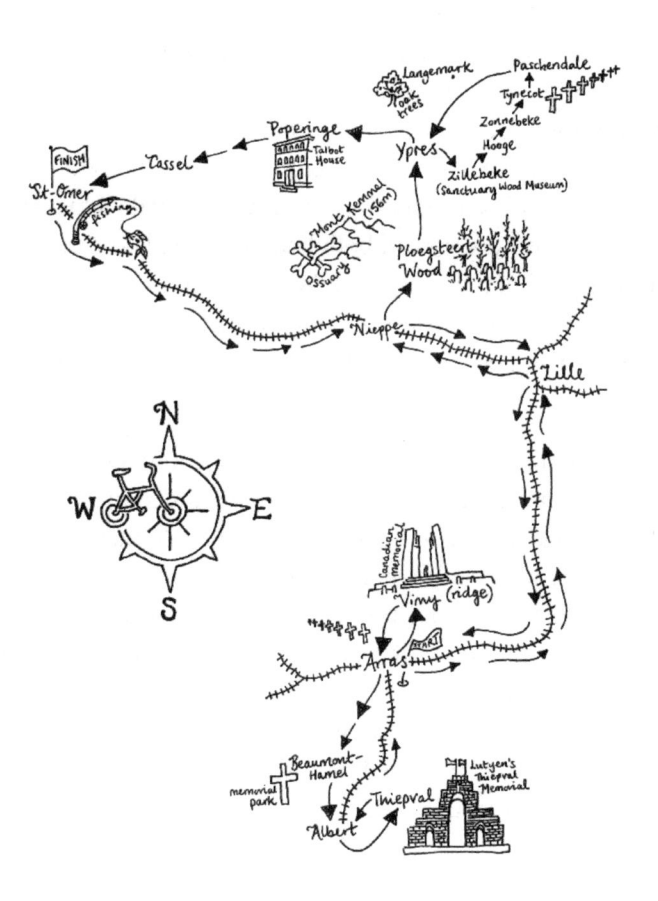

On a more sober note, though a Brompton trip is anything but sober and this one was no exception, if for a rather sobering reason, we thought it was time we visited the World War 1 sites. And what better way to do so than on a Brompton?

I have always had a fascination for the 'war to end all wars', and any literature or film on the subject. One of my favourite books is Vera Brittain's *Testament of Youth*, though I wonder if I could read it again without descending into severe depression. I do have a copy of the diary on which she based it (*Chronicle of Youth*) and feel I owe it to her and all who died or suffered appalling injury to read that, and to encourage others to read both books. Nowadays I am feeling similarly about the Second World War as it becomes as historic as the first war used to be if that makes sense. It's all because I'm getting older, I suppose. As is Modestine …

The cycling wasn't difficult on this holiday (September 2006) with the exception of the day we ended up at St-Omer. Picardy we found delightful, not unlike Wiltshire with its rolling countryside and charming villages. Flanders, straddling France and Belgium, is quite flat but has its own attractions, the town of Ypres being a notable one, and with both areas it is a joy to see how calm and peaceful it is after the utter destruction that was wrought upon them in that terrible conflict, followed only too soon by the Second War and the Nazi Occupation.

We left Eurostar at Lille Europe station, transferring to Lille Flandres and taking a regional train to the lovely town of Arras. There we stayed in Place des Héros in a room overlooking the Hôtel de Ville. The town hall was destroyed in 1914 and rebuilt in the Flamboyant style. Until 1917 Arras was near the front line and the town suffered heavy shelling as a result.

The owner of the hotel said he tried to run it like a *chambre d'hôte* and we think he succeeded. There were home-made jams for breakfast and butter straight from the wonderful market filling the square in the morning. Arras's other main claim to fame is that it is the birthplace of Robespierre 'The Incorruptible'. This brilliant lawyer's rise to fame in revolutionary France and his wretched attempt at suicide and miserable death by guillotine are well documented, so there is no need to write further about it here.

We spent two nights in Arras as we wanted to make a day visit to the Canadian memorial at Vimy Ridge, which overlooks the mining region of northern France and was the strongest defensive position in north-western France and therefore enormously important. About 66,000 Canadian soldiers died in the First War and they are commemorated on the memorial along with the 11,000 men missing and presumed dead. The memorial itself was being renovated when we were there and was shrouded in canvas but that didn't detract too much from the magnificence of the site. One day, perhaps, we'll return to see it. There was plenty of information about this amazing memorial, started in 1925 and constructed over eleven years in *trau* stone, a type of Dolomitic limestone. Young Canadians volunteering at the site took us on a tour and sheep were grazing mined areas where humans were forbidden to tread. We were assured they hadn't lost any, yet.

On our way back to Arras we stopped in a bar (of course), but we also visited a *nécropole*, as the French call their war cemeteries. It was huge, with long diagonal rows of white crosses on a slope. We noted several with the Star of David and reflected on how badly this sacrifice was rewarded in the next war.

Our next night was to be spent in Albert, the town nearest the Lutyens Thiepval Memorial to the Missing of the Somme. *En route* we stopped at the Beaumont-Hamel Memorial Park. In July 1916 the Newfoundland Division lost most of its men on the first day of the Battle of the Somme. The windswept plateau is topped by a statue of a caribou and is planted with the type of trees to be found in Newfoundland. The French donated this land so that a little piece of Newfoundland could be created on French soil for those who never went home. We walked in No Man's Land, feeling how privileged we were to be able to do so in peace and safety. In the visitors' centre there was footage of young men going into battle, laughing and smiling as they went to defeat the Hun. It was all deeply evocative and deeply moving, and I have never felt so glad to get back on my bicycle and feel the wind in my hair. To get back into a car would have been to carry the taint of death with me.

On the way to Beaumont, we had stopped for refreshment at a café with the intriguing name of Ocean Villas, run by an elderly English lady. We later learned that Ocean Villas was the British Tommies' name for the village of Auchonvillars.

And so into Albert, where we booked two nights in a *Logis de France* as we aimed to visit the Lutyens memorial at Thiepval the next day. Albert was almost totally destroyed during the Battle of the Somme in 1916 and the Battle of Picardy in 1918. Today it is a pleasant and well-planned modern town with an interesting museum in an underground air-raid shelter by the church. The exhibition describes the everyday life of the *poilus*, the French soldiers, during the First World War. The church (a basilica, in fact) is noted for the fact that a shell hit the dome during the war, causing the statue of the Virgin to lean perilously to one side. Nowadays it is restored to its upright position, and inside the 11th century Miraculous Virgin is given due veneration.

Arriving at Thiepval, where the Lutyens brick-built triumphal arch overlooks the valley of the river Ancre (the same river that runs through Albert), we happened on and chatted to the lady mayor who lived just by the memorial. The arch bears the name of the 73,000 British soldiers who died on the first day of the Battle of the Somme. Amongst this overwhelming number of names, Dahb spotted a Hugh Kennedy Birley who turned out to be a not-too-distant cousin of his grandfather who had also served on the Somme but never talked about it. At 48, Hugh was one of the oldest to die and was a medic like my husband which is unusual in itself as most of the family are teachers or farmers. We found out more about him in the visitor centre (and later through a family tree put together by an American David Birley) where we also saw a tear-jerking film which juxtaposed battles and present scenes and finished with a visual call of the fallen. I cried buckets.

Well, we obviously recovered after a good dinner and drink, because next day we visited the underground museum, then travelled by train and bicycle to Ypres, out of our French comfort zone and into Flemish-speaking Belgium! The town's Flemish name is Ieper, but it is better known to most of us as Ypres or 'Wipers', as the Tommies called it. We left the train at Nieppe, which was rather in the middle of nowhere, and cycled the rest of the way to Ypres. Mont Kemmel with its ossuary was to the west, and before that we passed Ploegsteert Wood which the Tommies called Plug Street. Vera Brittain's fiancé Roland Leighton sent her a poem about Plug Street Wood. He was killed soon after as were so many of her friends and her beloved brother Edward. They belonged to what she called the 'lost generation'.

Apart from thoughts like this we enjoyed our cycle ride and once in Ypres marvelled at the Mediaeval Cloth Hall, destroyed in the First War and its rebuilding finished only in the 1960s, and attended the playing of the Last Post at the Menin Gate which is somehow just one of those things one has to do. Dahb visited the Museum of Flanders while I walked round the walls, coming across various little cemeteries, the ever-present reminders of terrible times.

We stayed in the Old Tom hotel in the square and went for a day trip starting at the village of Zillebeke to the south-east of Ypres. Nearby is Hill 60 and the Sanctuary Wood Museum. Hill 60 is the name given by the Tommies to a piece of (not very) high ground giving an excellent view of the ground around Zillebeke and Ypres. The museum at Sanctuary Wood is privately owned and includes an amazing collection of 3-D photos. There is also a preserved section of British trench behind which cows ruminated contentedly in a field which was no doubt part of the battlefield.

Leaving Zillebeke to the north-east we passed through the village of Hooge, site of a vast crater that was blown by a British mine in July 1915. We went on to Zonnebeke and to Tyne Cot cemetery. This Commonwealth War Graves Cemetery and Memorial to the Missing is the largest cemetery for Commonwealth forces in the world, for any war. The location, on a broad rise in the otherwise flat landscape, was strategically important to both sides. The stone wall surrounding the cemetery bears the names of British soldiers missing in the Ypres Salient, also commemorated at the Menin Gate. The name Tyne Cot is said to come from the Northumberland Fusiliers who thought the German concrete pill boxes resembled the cottages of Tyneside workers.

On to Passendale, more familiarly known as Paschendale.

The Battle of Paschendale (1917), also known as the Third Battle of Ypres, is synonymous with mud and death but nowadays the village of Passendale is attractive and peaceful. We were enjoying our early evening beer when we were approached by a rather Teutonic lady on a bicycle (I suppose she was Flemish) who demanded to know what we thought of Passendale. Luckily, we were able to say we liked it very much; we would not have dared to say otherwise. After that slightly unnerving encounter it was time to head back to Ypres which meant we had to miss out on Langemark cemetery which is one of only four First World War German cemeteries in the Flanders region. Apparently, it is planted with oaks, the national tree of Germany, and in the Second World War was visited by Hitler who had been in action in the region in the earlier war, the one that was supposed to end all wars.

The next day we had quite an adventure trying to find somewhere to stay after leaving Ypres. We dawdled over to Poperinge, which is about 12km west of Ypres and the centre of the hop-growing region. We saw fields of hops growing up enormously long poles. During the First War the town was not under German occupation and was used to billet British troops and also provided a safe area for field hospitals. Being just behind the front line it formed an important link for the soldiers and their families, especially through the rest house known as Talbot House or 'Toc H', founded by the clergyman 'Tubby' Clayton. It was only about 4pm, too early to stop for the night, and in our naïvety we thought we would find somewhere to stay in Cassell, a lovely Flemish town that is actually back in France. We had, however, reckoned without the September wedding season – all the hotels in the area seemed to be booked. So we cycled on, and on, assuming we'd find a bed in the next town, but that hotel was also full. It was of course a Saturday.

On and on we cycled and finally arrived at St-Omer, about 30km from Ypres. We rushed up to a huge *Ibis* hotel with relief but no, all 90 rooms were taken. We were beginning to panic slightly (the hotel receptionist helpfully told us we'd probably find a bed in Calais, a mere 40km on), then found we had the phone number of a *chambre d'hôte* so we rang and were hugely relieved to find the *patronne* had room for us. When we finally found it, she told us that she had only just started up, so we were lucky in that no one seemed to know about her. We liked it so much we booked in for two nights and spent a war-free day pedalling around the marshes (many fisherfolk with wives reading books by lighted barbeques) and enjoying a delicious lunch somewhere or other, preceded by a beer by the river where merry St-Omer natives were playing games on the water. The next day was eventless and we took a train back to Lille and home.

Chapter 13
The Ardennes

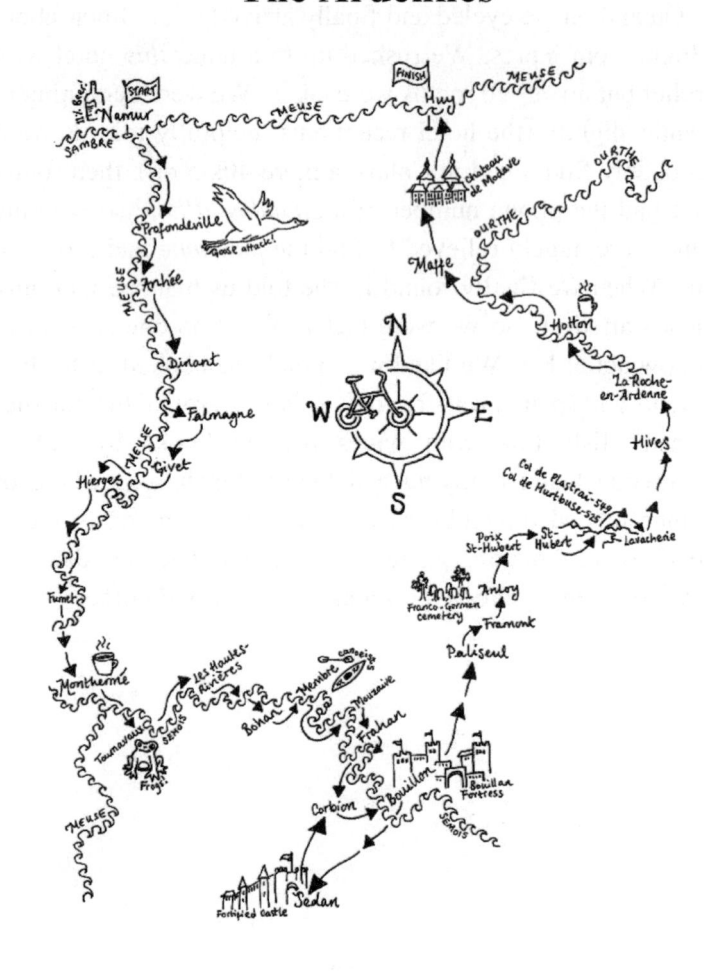

(The) Ardennes can mean the French *département* or the range of hills and forest which spans France and Belgium and through which the German tanks pushed to start their invasion of Europe in 1940.

On Saturday 2nd June 2007 we left Marsh Cottage at a civilised hour (8am) and, it not being a workday, didn't have to battle with commuting cyclists for space in the train's luggage racks. By 3pm Belgian time we were in Belgian Namur at the prebooked Grand Hôtel de Flandres, near the station. It was a very nice hotel, but we quitted it quickly to find Turismu where we bought a new large map of the area. We then stopped for a drink in the aptly named Rue de Brasseurs (brewers) and Dahb found he was drinking an 11% beer. It was lovely and warm and we watched a young lad being cellophaned to a lamp post by people we hoped were his friends. Perhaps it was art, perhaps it was a joke, perhaps it was a form of ritual murder – we didn't go back to find out.

We went up to the citadel where it's possible to have a decent walk through the ramparts. We came down a different way, to recross the Sambre river. Namur, regional capital of Wallonia (French-speaking Belgium), lies at the confluence of the Meuse and the Sambre. In 1815, when the English army heard that Napoleon had crossed the Sambre, they knew it was time to sharpen their bayonets.

We found a pedestrian street with several restaurants, but none had a table, so we went to a brasserie opposite Turismu and had decent salads and a very small plate of *frites*. We'd started with asparagus and found it very watery compared to our home-grown which is extremely tasty if not as abundant as we'd like. A wall thermometer showed the temperature to be 22 degrees which wasn't bad going for 10pm.

Sunday dawned absolutely beautifully, and after a good buffet breakfast at the hotel we were off before 9.30am (quite an early start for us), taking a cycle track to Dinant, 33km away. We survived a goose attack at Profondeville where there were many geese and cygnets (presumably adult swans as well). It was a fine stretch of river with limestone cliffs and climbers galore. We had a beer at Anhée where there were a lot of racey-type cyclists in the bar (you know, drinkers with a cycling problem) and before Dinant we passed the Abbaye de Leffe, home of the famous beer, though we couldn't see much of the buildings.

Over the bridge we went and into Dinant and it was lunchtime. We found a riverside café where there were no *frites* and they gave us omelettes instead of the *crêpes* we ordered but we had nice comfy chairs and sat watching a few boats and loads of *motos* which are usually a feature on Sundays. (If I haven't already explained, these are motorbikes. Actually, they are anyway.)

I ought to explain that last sentence. When a slip of a young thing, training in London to be a nurse, I sang with an occasional choir called the Glasshouse Singers. The very efficient organiser used to send us letters (remember those? Before emails ...) and once he wrote that we would be "staying with Ann, who is Lydia's mother if you know Lydia. Actually, she is anyway." My flatmate and I have never forgotten that one and refer to it whenever we meet.

After Dinant we followed a cycle track for a while, but it degenerated into a *Grande Randonnée* (long distance footpath) and at one stage we more or less went through the Meuse. Dahb had gone off looking for the track and was away ages whilst I discovered the path was just round a boulder all the time and sat watching people disappear past it and not come back.

So after a little paddle we eventually found a track winding its way up the forest, coming out at Falmagne where a hotel refused us a drink unless we had food as well, but did fill up our water bottles. We went on by road with big hills to start with, then up and down and back into France (there was still an old customs house) and then down into a village called Givet where there was a *Logis* with a room. We showered and nipped into Place Carnot for beers, to the sound of music from the next café. The Hôtel de Ville clock sounded tinnily every fifteen minutes.

We walked around a bit but couldn't see the way up to the citadel. We went back to the *Logis* for dinner; we were apparently on *demi-pension* and therefore could have only the *menu du jour*. It was a somewhat confusing system which had also confused a Dutch-American lady sitting at the next table. We decided to splash out a bit on the wine and were given a complimentary starter of fish soup and bits and bobs. All a bit odd.

The next morning, we tried to take a small road round the fort but weren't allowed to as it was a military training site. There was an exhausted lamb snoozing in a field. We went back to the main road by the river and eventually turned onto an attractive smaller one. We took a detour to see Hierges, which was a fine village overlooked by a ruined fortified château.

We took a canalside track and reached Fumay hoping to try some of the much-vaunted triple-fried chips, but although there was a van selling them there was a distinctly unsavoury smell coming from it, so we opted for lunch at the café. Lots of tripper boats were coming in to refuel. After lunch we found a road through some woods, joined a small road, and went down and down to Monthermé which is a small town on the confluence of the Semois and the Meuse. There was a *Logis* but it didn't open until 6pm so we went along the street and over the bridge where we found the Hôtel de la Paix, open and with a room. The room was huge and reached by going up to the first floor and down again. There were windows on all sides and two enormous beds, and a sort of lobby with table and chair on the way to the bathroom. It would have been ideal for staying several days.

We had a beer on the terrace, watching the local 'yoof', and lorry drivers coming in to stay. There were two French camper vans parked by the river, their occupants feeding cygnets, and we walked along the river, admiring the restored *girouette*, a weathervane which had once been at a local abbey. The bridge sported a memorial to the people killed defending it in the war. After this drama-filled hour we returned to the hotel for dinner and an early night. I hope I used the table in our room for catching up with the diary and writing a postcard or two.

We breakfasted at the hotel and drank our second coffee on the sunny terrace causing a big flurry of activity by the *patron* who decided it must be time to put out all the tables and chairs. The campers weren't up but I had heard one lorry leave at 5am and we saw the other go at 7.30am. We continued in an easterly direction along the Semois, pausing on a bridge at Tournavaux to try and catch sight of the frogs we could hear, always rather tricky. At Thilay we watched some fish, which were well away from some fisherfolk in their boat and saw a blue dragonfly. At Les-Hautes-Rivières we bought a picnic but failed to find any ice-cream.

By Bohan we had given up on ices and went on to a beer at Chez Willi. Then we went up and round and had our picnic on a rock overlooking Membre, with canoeists below waving cheerily. We saw a cat under a tree and some cygnets, the latter being the cause of the former's presence, perhaps? We continued along the river and took a track through a wood, coming out at Monzaive where I noticed, though he hadn't, that Dahb had a puncture.

He mended it on a pavement by the road with various people wandering by, including a Flemish couple who love coming into the Francophone zone for their hols. Puncture mended, we pedalled along, noting hotels as we went in case we had to come back to them. A bridge past Alle marked on the map seemed to be non-existent but we found a barely legible notice saying 'Frahan *par la passerelle*' (via the footbridge). The route was by difficult footpaths and some small bridges were broken but Dahb went ahead and eventually came back to say that there was indeed a *passerelle* to Frahan.

We took the road on the other side of the river (it would have been extremely perverse to have gone back over the bridge to the side we were on earlier) and after a climb up, arrived at Corbion at 7pm which was well past the yardarm stage. So we put that right. We climbed up again to get out of the village and then had a long descent into Bouillon. It started to rain so on went the anoraks and over the bridge into town we found Hôtel La Villa d'Este where we booked in for two nights, even though it wasn't the weekend.

Bouillon is in the lovely Semois valley and is overlooked by a fortress which was once the residence of Godfrey de Bouillon who, in the First Crusade, got to Jerusalem before anyone else but turned down a kind offer to be made its king. Bouillon itself was fought over many times over the years – not far from the border, you see.

As its name suggests, the hotel was run by an Italian family and after a warming bath we enjoyed pizza and Bardolino in the hotel restaurant. Stabling the Bromptons was a bit complex – up the street and through a side door into a corridor where we left them, returning to our room via a lift and an enormous function room.

We had a plan for the next day, Wednesday, which is why we booked in for two nights. We wanted to make the perilous journey to Sedan, which is *back in France*.

Disappointingly Sedan did not give its name to the 'sedan' chair, which is a derivation of the Latin 'sella' meaning saddle. It's a very important place, however. Its origins go back to Gaulish times, but three moments of history stand out. The Revocation of the Edict of Nantes in 1685 damaged the cloth industry which had been developed by Protestants. Sedan's capitulation in 1870, in the Franco-Prussian War, led to the proclamation of the Third Republic. And in 1940 a defeat at Sedan led to the fall of that Third Republic. The town was rebuilt after the Second World War, though there's a fair bit of old stuff around. The big attraction is the *château fort*, the largest fortress in Europe.

Breakfasting at 8am we were on the road for Sedan at 9.15am. The roads went up and down, as they tend to do, and after 15km or so we had arrived, tying up our steeds in Place de la Halle where we had an ice-cream in a café, feeling we deserved it as we hadn't managed to get one the day before.

We then did an extensive tour of the *château fort* which was certainly very fine. Afterwards we had a beer at the King's Head, a Whitbread pub, feeling it wasn't quite the authentic French/Belge experience. After a late lunch on the square, we went back to Bouillon via a couple of military cemeteries and the village of Illy. We crested the hill at a pillbox bearing a memorial to its defenders in 1940, and arrived at the same bar in Corbion where we'd had beer before going on to Bouillon. Naturally we had another beer.

We swooped down again to Bouillon with no rain this time and after changing into our evening clothes, walked around and went to Hôtel de la Poste for an outdoor meal. A coachload of Flemish persons seemed to be staying and I wrote that they were amusing to watch if I can't remember any details. But we're easily amused on holiday.

The next day we got the Bromptons through their side door then continued up that street and went via small roads and places until we reached Paliseul, which was big enough to have a Spar, where we bought our picnic. We had a beer in the square and a friendly local stopped to talk about bikes. We found an averagely good picnic spot on a track leading to a field and had just spread ourselves over the track when a tractor turned in. Flinging stuff to the side, we tried to clear the way then realised it was merely turning round. Panic over.

Between the villages of Framont and Anloy we came across a Franco-German cemetery (20-22 August 1914), very neat and backing onto dense woods. A Frenchman was working there – he lived in the Vosges but had a company that travelled a 300km radius to look after war graves. He asked if we could help his 17-year-old daughter who wanted to go to England to learn the language. We made desultory enquiries on our return but proved to be unable to help. She didn't want to be an *au pair* and we didn't know anyone who would just take in a French girl so eventually it all fizzled out. Her father had invited us to stay with them in the Vosges anytime but somehow we don't think we'll get in touch, having been so feeble about helping the girl.

We went on to Poix-St-Hubert where there was a station and plenty of trains to Namur and Arlon. On to St-Hubert itself where we visited Turismu for information, then found a room at Hôtel 2G, formerly Hôtel Luxembourg. It seemed a strange name change – perhaps there was something political about it. It was a huge place, and we had a French window overlooking the noisy main street, which we hoped would quieten down later.

We went over the road for a beer then walked to the library in pursuit of a railway timetable but, being Thursday, it was closed until Friday afternoon. Looking around for meals we decided that our hotel was as lively as anywhere else (or not) as two Welshmen and a dog were already there, and two Dutchmen came in later. There was no tap water available to drink – we should have grabbed a jug and nipped up to our room for some.

It might well be illegal to refuse tap water to diners, and I can't remember the reason they wouldn't or couldn't serve it. Restaurants are sometimes a bit tardy bringing water, or a bit absent-minded about it, but the one time it really was refused to us was in Rhayader in Wales. There was a notice outside warning would-be diners that they would have to buy bottled water, which we didn't quite believe. When it transpired that we knew the owners slightly, as they used to live in Swindon, we thought they might relent, especially as we were ordering a hearty meal with the usual accompanying fluid. But no, they remained firm – no tap water. What we should have done, of course, is either nipped upstairs to fill a jug, as above, or fetched our water bottles and slurped the contents surreptitiously when they were out of the room. We tend to judge a restaurant by its attitude to tap water. The Welsh one got *nul points*, but ten out of ten goes to those that are slapping down a chilled bottle of tap as we are heading towards our table.

We had a very short walk after dinner but made up for such slobbishness next morning by walking round the basilica and through the old *** ... woops, my notes have failed. The old what? And why did I write "another couple in there"? We went back to Turismu to find out more train times which were provided with some reluctance. We discovered that on Sundays trains ran hourly from Hotton to Liège but I'm not at all sure that's the information we were after.

We left the town upwards, reaching the Col de Hurtbuse at 525m. We tried to take a small road by an abbey and an airfield but were blocked by the military (did this really happen twice?) so went back to the N848 which was fairly quiet. At Col de Plastrai (549m) we turned off to a village called Lavacherie where several gardens sported plastic cows instead of gnomes, which we thought was a bit of a giggle.

We were now descending, following the river Ourther, and could see the Château de Celly above the road. For a while we cycled along a big dual carriageway, its hard shoulder being a sort of cycle track, and reached Tenneville, a village with no beer and therefore of no interest whatsoever. We went along a sort of top-of-the-world road to Erneuville which also had no beer, but the next place, Hives, had a bar where a huge Great Dane, a small black puppy and a black cat seemed to be living together in perfect harmony.

As we went down into La Roche-en-Ardenne, storm clouds were gathering. We found Hôtel Liège near an old tram station and secured two nights B&B for 40 euros in total. The Bromptons were quartered in a cellar round the back. We showered, then sallied forth for a late lunch at a crêperie and walked a little before coffee in a square over the bridge. We then visited the Musée de la Bataille des Ardennes which was very interesting. La Roche was liberated in September 1944, the Germans running away. They then turned round and reoccupied it and it was practically destroyed by the Allies trying to retake it in the Battle of the Bulge, which they did succeed in doing. This success was due to the Germans not thinking the Allies would attack. A population of only 1000 lost 114 dead and Nissen huts were hastily put up to shelter the inhabitants in a really vicious winter.

You come out of these museums and look around, unable to believe it could all happen. We walked around the town a little more, then as it was starting to rain, dived into Brasserie des Ardennes over the bridge. It rained and rained, really heavily and turning the stream brown, and we sat on the terrace for two hours, testing the Belgian beers. What else could we do? There was a German invasion of a more peaceful sort – a minibus of them seeking sporting activities. The rain eased enough for us to make it to a very nice restaurant a short walk down the quay.

Saturday dawned mizzly. A couple and a lovely yellow Labrador were also breakfasting and told us (yes, all of them) that the *météo* was forecasting more storms, especially this evening. The television was showing dreadful floods in France and Switzerland. It then stormed all morning, so we stayed in reading but at beer time it cleared enough for us to get to a bar in town. The sun was coming out so after a long hunt for a cash machine we headed out upriver, going up to 450m at Berimenil. At the Barrage de Nasramount, built in the 1950s, we found a café and had gweges and more beer on the terrace. We walked up to the barrage and looked at the lake beyond.

We'd had a lovely cycle circuit and went back to La Roche for yet another beer in a different bar in the square. The sun was lovely and hot (it is nice when the *météo* is wrong) and we watched paragliders paragliding from the hill opposite. We had *crêpes* for dinner, in the restaurant we'd had lunch in on the day we'd arrived. The waitress was somewhat aloof and once our savoury *crêpe* was served seemed to be determined not to catch our eye.

Sunday and time to start the journey home. We were off in good time and followed the Ourthe again, down, taking only one hour to do the 16km to Hotton where we had coffee. People were very much out and about, going about their voting business as it was the day of the Belgian parliamentary elections (and the French). We continued along the river, then left it to its own devices.

We lunched poshly in Maffe and had what we felt to be the best meal of the week on a 'terrace with flies' according to my diary entry. We were given gazpacho and coffee on the house. We continued along a road our map showed to be unmaintained, but it was tarred and very peaceful, and took us along a lovely route behind Château de Modave. Somewhere here we saw a huge row of cows with their noses in a trough and I took a photograph of their chunky bottoms. It's a good pic.

We were now descending on a rather busy road with lots of *motos* presumably going home after the weekend. We arrived at Huy and went to the station to check train times and to buy tickets. Then the hunt for hotels began. There were three in our guide, of which one was closed, by the fort. We found a

Best Western on the Quay de Compiègne but that was also closed. We phoned an *auberge* that wasn't on the map, though it claimed to be central, but there was no reply.

It took us a while to telephone successfully because we were using the French international code until we remembered we were in Belgium, for which we didn't know the code. After a long search through the Green Guide, which assumes you're already in Belgium, Dahb found it – 32 (France 33). We then decided to try the first hotel and hooray, they were open and had a room. Good. It's all very well having a train ticket but the satisfaction palls when you haven't got anywhere to spend the night.

Stuff dumped in room, we went out to explore Huy. The museum of the concentration camps had just closed, so we went straight down to the Grande Place for a beer on the basis that this is the best way to absorb the culture of a settlement. The square was full of life, a great place indeed. We had just finished our drinks to the sound of thunder when there was a heavy downpour. We had our brollies and watched with great amusement as all the diners scurried into various brasseries.

After walking around a bit more we settled on another café in the square and enjoyed our last dinner in Belgium. The weather had cleared, and seats were being wiped so that people could go back and sit in the square. Back at our hotel we had a short battle with the front door key but eventually effected an entrance.

After a noisy night (the hotel was by the main road but did have a good view of the Meuse), we breakfasted at 7am and caught the train back to Lille. I didn't record the journey home but presumably it was uneventful, and it is quite likely that we were home in time for pussycats and tea.

Chapter 14
Bordeaux to Mordagne
September 2007

On this trip we were very much in Hundred Years' War country, so I thought I'd write a little bit about it.

We started in the super region Nouvelle-Aquitaine. The Kingdom of Aquitaine was created by Charlemagne in the 8th century. The name is taken from Gallia Aquitania, a province of the Roman Empire, the name of which in turn is thought to refer to the wateriness of the area. Fast forward to Henry Plantagenet, son of the Empress Matilda, she who warred with Stephen over the English throne. She lost, but it was agreed that her son would succeed. He had married Eleanor of Aquitaine in 1154 and she brought as her dowry vast amounts of land in the French south-west. Combined with English possessions in northern France, this meant that by the late 12th century the western half of France, more or less, belonged to the Plantagenets and therefore to England on the accession of Henry as Henry II in 1154.

From then there was a general Anglo-French struggle, but the Hundred Years' War is considered to have started in 1345 in Aquitaine. One of the most famous battles in the war was early on, the Battle of Crécy in northern France in 1346 where a large force of French crossbowmen were made even crosser by being defeated by a smaller number of Welsh and English longbowmen. We visited the battlefield on a later trip and had to use all our imaginative skills to imagine the scene. Ditto the Battle of Naseby in Northamptonshire. Fun, though.

Another famous battle is Agincourt, also in the north of France, where Henry V defeated the French in 1415. Joan of Arc did her stuff after that, cheering up the French no end so that they were able to lift sieges and win battles and crown their king Charles VII in Reims cathedral. Sadly, she was captured by the other side and burnt at the stake in 1431. The war finished in 1453 after which the English gradually abandoned their French possessions. The last to be lost, in the reign of Mary Tudor, was Calais and Mary is supposed to have said that when she died 'Philip and Calais' would be found inscribed on her heart. Philip, by the way, was Philip II of Spain, her husband, who wasn't as loving as he could have been. I've always wondered whether anyone chopped her open to see.

There you have it, or at least some of it. The occasion for this early autumn Brompton trip was the wedding of a niece to be held at Mordagne in Tarn-et-Garonne, (for which see Chapters 2 and 8). We have rather made a habit of dashing back by cycle for this niece's significant dates, though admittedly the last time was her christening in 1980 when we dashed back from Africa, so perhaps it's not too addictive a habit.

On the last day of August, we boarded the 6.11am from Swindon and took a taxi to Waterloo for the 9.09am Eurostar departure. We had time for some lunch at Gare d'Austerlitz and on the café terrace chatted to an English woman who had a Dahon (American) folder and *lots* of luggage. The only tourist we've ever seen with a folding bicycle, she was going to Brive, which is east of Bordeaux, to visit a friend, and was then going to cycle around. She had pedalled from Gare du Nord and said it was fine, as Dahb keeps reminding me to try and make me do it. I should have cursed her and said, "May your Dahon park itself in the Place d'Étoile" but that would have been rather mean. The Place d'Étoile or Place Charles de Gaulle is that huge junction by the Arc de Triomphe. I would certainly never try to negotiate it on a bicycle having been driven over it in a coach on the way to a BBC recording at Radio France. It was petrifying.

Now we could have got the TGV to Bordeaux from Gare Montparnasse, rather than change at Limoges which we were just about to do, but it was hugely more expensive, silly money. I don't think there was a direct train from Lille at the time, as we would surely have taken that. Anyway, we had to get more tickets at Limoges but the 1.56pm TER we intended to travel on left while I was still arguing with the ticket machine. We learnt later that one *can* get on without a ticket but must then seek out the conductor to show one's good intent. No waiting for him/her to come to you. We eventually boarded the 6.12pm *Corail* (corridor train) for Bordeaux, which was very slow, getting us in at 9.02pm. The TGV from Gare Montparnasse to Bordeaux now takes just over two hours and I've just looked up the prices. Travelling today could cost from 65 to 165 euros one-way; I'm sure it was a lot more in 2007.

We took a taxi to our pre-booked Hôtel Choiseul in Rue Huguerie, north north-west of the station. The driver was Vietnamese, I think, and was very jolly, giving us a good guided tour past glorious buildings. He had to dump us at the end of the street as it was barricaded off for a cycle race. They were roaring round 60 rather boring circuits of an esplanade which seemed a bit grim to us, but there were lots of folk watching and everyone was having a good time.

Our hotel was very pleasant and the genial *patron* was just waiting for us to arrive so that he could go home. Oh dear, I might have said we were pitching up a lot earlier but had omitted to take into account a possible Battle of the Ticket Machine. We had a ground-floor room with a courtyard, especially for the bicycles, which had very high walls. The courtyard, not the bicycles. It was rather fun, and we could open the door and have lots of fresh air. We couldn't see the sky at dawn, though. Not like Teignmouth (in so many ways) where I could see the sea without lifting my head from the pillow. Now that's a sea view.

We had a very late dinner, feeling rather sophisticated, in a nice restaurant on the nearby Allées de Tourny. With two other streets, this avenue forms the Golden Triangle, so we were careful not to fall into it and disappear.

We had booked in for two nights as we wanted to see Bordeaux and it is so worth seeing. We were able to revisit 12 years later on our way back from the Biarritz area. A port city on the Garonne river, it is *chef-lieu* of the Gironde *département*, capital of the Nouvelle-Aquitaine region and hub of the famed wine area. From where the Dordogne river flows into the Garonne is the Gironde estuary, and the amazing Midi canal helps the Garonne to link the Atlantic and the Mediterranean. The area near Bordeaux is known as Le Bordelais and is at the heart of the ancient province of Guyenne. The city is also celebrated for its architectural and cultural heritage of which the Gothic St-André cathedral is a fine example.

After breakfast at the hotel, we hit the streets about 9.30am, walking down to the Esplanade de Quinconces, not at all far from where we were staying. On this vast area is to be found the Monument to the Girondins, the Bordeaux deputies who weren't sufficiently revolutionary for Robespierre and co., and who were guillotined for their lack of radical spirit.

We then played our favourite game of Hunt the Turismu which we found next to the Grand Théâtre in the Place de la Comédie, and which was crowded with tourists waiting for an open bus. We hoped for hotel guides, but they were only available for that *département* and we were going to be heading out of Gironde and into Dordogne and Lot, before getting to our destination in Tarn-et-Garonne. Not only travelling through several *départements* but into another super region, Occitanie!

Then we crossed the esplanade to the river where, sadly, there were no boat trips available. We walked along the embankment and through the Miroir d'Eau. This is the world's largest reflecting pool, granite slabs covered with 2cm of water and every fifteen minutes it creates a mist, which we just managed to avoid. A grateful dog was enjoying a drink and cooling its paws.

We got out our Michelin guide and started the green route of old Bordeaux, walking through lovely ancient and quiet streets at first. Everything got a bit busier near the market at St-Michel which itself was very busy. We found a bar in a cool square, and sat marvelling at the lovely weather. Down Rue St-Catherine to Turismu again trying but failing to find wine tastings. Ah well, nothing for it but to taste with lunch, after which we went to the St-André Cathedral outside which there was a skateboard convention.

Slithering round the exterior of the cathedral we found we were in the Quartier Mériadeck which was a bit seedy and difficult to get out of again. We felt quite at home, however, as it used to be a vast marsh seething with plague and other horrors. It is now a business district and somewhat 1960s modernist in style.

We went up the Rue des Remparts to Porte Dijeaux and lo and behold it was now beer time, so we had an Affligem. A busker busked and went round the tables. We then went back to the hotel for a quick change, the sophistication of Bordeaux clearly rubbing off on us, and pointed ourselves in the direction of the Chartrons district. This is north of our hotel and in the 18th century contained the mansions of the rich. It is now the centre of the city's antiques trade. On the quay is La Cité Mondiale, a 1990s complex which is now a business and conference centre.

We decided to walk through the Jardin Public. On the way we noticed a menu which proclaimed in English that you could 'make yourself your omelette'. I think it really meant you could choose your fillings for the dish. We exited the gardens just before the bell rang for 8pm closing. There were men on scooters rushing around closing the gates just before people got to them, but we made it by a whisker. After exploring Les Chartrons we wandered back to the old town where we found a modest establishment for dinner and enjoyed a glass or two of Pomerol, a red wine produced to the north-west of St-Émilion.

The next day, Sunday, we saddled and baggaged up and crossed the Garonne by the Pont de Pierre, turning right (south-east) to go along the river. We found a *piste cyclable* on an old railway line which – shock, horror – was full of other people! We left it at Créon which declared itself to be the capital of Entre-Deux-Mers, one of my favourite white wines. The name doesn't mean between two seas but is derived from *marée* or tide, and refers to the wine area's location between two tidal rivers, the Garonne and the Dordogne.

Créon was a fairly ordinary but pleasant place, so we rewarded it by having a glass of vin de plonk in a car-littered square. Then we rejoined the cycle track which led us to Gare d'Espiet, an old station converted to a modest but very good café with lots of shady tables. There we ate a 10-euros menu and drank 7 euros of wine, made friends with a French couple who owned a Yorkshire terrier which presumably was very fierce because he was tied up under a tree, and saw a cyclist who was with two non-cycling ladies. You really cannot beat our holidays for exciting experiences.

We stayed on the *piste* until Daignac, then left it for the small roads which took us to St-Émilion, crossing the Dordogne river on the way. We reached the town just before 5pm and got the last room at the Auberge la Commandole. Our room was over the street with a tiny window overlooking a brasserie garden.

There were quite a few English persons around, in fact it had been teeming with tourists when we arrived. We walked around and found it to be a truly lovely town, though there weren't many restaurants open in the evening with outside seating. We had an aperitif in a very pleasant courtyard and my Crémant de Bordeaux was very good whereas Dahb found his 9.50-euros-a-glass St-Émilion to be a bit *ordinaire*. We found a pizzeria by an old *lavoir*. Further into the holiday we might have rushed back for our washing. As we drank a *pichet* of very good rosé a cat came to drink at the *lavoir*, which made me think of D H Lawrence's poem *Snake*:

'A snake came to my water-trough. On a hot, hot day, and I in pyjamas for the heat. To drink there.'

I remember at school getting pretty muddled as to whether he was wearing pyjamas to keep cool or whether it was the snake who came because of the heat. I don't think there was any suggestion that the snake was the one wearing the pyjamas.

Back at the hotel we telephoned someone from our room. It was a terrible line so they probably never knew who was calling them and as we can't remember who it was it will have to be recorded as one of life's futile wastes of time.

The next day we cycled to Bergerac. Breakfast was recorded as being 'excellent' and 'fruity', and we left the town through an old gateway which led to a lovely road along the Dordogne, passing vineyards with châteaux galore. We passed through very few built-up areas, and it was easy cycling. At Le Fleix we found a café by the road with sunshades on its terrace and a really lovely lady in charge. We had the buffet to start, then a huge piece of pork followed by pud, all for 11.50 euros. There were some serious French cyclists who were also going to Bergerac, and a man and his son on oldish bikes. There was also an English couple who had come from the Midlands in a 4x4 – not quite so sporting.

We arrived quite early at Bergerac which is on the Dordogne; we had crossed it twice *en route*. We went to Turismu for some hotel lists and plumped for Hôtel de Family in the old part. It was small and French and 39 euros with a very pleasant *patron*. Although it was quite empty we were put on the second floor but the bicycles were put to bed in the bar, the naughty things. At least we didn't have to lug them up several flights of stairs.

We found a bar near a statue of Cyrano de Bergerac so while we're there I'll tell you about him. He was a real 17th century person but is better known as the subject of a French play of the same name written by Rostand in 1897. In the play he is a nobleman-soldier, is very good at duelling and is a gifted poet and musician. But – he has a hideously large nose which causes him problems with the girls, particularly the beautiful Roxane. Of course, she is in love with someone else and this someone isn't too bright, so Cyrano writes his love letters for him. Then the someone is killed so Roxane gets herself to a nunnery. Fifteen years pass and Cyrano tells her he wrote the letters. She says she loves him after all but it's a bit late as he is dying, having had an enormous log dropped on his head from a tall building. Honestly. And it just goes to show how you should look up as well as down when pootling about …

I read up on all this while Dahb went to the Maison du Vin for an exhibition and wine tasting which he declared to be very good, especially Côtes de Bergerac and Pécharmant. The latter is a little-known appellation within the Bergerac region and the name is given to full-bodied reds made from a blend of Merlot, Malbec, and Cabernets Sauvignon and Franc. Malbec is called Cot round here. I probably didn't drink this, preferring not to have bodies in my wine. We had our evening meal at quite a posh place called Le Richelieu just below the big square, sitting outside in lovely warmth.

The next day was Tuesday and we had arranged to meet

friends from home for lunch in Villeréal, which is halfway between Bergerac and Villeneuve-sur-Lot. We left Bergerac over a bridge, then found a cycle lane on the left bank of the Dordogne which got us out of town quickly. We climbed a hill – on a mule track – and gazed through some gates at the fabulous Monbazillac château. A famous sweet white wine is produced here and judging by the coach and car park we had passed, the *vignoble* gets a lot of visitors.

We were now in the Périgord, formerly a province and a natural region corresponding roughly to today's Dordogne *département*, still in the Nouvelle-Aquitaine region. There is now a Parc Naturel Régional Périgord-Limousin aiming to conserve the area's rich history and wildlife. Périgord is noted for its cuisine, especially its duck and goose products such as *confit de canard* and *foie gras*. It is also known as a truffle centre. It is divided into four sections: Périgord Vert to the north, Blanc in the centre including Dordogne's *chef-lieu* Périgueux, Noir to the south-east and Pourpre, the south-west part which includes Bergerac.

Into Issigeac, a typical *bastide* in which the buildings were gorgeously crammed. At 11.30am we realised we had one hour in which to cycle 14km as we were due in Villeréal at 12.30pm. The road was a good kilometre-eating one albeit with wonderful views, and we pounded along, screeching to a halt in front of the *halle* at 12.44 where our friends were waiting, he frantic because we were late and she laughing her head off at his anxiety. There then followed a long and liquid lunch, the first of two, but Dahb can't even remember the second one on the next day.

Villeréal is in the basic *bastide* plan, with eight main streets set at right angles surrounding the main square in which the *halle* is situated. This has an upper storey with exterior staircases, apparently an unusual feature. There was a very nice *crêperie* and lunch took three hours. We heard an extraordinary siren noise, the third time it had sounded, said the lady behind me. No one seemed to know what it was.

Eventually we parted, they to laze by the pool at their gîte near Monflanquin and we to that village which is very pretty and situated on the top of a hill with an extraordinary view of the Château de Biron. Try saying Monflanquin a few times: it is very good for practising the correct pronunciation of French vowels, especially after three hours of rosé-drinking.

Then we got on the road to Villeneuve-sur-Lot which we suddenly realised was a distance of 10 miles, not 10km, so we stepped on it a bit. We still arrived and had a hotel sorted by 7.30pm. It was a doubtful-looking hotel in a back street but actually very nice. You might think Villeneuve-sur-Lot is on the Lot and so it is, but it also looked doubtful though admittedly there were two fine bridges. We had beer in the main square which was also fine with arcades and fountain. After a wander we returned to the square for an outside dinner under the arcades, regaled by a group of noisy Englanders, the men with rather large tummies and shirts straining over.

The Lot river was originally called the Olt and rises in the Cévennes mountains so beloved of Modestine. After 485km it flows into the Garonne near Aiguillon, west of Villeneuve. Olt is also the name of a river in Romania which I think is a very useful nugget of information.

The next morning our hotel lady arrived to find us waiting in the lobby, all bright-eyed and bushy-tailed and ready for breakfast. This was served in a pleasant room and there were two other English folk there, very nice *motoists* who hailed from the north, as I do, but lived in the south, as I do because it's a darned sight warmer, in their case Kent. They were going to Lourdes for the procession (*moto* procession?). They reported that on Monday there had been heavy rain in northern France which pleased us somewhat.

The town looked much better by daylight, with the shops open and people bustling about. We decided we liked it, so Dahb paid it the compliment of buying a hat (see chapter 3).

We went over the bridge to leave the town and turned east alongside a picturesque electricity plant and aerodrome. Around 10am we rang our friends and arranged to meet for lunch for a change. The next bridge linked Penne-d'Argenas and St-Sylvestre and there were very pretty views but lots of traffic. We didn't cross but continued on the left bank, heading north until we crossed the river at St-Vite. We then followed a mainish and urbanish road to Fumel which was very attractive when we found the centre. We were now in the Lot-et-Garonne *département*. Finding a *crêperie* with a terrace, we telephoned our friends and settled down to another lovely long lunch with rosé.

Saying goodbye, we continued on the north of the river, crossing it again by an old-looking suspension bridge to reach Touzac, back in the Lot *département*. Are you keeping up? Dahb took a picture of the bridge, but I found later he'd missed the top of it, which was the distinctive part. This is odd, as I always think of him as a good photographer. Indeed, he used to develop his own and was fortunate to be able to use the darkroom at his old school. My brother also used to develop his photographs but in the only family bathroom, so you had to dodge strips of negatives as you performed your ablutions.

The Lot is very bendy at this stage. We went along through Vie-sur-Lot and on to Puy-l'Évêque, which had been recommended by our friends. It is a fine *bastide* with fine views, its situation at the neck of a long loop of the Lot being very picturesque. It is at the centre of the Cahors wine region and the name means Bishop's Hill. It was a Cathar stronghold but was taken over by the Bishop of Cahors in the Albigensian Crusade.

We found a two-chimney *Logis*, settled in (you can imagine it takes us ages to unpack), then pottered around. We had beer on a terrace by the river in the company of some more loud Brits, and some Dutch people with a huge dog, all of whom were quiet. We went back to our *Logis* for dinner, and I wasn't allowed to have ham and melon unless I had the 'menu'. This was somewhat odd as there was no one else there. The food was good, though, if the dining room was rather dismal.

We were due for one more night on the road before reaching the wedding destination. The morning was chilly as we set off along the Lot on a shady road with no sun. But at Grézels we turned into a sunny valley and started to cross the Quercy Blanc. Quercy is a historic and cultural region encompassing most of the Lot and Tarn-et-Garonne *départements* and Cahors is its traditional capital, though Montauban is the largest town. A distinctive part of the region is the Quercy Blanc (between Cahors and the southern boundary of Lot), characterised by its white limestone buildings. This is an undulating region of limestone plateau, cut by gentle, long and narrow hills known as *serres*, with fertile valleys between and stretching between the Lot and Aveyron rivers.

We had a lovely time going up and down these *serres*, reaching Montcuq for an early beer. This was another Cathar stronghold, and we liked it, though there was a lot of traffic. It had been a little tricky to get into as there were few signs. Perhaps this was to discourage cars – it didn't work.

We tried to extract hotel information from Turismu on Montpezat-de-Quercy, our destination at the time, but this was impossible as it was in the next *département*. Montcuq is in Lot, Montpezat-de-Quercy is in Tarn-et-Garonne. It is clear this frontier is not to be crossed!

Later we think we saw a crane and are sure we saw a red squirrel. A lot of houses looked like Dutch barns, and we do know a lot of Dutch people live or have houses in the area. We continued up and over the *serres*, having a picnic lunch and then an ice-cream at Castelnau-Montraher. I noted that there was a 'three-sided square with child with ice-cream "make-up" and a huge dog'.

Montpezat has been listed as a protected town, though on which list I have yet to discover. We got there just after Turismu closed. There seemed to be only very pricey *chambres d'hôte* which were far out in the country. I remember a lot of off-road vehicles. We had a beer and friendly locals said we'd find something in Caussade (we've heard that one before). We set off again, joining a main road (N20) which wasn't too bad as it had a hard shoulder and there seemed to be a new motorway running parallel (the A20 l'Occitane). The traffic was still bothersome but at least it was downhill nearly all the way.

Into Caussade and the first hotel was full. We then found a *Logis* and got the last room. They asked for 60 euros and were slightly apologetic that it was actually an apartment. It was huge! We had a lovely meal at a tapas bar, which felt rather exotic, then watched TV for a while in our vast sitting room. There was a homage to Pavarotti so we assumed he had died, which we later discovered he had, earlier in the day.

The next day we took a lovely route via St-Cirq. Near St-Antonin-Noble-Val we joined a main road for a time, then took an old and now one-way and deserted road into town. Freewheeling down we were able to appreciate the absolutely stunning white cliffs against a brilliant blue sky.

It was lovely to be in St-Antonin again. We had beer in a familiar café by the *halle* and leaving the Bromptons there had a potter around. It seemed to be full of Englishers. We had a really good lunch near the *halle*, served with lots of vegetables which is what Tiggers like. We had been warned the road we would normally take would be closed, which it was but not to us. It was a bit steep, but we got up fairly quickly, Dahb doing his manly thing of pushing both bicycles. At the top it was slightly rough, but we were soon through and were cycling along near the Grotte du Bosc when we were hailed by the occupants of a car who turned out to be our soon-to-be-married niece and a friend. The Grotte is described as one of Tarn-et-Garonne's geological treasures but I'm afraid we didn't drop in on that occasion, or on any others to date. Memo: in-drop next time in vicinity.

We went straight to the farm where we were staying and found the bride's mother there, dashing around with the farmer's wife doing flowers. We made friends with some kittens playing in the flower boxes, then went on to Mordagne where various people were gathered. We were set to work, then there was a great family-and-friends dinner on trestle tables outside.

Saturday and Sunday were taken up with the wedding, which was a splendid affair and seemed to involve a lot of washing up and furniture moving. We were very glad to be of help! On Monday we headed for Cahors where we aimed to pick up a train. Crossing the delightful river Bonnette we struck north-west via la Salle and Mouillac, and had a beer at Lalbenque. Now on the Causse de Limogne, somewhere or other we had a picnic of wedding leftovers, then dropped down to Arcambal, which is on the Lot, in what would have been a lovely valley had not someone built a motorway through it. We were right next to the A20 (the Occitane motorway again) but at least we weren't actually on it.

We then turned west along the Lot towards Cahors, finding some tracks in, and a local woman desirous of being helpful directed us along a goat track that was barely even a footpath. We did eventually emerge in the suburbs and found our way over a bridge to the centre, where we booked into an attractive Art Deco hotel.

Cahors is the *chef-lieu* of the Lot *département* and there are many monuments dating from Roman and Mediaeval times. The Santiago de Compostela path passes over the justly famous and quite extraordinary 14th century *Pont Valentré*, which has World Heritage status. The 'black wines' of Cahors wines are red which must contain at least 70%

Malbec grapes, known round there as Cot as they are in the Bordelais. They are also known as Auxerrois which is a bit irritating as Auxerre is in Burgundy. There is also a Cahors grape for which I read that one should see Jurançon which I can tell you, having cycled through it a couple of years ago, is a village just outside Pau near the Spanish border. No wonder we get confused and just sit down and drink the stuff.

We found the town very pleasant and had a good trog round, drinking beer in a square that was being done up and eating *crêpes* in a quiet street. In the morning, Tuesday 11th September, we bought tickets to Limoges where we would stay on the train, having a return ticket from there, and arrived home with no great incident. It had been a marvellous trip – lovely weather, beautiful scenery, interestingly varied terrain but nothing too difficult. And of course, meeting friends, then a superb French-style wedding. And what's more, our second Brompton trip that year!

Chapter 15
Champagne-Lorraine

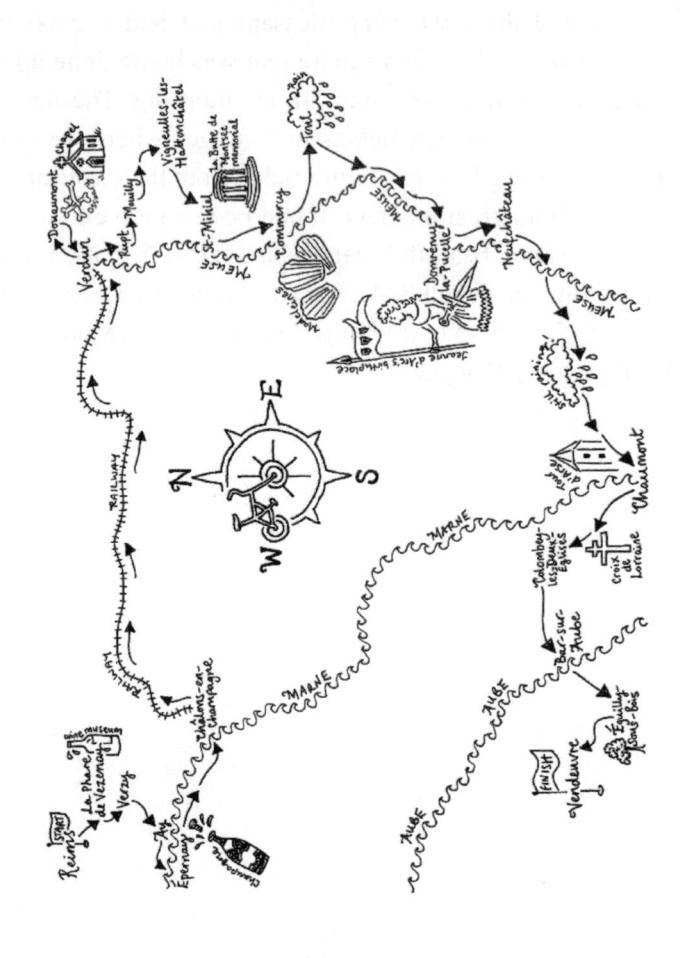

Calling this our Champagne-Lorraine holiday makes it sound like an official region, which it isn't, but we did a bit of regional boundary crossing as we went from Champagne-Ardennes to Lorraine and back to Champagne-Ardennes. These are now historical names, however, having been lumped together with Alsace into one new super region, Grand Est. Our Ardennes holiday of the previous year during which we were exploring a topography rather than a *département*, found us crossing back and forth over national boundaries which would have been very exciting if we'd had to go through customs barriers each time, which we didn't even once. We did see an old customs house, though.

The old Champagne-Ardennes region was made up of the Ardennes, Aube, Marne and Haute-Marne *départements*, and Lorraine of Meurthe-et-Moselle, Meuse, Moselle and Vosges. Lorraine's regional capital was Metz and that of Champagne-Ardennes was Châlons-en-Champagne. The chief town of Grand Est is Strasbourg.

The name Champagne has two meanings and in French two genders. The geographical area is la Champagne, and it's delicious bubbly product is the masculine *le* champagne. Champagne wines are popularly associated with Dom Pérignon (1638-1715) although grapes were being grown before the Romans arrived. The oldest recorded sparkling wine, by the way, is Blanquette de Limoux (16th century), which we discovered in the Roussillon area. We next found it in Aldi and after that in Tesco. The last time I looked it was out of stock, which is disgraceful. Luckily Vinceremos stock the organic version.

Anyway, Dom P. helped develop the sparkle of champagne and the fizz quickly grew in popularity. The main grape varieties used for champagne are Pinot Noir, Pinot Meunier and Chardonnay. The main area, centred on Reims and Épernay, was augmented in the 1920s by permitting the Côte des Bar, to the south-east, to call its wines champagne. Lorraine also has its wines which we tested carefully. If not the most celebrated wine area it has produced the lovely liquid since ancient times and there is some good stuff. Its wine economy suffered a great deal in all the wars that took place on the territory.

The *départements* listed above are mainly named after rivers and it certainly is quite a fluvial area, well-known ones being the Meuse which runs south to north through the Ardennes and the Netherlands (where it is known as the Maas) to drain into the North Sea, and the Moselle (German Mosel) which rises in the Vosges and then flows through Metz, Luxembourg and Germany to join the Rhine at Koblenz. The Seine rises in and flows through Champagne and thence to Paris, being joined just upstream of the capital by the Marne. The Vosges, which reach up to 1420m in altitude, form the border with Alsace to the east and several rivers rise on the watershed.

As departure time approached on Saturday 31st May 2008, I suddenly realised that Eurostar was due to leave one hour earlier than I had thought, so I forgot to take the plastic pots off the lettuce and spinach. By Thursday I had remembered this and fearing lettuce and spinach shrivelling in the heat, rang my neighbour – crisis averted. The last orders to the neighbours in charge were to eat the strawberries and asparagus. Robinson Cholderton, feline of the day, refused to speak as we left owing to flea medicine (he did attempt a polite refusal but was overwhelmed by opposing forces).

We left about 12.15pm, cycling to the station in about 35 minutes which is a lot quicker than I normally do it. Dahb called at Halfords for a bike lock to replace the one he had failed to pack, and at the pasty shop for a train picnic. It was a Chinese lock and as we couldn't crack the enigmatic instructions for changing the code, we left it at the one set which was dash dash dash dash.

We arrived in time for coffee at the new (for us) Eurostar terminal at St Pancras. We don't like it quite as much as Waterloo but we're getting used to it. Leaving at 4.25pm on the new route, mostly tunnel in the urban area so rather dull whereas previously we had a good view of St Thomas' Hospital where we had first met, we arrived in Paris around 7.30pm. We cycled round to the Gare de l'Est (the only bit of cycling in Paris I can cope with) and after checking the train time, settled comfortably in one of the nearby cafés. We saw a lot of Paris 'Boris' bikes and it was raining gently, having been lovely in Wiltshire and London. We suddenly realised what time it was and had to rush for the train.

The 8.50pm TGV to Reims, where it was raining even harder, took 45 minutes. We found our pre-booked Hôtel des Arcades with some difficulty, having been provided with a precise but inaccurate map. It is indeed in an arcade and once you have determined which street to look in, it is indicated but otherwise there is no clue. We arrived eventually, dumped our luggage, stuffed the Bromptons in the *sous-sol* next to the laundry, expecting them to be clean by morning, and went *brasserie*-hunting in a rather damp thoroughfare. In spite of the rain, Reims was very lively, and the *brasserie* was friendly and offered salads and *pichets* of rosé.

The next day, Sunday, dawned fair. We had breakfast in the hotel then headed out of town towards La Montagne de Reims. Dahb cleverly found a quiet way out through peaceful streets, and soon we were cycling through cereal country. Heading for La Phare de Verzenay (a strange location for a lighthouse) we found it to be a wine museum and brushed up our knowledge of French wine lore. There were lovely views from the lighthouse though we failed to see any ships. La Montagne de Reims is a regional nature park and its highest point is 287m, so perhaps calling it a mountain is pushing it a bit. But it's very picturesque and wild boar roam through the forested areas, allegedly. The vineyards are found on the north, east and south slopes.

We went on to Verzy and found a restaurant which had the audacity to be full. We desperately drank a can of beer in a rather subdued and foodless bar in the square. Not even a pack of nuts. Luckily in a nearby village we found an open *boulangerie*, unusual for a Sunday afternoon, so we acquired a pasty and ate it at the side of the road. Another crisis averted.

On the other side of the Montagne we arrived at Ay, famed for its viticulture but otherwise not looking up to much as we passed through, and finally reached the metropolis of Épernay which was much more like it with its champagne houses and an Ibis hotel I'd booked from home, easier to find than its Reims counterpart and equally pleasant and friendly. There was also more of an academic nature to it as the Bromptons were stabled in a seminar room on the first floor near reception.

We went forth to find a bar, and after refreshment we promenaded down the Avenue de Champagne which we had done earlier on a non-biking holiday, finishing with a tour and tasting at the De Castellane champagne house. It was all closed up now, so we went back to the centre to hunt down dinner. We found the Restaurant L'Ancêtre which was completely empty, so we bravely went in to start a trend though we failed to lure in other customers, doubtless scaring them off. Why do such places bother to open on a Sunday?

The food was on the pricey side but very tasty and we decided it would be churlish not to add a bottle of champagne. The *patronne* asked nicely if we could talk to her daughter who was studying Law in Strasbourg. She wanted to know the Latin phrase meaning one can't be retried once found innocent. We're not quite sure why she needed to ask English people but rang a solicitor friend who wasn't much help, probably also well through a bottle of something. She was talking about the law of double jeopardy and the Latin phrase is *ne bis in idem* which probably 'any fule kno' as Molesworth would say.

We ate breakfast to the accompaniment of highly percussive thunder and lightning, but it had cleared by the time we set off towards Châlons-en-Champagne, formerly Châlons-sur-Marne. Quite often we cycled along a canal path, eventually reaching the town's railway station. We bought tickets to Verdun, which is where we wanted to go, and enjoyed a glass of beer in a bar opposite the station, guarded by a charming Doberman puppy. We travelled in a one-carriage train through the Argonne Forest which was very pretty and the scene of much fighting during World War I as it was on the front line. I would very much like to return and explore the Argonne by bicycle.

Some aspects of Verdun need little introduction, the name being a byword for slaughter and bloody sacrifice. It was already a fortress in pre-Roman times and in AD843 the Treaty of Verdun split Charlemagne's empire into three and the town was ceded to the kingdom of Lorraine. It became part of the French kingdom in 1552. In 1870 it was occupied for three years by the Prussians. Between February 1916 and August 1917 the famous and very terrible Battle of Verdun took place all around the town. In less than two years, 400,000 Frenchmen died, almost as many Germans and several thousand American soldiers.

General Pétain was known as the Lion of Verdun for his command of the defence of the town in the First World War. With the German invasion in 1940 this hero of France, now Marshall Pétain, collaborated with the enemy and set up the Vichy government. After the war, aged 88, he was sentenced to death but because De Gaulle, for whom he had been a pre-war hero, considered him to be senile this was commuted to life imprisonment on the Île d'Yeu, where he died in 1951 at the age of 95.

Arriving at Verdun at lunchtime, we were soon eating a delicious meal in the centre. We eventually found the Turismu over the bridge, opposite the Palais de Justice (why is it so hard to find tourist offices?). We saw people coming out of the Palais but – and this is very interesting – we didn't spot any going in. Whatever was going on? There were people we took to be *fonctionnaires* (civil servants) on the steps, having a gasper. The Turismu gave us a rather pathetic map but luckily we found one we'd packed earlier. Our hotel, Le Tigre, was a little far out but very pleasant. It's an odd name for a French hotel but I suppose it's named for Clemenceau, the First World War French prime minister, as one of his nicknames was the Tiger.

The hotel was situated on Avenue de Paris, a busy road also known as the Voie Sacrée along which Pétain organised reinforcements and supplies to be brought in. However, our room was on the side of the building, so very peaceful. After changing we walked back into town. We were fascinated to see an invasion of camper vans, mainly French, parked just by the citadel. With our usual perfect timing we managed to visit this underground fortress during what proved to be a rare moment of sunshine.

Having waited for a long time for an English-speaking self-guided vehicle, we shared it with three American lads who were staying in Germany and had popped over for the day. In 1916-17 the citadel was used as a rest area for troops taking part in the Battle of Verdun. There are 7km of galleries equipped with arsenal, telephone exchange, hospital and kitchens – everything an army could require.

After the underground experience, we walked behind the Citadel towards the Cathedral and Bishop's Palace, still in full sun, and down the back streets to the Quai de Londres where we had a beer (of course). They have made much of the Meuse riverside and it is all very pleasant. After climbing up to the Monument to Victory, from which there were fine views, we returned to the riverside and ate on a restaurant terrace. I noted the wine: a tasty *Gris* (rosé) Côtes de Meuse Domaine de Muzy. We walked back to our hotel and were nearly sober on arrival, it being quite a long way.

The following day was sunny, which was something to be noted on this holiday. We cycled into town along the Voie Sacrée and then climbed up and out to the Memorial de Verdun which is a big war museum. Passing a statue of a lion *en route* (marking the most forward position reached by the

Germans) we saw the remains of the old station at Fleury village, destroyed in the conflict. We then went on to the ruined village of Douaumont – a chapel stands on the site of the village church which was completely obliterated during the initial German attack.

Before visiting the Ossuary, we fortified ourselves in a nearby restaurant, eating our lunch outside. We walked through the nearby *nécropole* where 15,000 Frenchmen were buried. Some crosses were a bit tatty, but that made the experience even more poignant. The Ossuary itself was built to receive the unidentified remains of some 130,000 French and German soldiers killed in the battle and is considered to be the most important French monument of the Great War. We looked in on the bones from the outside, and from the tower the views were fabulous.

On our way back to Douaumont village, we passed the Tranchée des Baionettes. In June 1916, two whole infantry companies were buried after intensive shelling of the trench they were in. The only sign of their presence was the tips of their rifles. We walked down the village's Grande Rue, where people's houses were marked by stones and details of their occupation given, and visited the little chapel at the bottom of the street. Then we went up to the actual fort, and again there were wonderful views. The sun was still shining but it was very wet and dank inside, and somewhat atmospheric.

We decided to take the long, pretty route back to Verdun *ville*, passing a very flooded campsite by the Meuse. We felt pleased with ourselves that we had a hotel and soon thought it even more, as it started raining. It then cleared and we saw a rainbow by Douaumont and a beautiful sky. As we reached the Voie Sacrée, however, the heavens opened and I couldn't see a thing because the rain got behind my spectacles. So it went on for one kilometre and we were somewhat dripping on arrival back at the hotel, greeted by Madame with a cry of horror and sympathy. Oh the bliss of not camping! We soon changed into dry clothes and whipped back into town for the usual refreshments and kept dry going back to the hotel and bed.

Wednesday June 4th dawned dry but as we left Verdun to the south-east it was doing its best to rain. We went up and over the Côtes de Meuse (vineyards!) and up a valley via Rupt and Mouilly. It felt good to be away from the scene of that terrible battle. Over a *col* we went, noting a Domaine de Muzy, the wine we drank in Verdun, then along a very orchardy track, with lots of mirabelles, to Hannonville where we picked up lunch in the *boulangerie* and *épicerie*. We ate it on the bench in the square by the boules pitch as it was not raining.

After a steep and winding road, we reached Hattonchâtel, a lovely village where a plaque informed us that a Miss Skinner, an American benefactress, had given money for a new school. The views were stunning and clear. The village ended in a private château and there was an odd-looking café with some revelling going on instead of opening, so there was *no beer* that midday. We eventually reached St-Mihiel, again on the Meuse, and our hotel we had prebooked over a beer. So, we must have found some somewhere – please forget my earlier complaint about not getting any.

The hotel was called the Rive Gauche (Left Bank) and there was a Bar du Centre there where we could sit outside. It was a former station with annexes, and a very long corridor to our room. The Bromptons were banished outside but we snuck them in later via the fire door. We went for a walk and saw a Dutch barge on the river, perhaps on its way home. We ate in the hotel, and I had two entrées instead of a main course, which is my idea of wild living. Our hotel was flagged up in the Michelin guide and this is one of the few if not the only time we have stayed in one of their recommended hotels, which are usually rather expensive.

As we left the next morning (Thursday) the Dutch barge was also preparing to go. We went under the arch by the abbey, through the old town, up and eastward down a wooded road with a view of the Butte de Montsec. The weather was dry but rather gloomy. The Butte de Montsec is an American monument standing on an isolated hill (275m) and was erected by the Americans to commemorate the offensive of September 1918 which enabled them to take 15,000 German prisoners. It was damaged by the Allies in the Second World War because the Germans mounted a machine-gun there. It was starting to mizzle, and I noted a woman sitting in a Dutch camper van while her husband went up to the monument.

Perhaps she had the right idea.

Passing through various villages and always within reach of the Meuse, we eventually reached Commercy. It was now raining but we found a lovely restaurant (Le Fer au Cheval) where the meal was excellent and the people friendly, and we were warm and dry. Nearby was the Château Stanislas, built in the early 18th century as a hunting lodge for the Dukes of Lorraine before becoming the property of one of them, Stanislas Leszczynski, deposed king of Poland and the father-in-law of Louis XV. Commercy stands on the west bank of the Meuse and its strategic position meant it lived under the threat of invasion for a long time and there are many fortified churches and houses still standing. A Proustian note: Madeleines are a speciality of the town.

We continued wetly along our chosen route, eventually reaching Toul by an excellent canal path. It was downhill with lots of locks, and the same barge going through the locks keeping more or less abreast with us. The rain had been very heavy, and it was still raining when we got to Toul. We whizzed into the town centre via the old Vauban ramparts, finding a hotel (the Lorraine) with one room left which we grabbed. It was a lovely hotel, and the bicycles were allowed into a (leaky) garage which we failed to open initially because you had to push, not pull. *Très technique*. We changed into dry clothing and went out again into the rain for beer and food. Toul is on a bend of the Moselle River but I can't tell you much more about it as it was too wet for exploring. It was still raining as we went back to our hotel.

The next day we achieved our aim of visiting Joan of Arc's birthplace at Domrémy-la-Pucelle, back in the Meuse valley. It was probably appropriate that we did so on a Friday, her being a bit Catholic in her leanings. It was fascinating to be able to see the actual house where she was born in 1412 (now a listed historic monument) and the excellent exhibition about her. We came out into the drizzle, but it was petering out and we arrived drily at Neufchâteau, soon finding Hôtel Le Rialto which I'd booked by phone earlier in the day. Situated at the confluence of the Meuse and the Mouzon, it is a lovely old town with some beautiful houses but not much in the line of restaurants. However, we were able to eat in the hotel and it was very good.

It was raining a little at breakfast but dried up and stayed dry, if rather dull. It turned out to be one of the greyest holidays we have ever had (I wore gloves quite often) but it was still packed full of interest. We were a bit unlucky on the lunch score that day but managed to buy some crisps and a bit of fruit cake, eating them by the side of the road at about 4pm. At least this was lunch and not breakfast viz the Montagne de Lure crossing in Provence.

It was very bleak on the heights, and there was *colza* (oilseed rape) everywhere. We passed through many a forest, eventually reaching Chaumont via a canal with a cycle track, and tried to find our pre-booked *Logis,* which we discovered was a motel well out along the main road. We found a room at Hôtel Terminus de Gare and rang to cancel the *Logis.* The bicycles went into a room that seemed to be garage, shed and laundry. They were clean anyway, owing to the amount of rain.

Chaumont is on the edge of a steep plateau separating the rive Suize and the Marne and has retained much of its Mediaeval character. We liked the town very much, with its viewpoint, *donjon* and pretty turreted houses. There is also a hexagonal 13th century tower delightfully named the Tour d'Arse. We found a bar for beer and stayed on for a meal. We walked a bit more and then went back to the hotel. All very satisfactory.

The next day was Sunday so starting late wasn't too wicked. We had to begin on a *route nationale,* but it was fairly quiet presumably because it was Sunday, and we were soon onto the small roads. We saw some sun at 10.45am and my diary says it was over four days since it was last seen by us. It then went in again.

We were now achieving a long-desired aim, a visit to Colombey-les-Deux-Églises and the house of General de Gaulle. We saw the Croix de Lorraine memorial to him from a distance and had a lovely meal in an empty restaurant in the village. The one next door, the first we tried, was heaving with a coachload. In De Gaulle's honour we drank Champagne de Haute-Marne which was delicious – rather appley. We then went to see that great Frenchman's beautiful home.

I can't remember now whether I saw Churchill's house, Chartwell in Kent, before seeing La Boisserie, but the feeling of homeliness is the same (and that can be said of Kipling's Batemans, too). We bought tickets then walked down the drive to the house as if we were calling for tea. It was sunny and warm! Apparently the only foreign statesman De Gaulle welcomed to La Boisserie was Konrad Adenauer, and I think that was a wonderful gesture of reconciliation. Not many rooms were open to the public (the house is still owned by his son Philippe), but it was enough. Although we couldn't enter the study, we could see into it and the view that De Gaulle looked onto as he was writing his memoirs, hoping that France would need him again, as indeed it did in 1958. There were lots of mementos and photographs, all fascinating stuff.

I admit to being a fan of both De Gaulle and Churchill, faulty as they were and undoubtedly awkward so-and-sos. But they were surely Great Men and they certainly had great houses.

After seeing the garden (again, wonderful views) and the bridge table at which *le Général* died of an aneurysm, we went back to the village and visited the cemetery by the church. There we saw the grave of the man and, alongside as he had wished, that of his daughter Anne, who had Down's Syndrome and died of pneumonia in 1948, aged twenty. De Gaulle was devoted to her. His wife Yvonne is also buried there.

Then, as it was *en route*, we climbed up to the Croix de

Lorraine Memorial, at 398m pretty high for round there and huge. There was an exhibition about de Gaulle's life and photographs of Chirac, Villepin and (according to Frenchmen who told us), Philippe de Gaulle and the General's grandson Jean. There were also pictures of 'Tante Yvonne', showing what a lovely young woman she was.

We were now in the Champagne de Bar area and took a lovely route through the wine villages and into Bar-sur-Aube, eventually finding a hotel that was open and not full. There were two rooms left and we got no. 27 overlooking the garden. It was a rambling place and the Bromptons were given shelter in a garage round the back.

We found beer in a bar behind the Hôtel de Ville, sitting *outside* if not in the sun. We found Tuesday's train times (changed because of strikes) and decided we could probably get back to Paris. After an excellent meal we went back to the hotel – there was a bit of thunder and lightning and some rain, but it was a dry walk back.

Monday 9th June dawned, as days tend to do. We had breakfast at 8am and found there wasn't a room for the next night as there seemed to be a lot of commercial travellers and people coming to a film festival. So, sadly, we said goodbye and aimed for Vendeuvre which had a station to Troyes and Paris. Again the route was lovely (the Côte des Bar is well worth exploring and there are woods as well as vineyards) and we even sought shade for our picnic and beers and cafés. In the distance we could see the Croix de Lorraine. A particularly lovely champagne village was Éguilly-sous-Bois

– it seemed familiar, and I wondered if I had visited it earlier with a musical group. A friend used to organise *La grange musicale itinerante*, chamber music holidays in various places. I went to one in Champagne and one in Auvergne. Not on a bicycle, I hasten to add, as it's not easy to carry a viola as well as other luggage.

We cycled up a 1 in 20 gradient to a crossroads at the top, then over Autoroute 5 with Vendeuvre in the distance. We saw a hen harrier quartering a field for its prey. Reaching the park of the Vendeuvre château, we shot down the Grande Rue; no hotels in sight, no directions to the station but we did find an information board by the Hôtel de Ville and thus found La Côte d'Or which did have a room. That was a close one – a small storm was breaking out as we esconced ourselves.

After a struggle to work the shower, which seemed to us as complicated as Concorde, the name we gave to my mother's new electric cooker which was impossibly over-buttoned, we found a beer in the sun and having walked round the château we headed back to the Grande Rue and the Café de Paris, and then the hotel for dinner in a sepulchrally cold dining room, but of course it was lovely as all our dinners are in France. We had an early night and I noted that the church clock didn't strike eleven or more, but started again at 7am.

Naturally our last day (Tuesday 10th June) was glorious. We apparently made history by asking to have our breakfast outside and it was excellent and even the coffee was hot. There was a beautiful yellow-orange rose in the courtyard but no one knew its name, and a mound area which was reserved for more roses. We did some basic shopping: *saucisson*, garden string, carrots, Chaource cheese for the neighbours and Robinson Cholderton (our cheese-eating cat of the unwanted flea treatment) and some *croutons* for us, and a new holiday notebook. I wonder why we bought carrots – perhaps I meant to write carrot seed.

We took the 9.57am train for Paris, sitting in the sunshine waiting. We must have got home without undue delay, as I wrote nothing else in my diary. I wonder if it was rush hour, in which case we probably had trouble getting our bikes and even ourselves on the train and doubtless someone stood on my toes from Paddington to at least Reading.

Chapter 16
From the Marsh in which we live, to the marshes of western France (Charente)

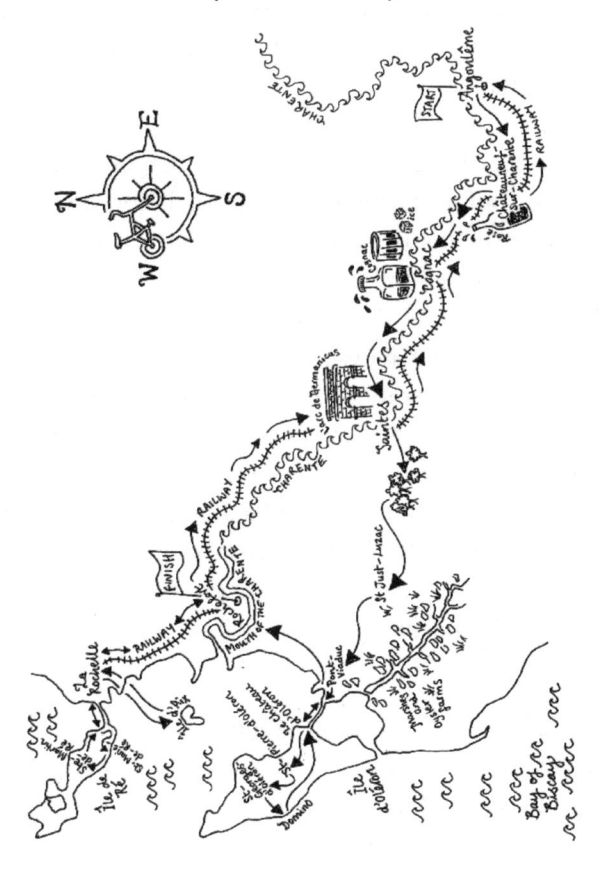

In 2010 we visited the region of Poitou-Charentes (now part of Nouvelle-Aquitaine), passing through the *départements* of Charente and Charente-Maritime which are separated by the green and placid valley of the Charente river. The area visited included the ancient provinces of Angoumois, Aunis and Saintonges, centred on Angoulême, La Rochelle and Saintes respectively.

The Cognac country is to the west, with cereal-growing in the Angoumois. Charente-Maritime, as its name suggests, faces the Atlantic with rocks, dunes and sandy beaches, and forests and plains inland. The Charente river rises in the Limousin and flows westward through Angoulême, Cognac and Saintes before turning north to Rochefort and reaching the sea opposite the Île d'Aix. Other nearby offshore islands are the low-lying and sandy Oléron and Ré, nowadays reached by viaducts. The coast is unusual in that alluvial deposits from the Charente and Seudre rivers (the latter reaches the sea just south of the Île d'Oléron) have combined with marine currents to form an area of marshland not unlike the Marais Poitevin in the old Poitou province. Most has been reclaimed as polders, low-lying land protected by dykes and familiar to visitors to the Netherlands, on which crops are grown or which are transformed, for example near Marennes, into shallow basins in which mussels and oysters are farmed.

Leaving home at 7.25am on Monday June 14th and cycling to Swindon station for the 8.11am train, we arrived at Angoulême just before 8pm, having changed at Lille for the Bordeaux train. We could see our prebooked hotel from the station so didn't bother to unfold the bikes. It was a nice hotel, very reasonably priced. We found a pleasant restaurant in the old town and ate rather too much pizza. The trains were noisy, but I slept well once back in bed having had to get out and turn off Dahb's light as he'd fallen asleep over his book. He can fall asleep anywhere and has clearly been a cat in an earlier life.

Angoulême is the *chef-lieu* of the Charente *département* and we went there because friends had said it was lovely. We weren't overly impressed, but it was handy and there was plenty of interest. It is on one of the main routes to Santiago de Compostela. A citadel town, it occupies an impressive site above the river, with an upper (old) and lower (newer) town. The upper town is ringed by ramparts and the oldest part is a maze of narrow streets that have been sympathetically restored. A famous native is Marguerite de Valois, born in 1492 and sister of François I. (He's the one who met our Ennery the Eighth at the Field of the Cloth of Gold.) The author Guez de Balzac, one of the founding members of the Académie Française, was born here in the 16th century and Honoré de Balzac (1799-1850 and no relation, as far as I know) was 'adopted' by the town which he described in *Les Illusions Perdues*. Another claim to fame for Angoulême is the Centre National de la Bande Dessinée et de l'Image, the Comic Strip Centre, which was closed while we were there, naturally.

After breakfast we reserved a room for the following Monday, then went into town and tied up the bikes in the

Place des Halles, assuring them they wouldn't be slaughtered and sold as cheap meat. The Turismu was able to give us accommodation guides for Charente and Charente-Maritime – rare nowadays to be able to get so much information in one tourist office. We filled in a questionnaire and gave full marks, which certainly pleased the Turismu Madame.

We started walking the ramparts in an anti-clockwise direction and failed to find the Ladent Tower from the top of which a General Resnier, born in the town in 1728, had launched himself in a flying machine of his own invention, with the plan of an airborne invasion of England by Napoleon's army. He didn't make it to England, or indeed anywhere, but crashed and broke his leg, after which he abandoned his invasion plans. He was 78 at the time – they don't make them like that anymore.

We left the ramparts at the Cathedral and walked back to the centre to fetch our bikes and baggage. Getting out of town wasn't very easy. It was fun at first, but we were forced onto a busy road and I was knocked off Modestine at a roundabout. The driver doing the knocking said he thought I was going on, in spite of all signs to the contrary. So at least I was stationary when hit and there was little damage to me or the bicycle; I'd bumped my sacrum and was a bit botty sore for a while.

Eventually and with relief we were in the country, at which point the rain started so we donned waterproofs, finding that we had left the trousers at home. We battled on to Châteauneuf-sur-Charente and found a café serving food and an excellent Châteauneuf rosé. Dahb was able to catch up with the SA World Cup scores.

We went out into light rain and set off for Cognac. The country was rather flat and dull but would doubtless have been more interesting in better weather. After an uneventful afternoon we cycled into Cognac around 5.30pm, in rush-hour traffic, but were lucky enough to get the last room (allegedly) in Hôtel La Résidence, a big family room we were given for 65 euros rather than the normal 72 (allegedly). There was a good heater in the bathroom which was useful for drying clothes so after changing we sallied forth with brollies (carrying one each this time) to explore the Old Town in the rain. We checked up on the start of the Hennessy tour in the morning and found a nice *crêperie*. Back at the hotel we saw the *météo* – not very encouraging.

Cognac is the birthplace of François I and is described by the Michelin guide as a peaceful little town, which I think is a fair description. We liked it, despite the rain. Michelin also says that 'the buildings around its famous cellars and stores have been darkened over the years by the microscopic fungi which thrive on the alcohol fumes'. Golly.

Cognac town is surrounded by vineyards devoted to the production of Cognac brandy and is the capital of the 'Champagne' Cognac area, thus named because the soil is similar to that of the champagne Champagne. I must say for a long time I thought that Champagne Cognac was made from champagne which seemed an awful waste. I know what I'd rather do with champagne. Cognac is a distillation of white wines produced in the region, mainly from the Ugni Blanc grape which is grown in Italy as Trebbiano. The vineyards were ruined by phylloxera in the 19th century and were replanted. The good burghers of Cognac got through this crisis as they had huge stocks in store for ageing (we were to see such stocks on our tour). Wine experts consider Ugni Blanc an important but mediocre grape, producing thin and tart wine. Clever of someone to find such a use for it, indeed its acidity is said to be important for making brandy.

Sure enough, it was raining in the morning. We went to the Hennessy premises and joined a Francophone visit with two Belgian men who were going on to Bordeaux later in the day. The blonde lady guide spoke very clearly, and we were able to understand most of it. The tour started with a boat crossing of the river and was very interesting. The Irishman Richard Hennessy spent 12 years in Louis XV's army then decided to settle in Cognac, attracted no doubt by the fungoid alcohol fumes. He started trading in 1765 having tried out the product on his family in Ireland. Their fate is unrecorded. In 1971 the company merged with the champagne house Moët et Chandon to create Moët Hennessy. Then in 1987 it merged with Louis Vuitton to become LVMH or Louis Vuitton – Moët Hennessy. Kilian Hennessy, a fifth-generation direct descendant of Richard, remained on the company's advisory board until his death in 2010 at the age of 103. That fungus must be good stuff. The chief brandy taster is similarly descended – it is good to hear of such continuity.

There were astonishing numbers of barrels in the *chais*, as *caves* are known in Cognac, apparently one billion euros worth. The oak barrels were beautiful and the process of making them fascinating. At the end of the visit we enjoyed a sample, then left to cycle on in the rain which was not as heavy as earlier in the morning but still wet. Still, not bad timing on the whole.

We left Cognac to the west, through countryside which wasn't particularly interesting but there were some nice villages. Reaching Saintes at about 4pm, we went into the centre to look for hotels. There were none to be seen until we spotted Les Messageries and booked in. We changed and exited, and started a game of Hunt the Turismu which had changed sites since our guide was printed. Fortifying ourselves with tea and toast in a *salon de thé* and sorting out our plan for the next few days (in severe danger of being organised), we eventually found the new Turismu and a very helpful tourist lady who rang hotels in Île d'Oléron and La Rochelle to book us in for Thursday, Friday and Saturday. I wonder if she would do this today? Often we are told they can telephone only in the town itself, but they will look things up and give out numbers which is when you find you have no signal for your mobile.

Feeling very impressed and grateful we went out again into

the rain, inspecting the cathedral and following the tour in the Michelin guide. There are local monuments dating from every period since the Romans and, like Angoulême, the town is *en route* for Santiago de Compostela. A famous resident was Dr Guillotin (1738-1814) who, in the interest of equality at death (beheading was until then reserved for those of noble birth), invented what came to be called the 'guillotine'. He wasn't thrilled with the name and might well have thought it was a little over-used in Robespierre's time.

The cathedral was damaged by the Calvinists in 1568, as was that of Angoulême. I didn't know they were so destructive. There is a Roman amphitheatre, but we didn't get there as it was a little way out. A Roman arch – l'Arc de Germanicus – was moved from a bridge that was about to be destroyed and rebuilt on the east bank. The Inspector of Historic Monuments who saw to it that the arch was saved was Prosper Mérimée, author of the Carmen story set to music by Bizet.

We took to Saintes, there being something very attractive about it. After the tour it was time for the evening beer and salads and *crêpes*, again with good *vin de pays*. It had been raining for 32 hours non-stop so we thought the weather could only get better.

And we were right. In the morning it was dry, and we left in good time and cycled through gently undulating and wooded country, getting warm enough for us to take off our jerseys. We were delighted to see a stork (unless it was a crane in which case we would still be delighted) on a stork chimney and one in a field (yes, that one was definitely a stork). Passing a *café fermé* we went on to St-Just-Luzac hoping we could stop there as we were so fond of the Cornish St Justs. We did find a very nice restaurant and actually ate outside. However, just as we were setting off it started raining again. I don't wish to grumble; as I write this there is a snow blizzard in the English Marsh!

We were now approaching the Pont-Viaduc, the bridge built in 1966 and the longest in France at just over 3km, joining the mainland to the Île d'Oléron. We were forced onto a beastly dual carriageway leading up to it. There was a narrow cycle lane, but it didn't help much. The viaduct is 5km long and we'd had quite enough of it by the time we got over. As soon as we could we forked right onto an Oyster tour road, according to a sign, which led to a pleasant village, Le-Château-d'Oléron. We continued on a coast road which wasn't very salubrious with lots of *ostréiculture* and a fair amount of traffic. It was very built up. I think *ostréiculture* is the word for oyster growing – we certainly didn't see any ostriches.

The Île is, apart from Corsica, the largest of the French islands being 30km long and 6km wide. For a long time it was disputed between the English and the French, the English finally abandoning their claim in 1372 and spitefully taking away all the official documents. It was occupied by the Germans in 1940 and not liberated until May 1st 1945, and then with great difficulty, so stubbornly did the occupiers resist.

In St-Pierre-d'Oléron, which is the administrative capital and quite a big place and full of tourists, we got stuck in a one-way system so went round in a large circle. The next place was St-Georges-d'Oléron which was quite pleasant and had a Turismu which, although closed, sported a map. We located Rue de l'Océan, where our hotel was, and thought how efficient we were. A sign pointed to hotels, so we set off to find ours.

We got to the end of the street with no hotel in view, so we knocked on a door to ask for directions and found some very friendly people who couldn't have been more helpful and offered us water and the use of their loo (phew). They told us there were lots of Rues de l'Océan, which is fair enough, and our hotel was in Domino which was about 7km to the west (it was in the address, but we hadn't a clue what it meant). They offered to drive us over which was super of them, but we turned down their offer and battled on, at first through some rather boring built-up areas and then on a lovely cycle track to Domino, at which point signage to our hotel began. We were nearly there when we found a man who had fallen to the ground, but we left him to some French people who were trying to help him. We suspected he was a tad tipsy and had fallen trying to get into his car and no doubt drive drunkenly all over the island.

At last we were at Hôtel la Petite Plage which was very smart. We changed into our evening suits and had a drink sitting on a comfy sofa, shuffling into the restaurant for a (for me) fishy meal. We'd cycled more than 80km from Saintes but the Oléron wine suffused us with energy so we went out after dinner for a walk on the beach. We met a couple who'd also been dining and whose language we'd been trying to make out. They had been doing the same, wondering if we were American. She was German, he was English, a Chichester man who had taught in Switzerland and Germany. We chatted for a while on the beach, then went inside to bed.

We had a late breakfast because the bread didn't arrive until 8.30am. Then we headed down the west coast which we felt was nicer than the east, but even so there was almost continuous development. We stopped at La Cotinière for coffee, and sat people- and bike-watching in this busy and attractive port. There were one or two 'faces', and two dogs in bike baskets. There was a tandem, the front of which was semi-recumbent. I've never really fancied recumbent bikes as I like to peer over walls into people's gardens rather than count the hub caps on passing lorries.

We carried on down the coast, quite a bit of the time on cycle tracks. The houses were rather smart. Eventually we reached the viaduct again and over we went. The tide was in (it had been out the day before) and there were oyster-fishing boats pottering around, so it all looked much more interesting. Just over the viaduct was a very nice restaurant, although we were the only ones there. Madame was horrified when we ordered a whole bottle of wine, probably thinking we were driving, but she was quite happy to take a large tip by mistake. There was a time when I was slightly shocked at the notion of quaffing a bottle between us but nowadays it seems to be quite easy.

We made our way through some dreary back streets and reached Hiers which was much nicer. And there was a *hill* up to it, after which we were on a rangy marsh road. (In *Beyond the Fringe* the eastbound Central line is described as passing through places uninhabited except by rangy marsh birds.) It was pretty countryside with a fair sprinkling of wildlife. We saw storks, rangy marsh harriers, a kite, egrets, heron and dykes with water. There were storks on chimneys, and in trees. We thought we saw an otter though it was quite likely a coypu, a large herbivorous and semi-aquatic rodent introduced to Europe from South America. It lives in burrows by water and is considered an invasive species. I saw one once in Paris and it was messing around quite happily on the banks of the Seine while people gathered round it declaring they didn't know what it was but that they could tell '*ce n'est pas un rat*'. I should hope not, the size of it.

We were aiming to use the Pont Transbordeur de Martrou which was marked on the map as a way to get over to Rochefort. This iron transporter bridge is described by the Michelin guide as a splendid example of industrial art dating from 1900, and is 176m long, standing at more than 50m above the surface of the Charente river. Other examples can be found in Marseille, Brest, Nantes and Rochefort, the excessive height allowing ocean-going ships to pass under pedestrians and vehicles. A new bridge for traffic was opened in 1991 but cyclists and pedestrians are still able to use the old bridge except that, typically, when we arrived we found it was being repaired so we had to backtrack and use the main bridge. We survived it, just, but were agreeably impressed by the cycle ways in Rochefort.

Rochefort has a great maritime past and there is a fine arsenal. Colbert, the minister in charge of Louis XIV's navy, chose the port as a base from which to fend off the English. General La Fayette sailed from the port in 1780 to help the Americans in the War of Independence. In 1816 the frigate *Medusa* set sail for Senegal and was wrecked off Mauretania. The artist Géricault painted the event as *The Raft of the Medusa*, and it felt exciting to be in the ship's home port because some years ago I sang in the oratorio of the same name with the BBC Singers (written by Hans Werner Henze as a requiem for Che Guevara). It was great fun to sing, and we all had tiny solos as we died after which we had to cross the floor of the Barbican concert hall to join the dead souls on the other side. Being choral singers, we weren't used to moving around much but we all got over without anyone falling flat on their face.

We found the station, tucked the Bromptons into themselves, and took the train to La Rochelle. On arrival Modestine was resisting her seat going up again so Dahb rode her for me, trendily low, looking rather like Groucho Marx. We passed the Vieux Port and reached Hôtel de Paris, booked for us by the lovely lady in Saintes. The bikes were stabled in the courtyard, and we changed and popped back to the Vieux Port for drinks. What a lovely town it is, and such good cycle lanes. I think it was La Rochelle that pioneered 'Boris' bikes, bikes for hire on the streets. They were white and it might have been Rochefort, but we didn't see any anywhere so perhaps they had all been stolen. Back in the pedestrian area we found a *crêperie* at a crossroads where we could do great people watching. We decided it must be a university town as there was so much 'yoof', and indeed it is.

The next day (Saturday), Dahb managed to mend my bent seat tube using the handle of a hoe, so I suppose I should add hoe-handle to our what-to-take list. We were going to the Île de Ré and set off down the coast, having found a cycle track. On the bridge there was a barrier between us and the traffic, much better than the Oléron viaduct.

On the island we found a back street and then a road to Ste-Marie-de-Ré where we had a beer with a crinkly-faced dog which made the most extraordinary noise when its owner left it to go to the loo. We went on to St-Martin-de-Ré which we entered through the ramparts. It was very touristy but rather pretty and there were plenty of restaurants. With lunch (sitting outside) we had some Île de Ré wine, which wasn't at all bad.

We debated whether to explore the island further but the weather was looking a bit grim and the wind getting up, so we decided to turn back. It was quite tough going getting up to the bridge, but once over Dahb found an excellent way back into town, straight down to our hotel street. It was much quicker than the coastal track we'd taken in the morning and very quiet, with cycle lanes as we approached the town. We got in at 7.30pm so changed and went out again, finding beer by the harbour at a bar with big comfy chairs, soft-seated. We people-watched for a while, then walked round to the other side where there were quite a few restaurants, some with pouncing waiters. Those are the ones we usually avoid as we wonder why people have to be lured in. We had cycled about 60km so went to bed pleasantly tired.

We had decided to stay another night and take a boat to Île d'Aix, without bikes as it is tiny. The crossing took an hour and was fun, going round Fort Boyard which was started at the time of Napoleon Bonaparte but finished by his nephew Napoleon III by which time it was militarily out of date. We landed just outside 'the' village and walked through streets that were seething with people. We went round the island in an anti-clockwise direction and the weather was good to us. It was a very pleasant walk, and we took in Fort Liédot which had housed Russian prisoners in the Crimean War and First World War, and Prussian prisoners in the Franco-Prussian War of 1870. We lunched in the village and owing to some misunderstanding about where we paid the bill, we nearly missed the boat. Dahb raced on ahead and we made it just about on time, the boat being a bit late anyway.

Back at our hotel we changed and went out towards the area

known as Les Minimes, searching for La Ville en Bois where the Michelin guide said we could see picturesque wooden shacks. We hunted around but they seemed to have been cleared up to make way for modern buildings. There were lots of boats, but they were rather gin palacey – very few that interested Dahb who is a dinghy sailor. We found a bar on a sunny street, in blissful heat. After dinner on the quay, we collapsed exhausted into bed, again.

The next day was Monday 21st June and Midsummer Day and knowing our record the temperature would drop several degrees and we would have to battle through a snowstorm. Whatever, it was time to get back to Angoulême in order to catch the return train on Tuesday. Although it was still cool (I told you so), the sun was shining brightly (oh) so we decided to cycle back to Rochefort and take the train. Part of the road went alongside a canal, and we went through an attractive marsh area where there were special-looking cows including Herefords. It was very easy getting into Rochefort thanks to the cycle tracks and in the centre, we found a shady table in Place Colbert (gosh, needed shade?) and enjoyed a salad and some Charentais rosé.

Back to Angoulême by train and to Hôtel d'Orléans again, even to the same room. We changed and went out to explore the old town where the best bit is by the cathedral. We could hear bands playing and when we got to the maze of streets starting at Rue du Soleil we found more bands and hordes of people. We made our way, with difficulty, to Place des Halles where a rather poor band was playing on a stage. Still, we got beers and enjoyed people watching. Then we squeezed back down Rue Massilly where there were drummers drumming, and found a very good restaurant, though there was nowhere to eat outside. No matter, we could hear the drummers perfectly well even with the door closed, which sounds as if we were trying to, which we weren't. We asked the waiter what was going on and he told us it was the Fête de la Musique (which much was obvious) and that it happened everywhere in France on June 21st. Why had we never encountered it before, we wondered? We squeezed through the crowds to get back to the hotel – there were bagpipes in Place Marengo. We slept like logs so presumably the Fête didn't reach the station quarter.

We had an uneventful journey home via Lille and I managed to finish *The Girl with the Dragon Tattoo* which was all the rage then. We had lunch at Lille and were home in good time, walking into the usual feline 'And where do you think you've been don't you realise I haven't had a thing to eat all week?'

Chapter 17
Roussillon

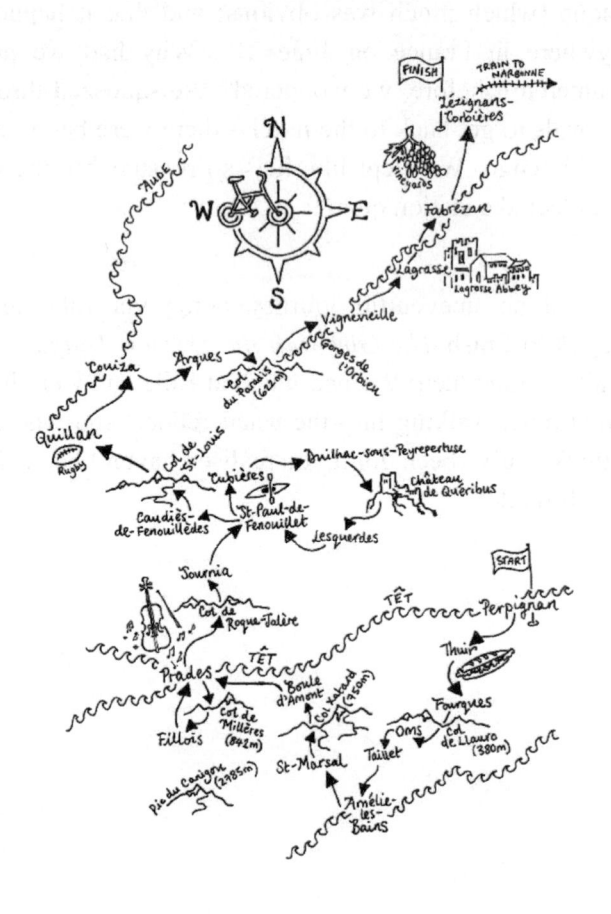

In 1998 we had had a long and eventful holiday in Languedoc and in 2011 were preparing to visit Roussillon, the other half of the former region. We had just touched the Aude *département* at the end of the Languedoc holiday, Carcassonne being its *chef-lieu*.

Roussillon is one of the historical counties of the former principality of Catalonia, corresponding roughly to today's Pyrénées-Orientales *département.* It may also refer to Northern Catalonia or 'French Catalonia'. Michelin describes Roussillon as resembling an enormous allotment with its orchards, market gardens and vineyards. There are certainly vineyards – Côtes de Roussillon cover the southern slopes of the Corbières *massif* which is bounded to the west and north by the Aude river and by the sea to the east. There are also fine beaches with tourist resorts and never far from view is the magnificent Canigou (2784m), a mountain peak revered by both French and Spanish Catalonians. On Midsummer Eve bonfires are lit on its summit.

We left home by bicycle on Saturday 4th June and just missed the train we were aiming for. The next one was cancelled. Feeling a bit rushed when we got to Paddington we found there were no tubes running so we hopped in a taxi which got us there quickly and which we thought good value at £13.60. (The next time we decided to treat ourselves to a taxi we found they had relocated the taxi rank and we felt we had walked as far, if not further, than we would have done if we'd taken the underground. Or even walked to St P.) At St Pancras we headed for the ticket machines to get our internet-booked tickets and the machines worked, with help. Then we shopped for lunch and supper, as it was to be a long journey, and went through to get the 12.28 Eurostar. Our seats were not together but a nice man swapped.

We crossed Paris on the RER to the Gare de Lyon and had time for a beer there before the Perpignan train left at 5.20pm. It was a lovely quiet train with lots of luggage space, but it stopped in the middle of nowhere (possibly Beaujolais) and thus ran 55 minutes late. We rang our hotel to tell them, the man answering sounding very uninterested. We did find later there was a night porter, but it wouldn't be the first time I'd arrived at a hotel to find someone else in my room.

From Valence the train stopped at a lot of stations including Montpellier, Béziers and Narbonne. At 11.15pm we rolled into Perpignan to find armed guards closing down the station. We cycled through town to our hotel which was a one star and very much our type. No faff, but everything we could need including a simple shower that worked well. There was a wonderful terrace, very scruffy with a superb chair with a painted back and crumbling seat.

We had booked for two nights so after breakfast at the hotel with some dreadful coffee that we finally persuaded Monsieur to reheat (but the croissants and tartine were fine), we set off to explore the town. We found a lovely way in via a canal, with flower borders and oleander alongside. We also saw bougainvillea and jacaranda. After a short game of Hunt the Turismu we found it, and I asked for the accommodation guides I'd emailed for and been assured would be waiting for me. The lady knew nothing of my request but seemed to have the information anyway. Then I asked if the Narbonne office had sent the Aude information as I had asked but that hadn't arrived. She said it wouldn't have because Thursday had been a bank holiday. She then said she had loads of information on the Aude and produced a great pile of stuff that was about everything except hotels, apart from some in Narbonne. They seemed to be determined to get us to Narbonne. She did assure us that Quillan, and Limoux had plenty of accommodation and we hoped this was more accurate information that we'd been given that time in Portugal (it was). As we had all the Turismu numbers for the two *départements* we'd be visiting we left it at that. As usual, only too willing to help but rather lacking the essential information.

Perpignan was once the capital city of the Counts of Roussillon and the Kings of Majorca and is described by Michelin as an outlying post of Catalan civilisation north of the Pyrenees. Lying on the river Têt, its economic dynamism is due to the export of fruit, vegetables and wine from the hinterlands. The city batted back and forth twixt Spain and France for some time, with various attempts at autonomy, but with the Treaty of the Pyrenees in 1659 it became French once and for all.

We went to the Parc des Platanes where there was a big market, always fun to explore, then at Place de la République we had a Leffe beer and some nibbles. We sorted our Turismu stuff into keep and chuck piles, most going into the latter. After a bit more pottering and lunch outside – very pleasant and with a carafe of rosé – we went to visit the cathedral which was, unusually for us, open, if somewhat grim inside. We were unable to get to the cloister cemetery (I just *lerv* cloisters) because they were setting up for a concert. We then walked round the citadel which was a long way but there were lots of interesting things to see and fine views towards the Canigou, which was shrouded in cloud.

We then went to the station, which was quite a distance, to check that our return TGV stopped at Narbonne, which it did, so we thought we would aim there for our last night, as the Turismu people seemed so keen to get us there. Back to the centre for evening drinks and I had a big glass of sangria at the first decent place we came to. It was lovely, sitting in the hot sun and being served by a very jolly waiter. There were cars with North African men roaring around waving red flags and hooting and shouting. Our waiter told us that Morocco had just beaten Algeria 4-1 at football. We decided the men behind us must be Algerian as they were looking very glum whereas a group near the restaurant were clearly rather pleased. It was so pleasant where we were that we decided to move over to the tables set for dining and have our meal there. We had pizzas and carafes of red and rosé wine and watched the people around us. There were two thin girls next to us who spent their time looking at their phone cameras and picking at their food, leaving quite a lot of their main course. This is an abomination to us and we felt like offering to finish it, but we were rather full of pizza. We walked back to the hotel along the canal and so ended an amusing day in Perpignan. Time to saddle up and move on!

We had more tepid coffee the next morning – I really think we should take our own coffee cosy with us. The only time we get hot coffee is when we're in a hotel with a bar and the coffee is made in the bar machine. Then Dahb led us out of town on a good route, over the Têt and through the suburbs. Soon we were on pretty quiet roads passing by fruit farms, some sadly derelict. Nectarines were being picked and we thought 'yum' and then wondered what was sprayed on them. After about 25km we reached Thuir where we hitched the steeds and went lunch hunting. We got gweges at a *boulangerie* and some sweeties at a paper shop, then had a beer on the terrace of Le Café Bleu. The weather was warm but getting cloudier and the *météo* forecasted afternoon shower activity.

At Fourques we shared our gwege with a very hungry cat, and then climbed to the Col de Llauro (380m) going on to Oms where we met a couple with a mule. Then a lovely little road to Taillet and on a bit, still on tarmac, but after passing a man and his dog we found the tarmac had run out. We went quite a long way downhill on a very rough track, hands hurting as we held the brakes. With relief we reached the tarmac again, crossed a river, contoured up again then enjoyed the descent into Amélie-les-Bains which lies at 300m. Amélie is the southernmost spa town in France and owes its development to the opening of a military hospital there in 1854. It is joined with Palalda, a Mediaeval town we managed to miss.

We found a street with several hotels and chose a very nice one-star, Hôtel des Combes. After changing we drank beers just across the road, then hunted for dinner spots eventually finding Au Poivre Vert which was empty and quite pricey. But it was good and the waitress was very pleasant, and we had the *cuvée maison*, a Côtes de Roussillon rosé. The weather had stayed mainly dry with just a little rain in the evening.

Breakfast was self-service and there was a machine for making coffee which was fine if drunk immediately. We went to look for picnic stuff and followed signs to Casino but discovered it was a gambling sort of casino, not the chain of little Casino shops. But there was a Spar, a *boulangerie* and a market so we got what we needed, including radishes which we find very tasty for picnics especially if I've remembered to bring some salt.

We started off on the road we'd come in on, then carried on up, higher and higher to Taulis (500m) where there was no café. We went down to cross a ravine, then up and up to St-Marsal at 700m. There we were overtaken by a group of German *motoists* who, like us, headed for La Casa Syldie. It started to rain so we all dove indoors, where we had galettes, *crêpes* and some rosé.

It was still raining when we'd finished so we togged up and set off up the road to Col Xatard (750m), eschewing a higher route via La Bastide. We zoomed down via Boule d'Amont, the Canigou now behind us and looking snowy on top. We then had to join the main road, which was horrid. We tried a deviation but we just found ourselves in the middle of maize fields, so we tackled the main road again. It wasn't too bad as there was a bit of a hard shoulder, though that was liable to disappear at times. It was raining very heavily but we reached Prades at last. The first hotel seemed to be closed, in spite of a number of foreign cars in the car park, but the next one (Hôtel Hostalrich) was open and had a room, the bicycles being stabled in a huge dining room and guarded by some tubby cats. Our gear was extremely wet but we ourselves were dry.

The room was fine so we booked in for two nights. As it was quite late we hit the town and found a café in the square by the church with comfy soft-cushioned chairs into which we collapsed gratefully.

We had a delicious meal accompanied by an organic Catalan white wine made in a vineyard formerly belonging to Maréchal Joffre. Dahb impressed me by immediately sniffing out the 80% Muscat, the rest being Viognier. We could hear some English voices in the corner. All very pleasant, then back to our hand-held shower and bed. Joffre, by the way, was Commander-in-Chief of the French forces in the early part of World War I. He is best known for defeating the Germans at the Battle of the Marne in

September 1914.

Prades lies right at the foot of the Canigou and its chief claim to fame is that the renowned cellist Pablo Casals, a Spanish Catalan, made his home there when he left Spain at the outbreak of the Civil War. He was an ardent Republican and after the defeat of the government in 1939 he vowed not to return to Spain until democracy was restored. So opposed to Franco was he that he refused to perform in countries recognising the Francoist regime. He died in 1973 at the age of 96, just two years before the end of the Francoist state and was posthumously honoured by the restored monarchy.

We got up quite late the next day (Wednesday) and had breakfast in an enormous dining room full of strange things. One of the tubby cats came in to say good morning and the coffee was fairly tepid. We wandered around town for a while and tried to get information about St-Paul-de-Fenouillet from Turismu as we thought it looked like a good place to aim for on Thursday. Alas, they couldn't help as St-Paul was in a different *secteur* although it wasn't many miles away.

Off we went and after about 100m I had a puncture. Dahb mended it in a public park, finding a tiny piece of wire in the tyre. Off we set again, but my tyre was still deflating. We borrowed someone's parking space to change tube and tyre, Dahb struggling titanically with the Schwalbe tyre. Off we set again, and all seemed well. It was now dangerously close to beer time but in spite of following signs to Codanet *centre ville*, not a bar was to be seen, so we had to proceed beerless up the valley.

We passed the lovely abbey of St-Michel-de-Cuixa where the Pablo Casals music festival is held, and went on to Taurinya which was again beerless. Up and up, we went to the Col de Millères (842m) and the views of the Canigou would have been superb had it not been obscured by cloud. The scenery was stunning anyway and descending to Fillols we found *two* bars. The village dogs provided entertainment as we enjoyed our welcome drink and there was one character, rather like the Tramp from that lovely film, *The Lady and the Tramp*, who was clearly at a bit of a loose end.

It was now chilly as we went down so we donned anoraks and set off back the way we came. Back in Prades it was cool with very light rain. After changing and buying the next day's picnic we had our evening beer and then a meal in a restaurant that was packed with foreigners – North Americans, a group of German men, a group of Dutch or Danish and another couple whose identity we couldn't make out. We had a delicious meal accompanied by Marshall Joffre's red wine this time. Full of food we went back to have an early night and thus an early start.

The next day we were up with the 8am lark and leaving town by 9am which is what constitutes an early start nowadays. Setting off on the D619 we soon branched off to the right and, climbing quite a long way, passed a St-Jacques chapel (we were on a Santiago de Compostela route). There were some wonderful views of the Canigou when the clouds lifted as they did from time to time. We arrived at the Col de Roque Jalère around 1pm, at 991m. Prades is at about 320m, so we had gone up quite a lot. We swooped down to Saunia which was quite a big place with shops and an *auberge*, but no bar. We carried on for a while then decided to have lunch before beer and ate our picnic by the road. The cheese was a bit hard, but the radishes were still juicy. A lady with an old man walked by and said we were *de bon courage*. Continuing down we think we saw a hoopoe and there was still no beer at the next village. Things were getting desperate as we were having to climb quite a bit which is not good for the digestion. At the next village, le Vivier, there was no beer. This was getting depressingly repetitive.

On the way down we caught a glimpse of the Canigou and there were quite a few vineyards around. There were good views of the valley as we descended and went through the Clue de la Fou gorge to reach St-Paul-de-Fenouillet. It was a bit doubtful looking but there was a Turismu, and they booked us into Chez la Mère *chambre-d'hôte*. They told us it was the best place, although they weren't meant to say that. It had an Accueil Paysan label, which put emphasis on home products and meals served in the house.

I think it was one of the best places we'd ever stayed in. The very friendly Monsieur and Madame welcomed us and showed us our room, first storing our cycles in the most wonderful glory hole of a garage. Our room was over the road from the main house, up some steps and was the most wonderful set-up. Madame said dinner would be served at 8pm so we nipped back to the square and had the long-awaited beers, Dahb managing to swig a 50cl without anyone telling him off. The sun came out for about five minutes and a group of English persons arrived for drinks.

Back to the ranch for dinner and it was a splendid evening with great food and liquor to match. There was a French couple who lived near Aix-en-Provence, a quiet man whose name we didn't catch, and a voluble man called Albert who didn't seem to come from anywhere special but was very friendly. He and our Monsieur, Claude, talked the hind legs off several donkeys and nearly all the conversation was about food and therefore very interesting. Our hosts were strongly accented, Albert less so, but a very rapid speaker. The party broke up about 10.30pm and it was quite hard work getting our stuffed tummies back to our room.

The Fenouillèdes, by the way, is the name given to the area between southern Corbières and the Conflent which is the part of Roussillon through which the Têt flows. Prades is in the Conflent. We had booked in for two nights so that we could do a *Pays Cathare* circuit. We wanted a closer look at some of the main 'Cathar castles' which are actually castles built by the French after the Cathar or Albigensian Crusade to defend the new border with Aragon. Carcassonne was a major one and Peyrepertuse is known as one of the five sons of Carcassonne, another being Quéribus.

We started off through the Galamus gorge, which was really impressive, the rugged road being carved out of the rock. We could see over to l'Ermitage St-Antoine-de-Galamus, but goodness knows how one got to it. We met an American who was in a *moto* group with a support vehicle – he said he thought we were insane (you too, chum). A pair of cyclists passed us on *VTT*s, carrying rucksacks on their backs (*that's* insane). Albert had told us about the terrible wind in the gorge and there was certainly quite a bit of it, but not all the way through. We could see canoeists on the river below – it looked horrible and freezing. We stopped for an expensive and indifferent coffee at le Vieux Moulin and met a French woman who asked if the gorge was vertiginous as her husband had vertigo and he was the only one who could drive their big car. We recommended they took another route.

The next place was Cubières, a nice place with lovely gardens. In Duilhac-sous-Peyrepertuse we found a pleasant *auberge* for lunch with great views of the château, amazingly built into the rock. Michelin says it is one of the finest examples of a Mediaeval fortress in the Corbières and the outcrop has been occupied since Roman times.

We went downhill then up again, taking the road to Château de Quéribus which as late as 1241 was still providing refuge for the Cathars. It fell in 1255 and became a royal fortress. Time was getting on, so we didn't go right up to it, but we had had a superb view of it for quite a while. As we munched some cherries, the rucksack couple appeared. He still had his, but she'd managed to ditch hers which was rather curious, and I wondered if I could do the same, having taken out all my belongings and stuffed them in Dahb's bag, of course.

There were fantastic views of the Canigou as we swooped down to Maury through a lovely valley with vines. After crossing a busy road, we took a little road up to Lesquerdes, which we liked the look of. Then we went down and so much into the wind that we had to pedal at times. Going through the Clue de la Fou again we arrived back in St-Paul at 6.45pm so stabled the beasts, changed, and went to the square for a beer again. We sat outside at the same table, but it was cool so we wore anoraks. The weather had been dry all day if a bit cloudy and windy.

Then we had another lovely evening Chez la Mère. The Aix couple were there again, and the little man, but instead of Albert there was a young chap with a Renovato Auto polo shirt and a similarly marked van outside. He was very nice and friendly but totally incomprehensible. We had another delicious meal, accompanied by red wine (having started with Muscat as we had done the day before) and I heard the little man speak once but he was ignored by the company. To be fair, I don't think they heard him.

We left our Acceuil Paysan with some regret and after buying a picnic in the square fought our way along the main road for a couple of kilometres into a strong wind and turned off gratefully towards Prugnans, up a pass to a mini *col,* de Parable (320m). We saw a train on the tourist railway. Down to Caudiès-de-Fenouillèdes, 'gateway' to the Fenouillèdes (or in our case gateway out of it) where we had beer inside a café by the main road, the Bromptons occupying a terrace round the back that was too cold for us.

We flogged up to Col St-Louis (687m) and the road really did tie itself in a knot under a bridge, just as it showed on the map although it seemed very unlikely. We had lunch at the *col* on an unfinished picnic site, and out of the wind it was quite hot. However, we donned jerseys for the descent, followed soon after by anoraks as the wind was still cold. It was a lovely gradual way down, ending up in Quillan, apparently a major tourist centre, where we found all the hotels clustered on Boulevard Charles de Gaulle. There was a car-racing competition in progress resulting in lots of noise and cars roaring up and down the boulevard – hardly what we would have chosen for our overnight stop had we known. Quillan is really keen on rugby, apparently, since the decline of the hat-making industry (strange replacement).

It was Pentecost so the first hotel was full, but we were lucky to get a room in the next one we tried. Away from the ring road, where all the cars were, it was quite a nice place. As we sipped beer in the Place de la République we were approached by an English couple who had hired a car but had no map – did we know where such-and-such a place was? We found a pleasant pizzeria for dinner, quite a lot of its tables being reserved. The people-watching was good. There were several French families whose children were given adult-sized pizzas and didn't eat them. The mothers didn't seem to eat much either – probably longing for a ciggy. There was a table of Englanders next to us, none of whom were drinking wine. Dear me.

Having breakfasted and bought bread, we set off on a very nice little road between the river and the railway. After Cuiga we turned east and did a very gradual climb to Arques which sported a fine château and where we had beer and little crispy things. Then we flogged up and up to Col du Paradis (622m) – at this stage I was wearing only a vest t-shirt. We went down again, hunting for the perfect picnic spot and eventually finding a meadow in which to have lunch. There were lots of cornflowers and butterflies.

We continued down, through the very pretty Gorges de l'Orbieu, down to Vignevielle after which we had a very good sight of Château de Termes which was up on the other road. Still descending we had a lovely view of Lagrasse Abbey and finally reached the village itself to find that the *Logis* was full. On a Sunday, for goodness' sake, but then of course we remembered that it was Pentecost and Monday was a bank holiday.

The *Logis* Madame directed us to a street where there were *chambres d'hôte*. We tried one but got no reply and the second was fenced off. We asked a passing lady if there was another and she led us to one but there was no one there. She then asked another passing lady for help and the latter took over as guide. She took us to a lovely-looking place which was full, and where the lady owner was weeping copiously. Then our hard-working guide led us to Les Trois Grâces where there appeared to be no one, but a boy appeared and went to find his father. To our relief he had a room and it proved to be a really nice place.

We fell completely in love with Lagrasse and its abbey, historical houses, and bridges over the river Orbieu. No wonder it is one of Les Plus Beaux Villages de France. It is very old – it was Charlemagne who gave permission for the construction of the abbey. It lies plum in the Corbières wine area, and the region is renowned for the wine produced in the surrounding hills. It's the largest wine-producing region in France.

We pottered around the beautiful streets then found beer on a bar terrace in the main street. It was so pleasant we decided to stay and eat. There were two tables of English persons and at one of them a girl was speaking loudly in that annoying public school way that makes you want to trip them up. There was an interesting family to Dahb's right; we couldn't tell if they were speaking English or French or both. He looked Spanish (and didn't actually speak), she was North African or even perhaps Indian. Both she and the children were very dark. The latter seemed to be sharing a starter unlike the little English boys next to them who each had a bowl of mussels. We couldn't quite make out the hippy types behind me – one was speaking in Estuarine. Lagrasse is quite an arty place – lots of pottery and potters about. After a lovely meal and very local wine, we made our way back to Les Trois Grâces to be met by a yellow Labrador hoping we'd brought home a chop.

Wonders will never cease – next morning the coffee was hot, being served in a thermos flask. After a good breakfast we went out for a walk, crossing the Orbieu with an excellent view of the Vieux Pont but finding the Abbey not quite open. We wandered back through the Mediaeval streets and past the 13th century market hall. Then we set off up the valley and went up and down dale, needing shade for our beers in Fabrezan. We crossed the Orbieu again and took a road through the vineyards, arriving at Lézignans-Corbières ('halfway between Carcassonne and the sea') where we had quite a job to find the station. When we did we found that most trains weren't running because it was a bank holiday. But we needed only one ...

We went back to the town centre and enjoyed a leisurely lunch and leisurely coffees afterwards. Then back to the station for the 5.27pm to Narbonne where we secured a room at Hôtel d'Alsace, a very nice two-star near the station. We dumped our stuff and changed and went out to explore. Narbonne has been a busy place since before Roman times and its flourishing port with imports and exports caused Cicero to call it "the boulevard of the Latin world". By the 14th century the bay had silted up and Narbonne ceased to be a port. There is a fine cathedral and an archbishop's palace which looks onto Place Hôtel de Ville where we had drinks, served after quite a long wait. After a bit more walking we found a pleasant restaurant on Cour Mirabeau, by the Robine canal. We had an aperitif of Blanquette de Limoux, then a wine that was a blend of Fitou, Carignan, Grenache and Syrah. After dinner we took more small streets back to our hotel and agreed it was a very attractive town.

We had a bit of time before our train the next day (Tuesday 14th June) so took another look at Narbonne and bought some lunch for ourselves and presents for the neighbours at an organic shop. We went back to the hotel to get our luggage and to pay, and became a bit worried about missing the train as Dahb's card wouldn't go through the hotel's card machine. After absolutely ages Monsieur managed to get it working, and we caught the 10.52. The train was very full as the Dijon train was very late, so the passengers from that one piled in with us. Apparently it was going to stop at Lyon which it didn't normally do. We got some beers for our midday fortification then Dahb gave up his seat to an elderly lady, so we had to wait until the train was less full to have our lunch. I could see Dahb chatting away to people in the vestibule – good French practice. We were due to arrive at Paddington at 7.05pm and as far as I can remember, we did.

Chapter 18
Provence yet again part 1

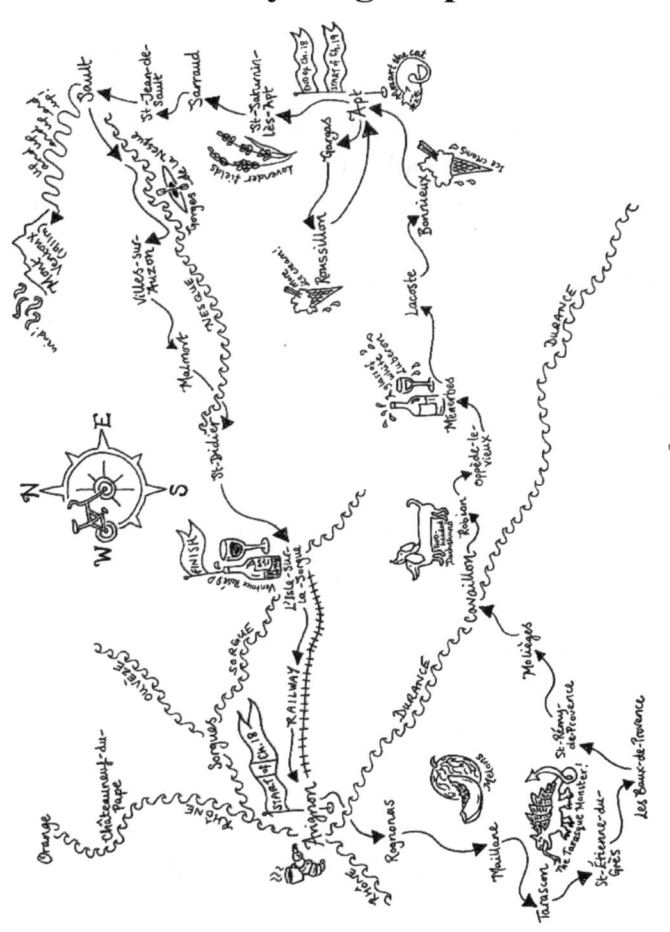

Earlier chapters described holidays taken in Provence in 1996, 2000 and 2006. In 2013 we set off again for that lovely region of France. On Monday 10th June we cycled to the station and caught the 9.11am to London. The weather was cool and grey, having been so far a lovely June, and the roses were just coming out.

At St Pancras we managed to get our tickets out of the machine unaided and headed for our favourite Le Pain Quotidien. This is the point at which we feel the holiday begins – ready to board Eurostar but with time for coffee and croissants. As in too many French hotels, the coffee was weak and tepid, being served in large open cups. On holiday indeed! Someone was playing horrid music on one of the honky-tonk pianos that are there for the public and there was a crooner and drums. But probably someone liked it and it didn't do us any harm.

Checking in to Eurostar, Dahb managed to cause general chaos by failing to remove his money belt before going through the X-ray which meant he had to go back against the flow to put it on the conveyor. But at least no Semtex was suspected (odd, as we had the same oil container we carried when suspected of terrorist intent on an earlier occasion) and we got through and had time for a beer before boarding.

We had a fairly quick change at Lille, so ate a home-made picnic on Eurostar, and had time for a coffee at Lille. Then we tried to get on the TGV. Our tickets showed two train numbers with our seats in coach 8. Coming out of the lift down to the platform we found ourselves by the nose of the train so made for the rear end near which there was an information screen showing us we should be at the front. Slightly confused, we went back to the train's snout to find another train had just been attached to it and of course coach 8 was right at the other end of the second train. Feeling in a bit of a rush but grateful we weren't completely geriatric, we finally found our seats, though not before I noticed that Dahb had dropped the green toy bag he had been carrying separately (it usually goes in his front pannier and he was gallantly lightening my load). We found it and climbed aboard.

Nothing to do now until Avignon in four hours' time. We were amazed to find we had smashing seats, by a left-hand window in a forward direction. Usually, we travel backwards in those seats that have no windows. There were lovely views going through Burgundy and Beaujolais, then alongside or near the Rhône, with superb vistas of the Vercors, the left side being the right one to be on, if you get my drift.

It was all so pleasant and comfortable that four hours didn't seem very long at all. Soon after 8pm we were standing on the platform at Avignon's TGV station, which was just where we expected to be, having checked it out beforehand. We didn't really know where the Avignon TGV station was, however, our maps being too old, but there was a shuttle bus outside which took us into town and dropped us at the post office, very near our prebooked Hôtel Alizéa.

We had a very pleasant room with plenty of space for the Bromptons to doss down with us. It was on the fourth floor but there was a lift (unlike the delightful Hôtel du Levant in Besançon where we were given a room on the fourth floor and had to carry everything up, including the bicycles). We went straight out again, up the street to Place de l'Horloge and ordered two medium Leffes at Lou Mistral which turned out to be 50cl, so thank goodness we didn't order large ones. We stayed there until about 10pm then hunted for somewhere to eat as we could see places shutting down. We found a pizzeria with a sheltered terrace, a very nice waiter and excellent fodder accompanied by a red Ventoux. So ended the first day.

When I went out for a pre-breakfast walk, the temperature was already eighteen degrees. I found a lovely square and some sweet-scented limes, and the Impasse des Abeilles where we'd stayed in 1998. *Chambres d'hôte* were still available there. I went back to collect Dahb, and we walked through the pedestrian area to Place du Palais (des Papes, along a lovely street cut out of the rock behind the Palais). No suitable cafés so we went back to Place de l'Horloge where we'd previously spotted a *salon de thé* in which we got excellent double coffees and croissants. We bought a picnic, including radishes, in the magnificent *Halles* and having booked our hotel again for our last night (the 20th) packed and set out on our adventures. This hotel was not only pleasant and friendly but, at 67 euros, the cheapest we saw in Avignon.

Big cities can be difficult to get out of and Avignon proved to be no exception, although we had got a Vaucluse cycle map which showed a cycle *piste* to the station, where we were going. The *piste* was shown starting from the Palais and following the Rhône right round. We had considerable trouble crossing a boulevard but could see some sort of track or path by the river. Dicing with death, we crossed the road and made it to the Rhône by which time there was a track which wasn't obvious for cycling but was wide enough, though cluttered a bit with pedestrians.

But there was a strong warm north wind which was perfect, so we had a good start, until the track degenerated into a footpath and a small ravine to cross, then all we had was a footpath by or on the road, *just* away from the traffic. Eventually we found a proper *piste* which might or might not have pointed to the TGV station (we wanted to check where it was) and it was pretty well all right up to the station except for the occasional step and a crowd of Health and Safety people cluttering up the path and who appeared to be learning how to use a lawnmower, presumably healthily and safely.

The TGV station was and presumably still is a vast ghastly building in a huge industrial zone which was shown as marshland on our map. The *piste* petered out behind it and we couldn't see how to get to a huge new bridge over the river Durance. Not that we were keen to get up there with all the traffic but there seemed to be no other way of crossing the river. Eventually we took a road back and round and went up the slip road which had a wide hard shoulder, almost serving as a *piste*. Up and over we went, very high and windy though at least the wind was behind us. There wasn't too much traffic, but it was very fast and much was HGVs, but we were finally over and at a roundabout took the road to Rognonas, still a bit busy but with a 30km limit in the village. We had a look around and found a modern café in a square with a market packing up. We sat on a sunny if windy terrace and bought two Affligems from a jolly Madame. The loo was frightfully smart though lacking any loo roll.

It was lovely to be out of the urban area. We were going through flat agricultural country with polytunnels of melons, attractive houses and farms, and easy cycling with the wind still behind. Outside Graveson we had our picnic on a bench by a road and a canal, then went on to Maillane where Mistral was born, lived and died.

Frédéric Mistral (1830-1914) was a French writer and lexicographer of the Occitan language. He cofounded the Félibrige literary and cultural association which promoted the Occitan language and received the 1910 Nobel Prize for Literature. A lovely lady from the adjacent library let us in to the museum, that is, his gorgeous house and pretty garden. There were lots of pictures of famous people and letters too – amazing who he corresponded with. Then we went into the attractive village and had good coffee and water sitting on sofas on a shady terrace – very luxurious.

On to Tarascon, Dahb examining apples (on trees) and myself looking at some Camargue white horses, the ones we didn't see when we cycled in the Camargue in appalling weather many years ago. There was also a field of little black bovines which we supposed were matador-fighting bulls. Dahb had found a good approach to Tarascon, just one tricky road to cross then we were in quiet old streets leading to Place des Halles and the Hôtel de Ville. We had torn out some sheets from our 2005 hotel information and found a couple of two-star establishments: Le Provençal on Boulevard Victor Hugo was a bit pricey, but the cheaper Le Castel over the road wasn't open until 6pm so we booked in to the first one. The patron said it was the last room, so we felt pleased (though we do sometimes wonder if they always say this).

The steeds were enstabled in the garage behind, their riders coming back to reception through the kitchen – most thrilling. The *patron's* English was excellent; chatting to him we learned he had worked at the White Hart in Sonning, near Reading, one of the many English pubs we've had a drink at whilst cycling. Our room was marvellous, with a shared terrace which no one else used. As we headed purposefully out the *patron* warned us there were not many bars and suggested trying the station restaurant. Naturally it was closed on Tuesday evenings, but we found somewhere else and, after drinks, stocked up on a 25cl *plastique* of red wine as we felt we ought to have a nightcap on our terrace. Then we did some exploring in the old town, with its narrow streets and fine castle built sheer into the river. The guidebook says it is in an exceptional state of preservation and thus one of the finest Mediaeval castles in France, but because we were in town it was closed (to be fair, it was evening).

For some 2000 years Tarascon, a pre-Roman trading post, has been linked with the Tarasque monster, an amphibious creature which, according to legend, climbed out of the Rhône from time to time and gobbled up little childer and cattle and killed anyone trying to cross the river. But to save the town Ste Marthe popped over from Les-Stes-Maries-de-la-Mer and subdued it with the sign of the cross so that the townspeople were able to catch it, the monster being now one big pussycat.

We went through some arcades, which are apparently unique to the region, and in l'Antre (the lair) du Tarasque saw a model of the monster in the window. He's brought out on special occasions. As with bars, there weren't huge numbers of restaurants but back at Le Castel we had an excellent meal, although we were the only customers once a solitary man had exited, perhaps finding it had suddenly become rather crowded. We drank a *pichet* of Gard Beauvais rosé and for nibbles were given olives and pappy bread triangles with anchovy paste which were delicious – I made a note to do them at home. I had to ask for a key to use the loo; apparently if they don't lock it people just wander in and out using them as a public convenience. Back at our hotel we sat on the terrace with the unpromising sounding plastique of 'Vin de France', but it wasn't bad at all.

The temperature had been wonderful all day, lots of sun but enough breeze to keep it sufficiently cool. There had been superb views *en route* of La Montagnette, a range of low hills paralleling the Rhône to the east, and the Alpilles to the south. The Alpilles are loftier and are in the direction we were heading the next day, south-east of Tarascon, as we now had a plan to revisit Les Baux-de-Provence.

The sky was blue first thing, and the *météo* on the enormous TV in our room showed fabulous sun over Provence all week with the rest of France and the UK often somewhat indifferent. This pleased Dahb hugely – he can't bear to think of anyone else having good weather when he's not there. I must say I like to see a bit of rain falling at home but that's a gardening matter rather than curmudgeonliness.

He took a picture of me sitting on the balcony writing the diary and I took a picture of Le Castel opposite, though I will have to look at the pictures (if I can find them on my computer) to find out why. You know, digital cameras are all very well, especially the way the date is on the pic so that you can remember when you took the photo even if you can't always remember where you were at the time, but we used to take about one film's worth a year and the excitement when we got that film developed and settled down to look at the pictures cannot easily be replicated. Although the feeling I have when I see a full glass of plonk coming my way is pretty near it.

Panic ensued when we realised the camera wasn't working because there was no battery. Dahb had charged up the battery before leaving home. Q: where was it? A: still in the battery charger. Luckily, we had brought a spare by accident. By the way, Dahb used to carry the camera, but I now take it as he could never be bothered to take any photos. Now that I carry it, we get a few more though I do agree that it is often a bit of a bore stopping and taking it out of the pannier just in front of me and switching it on.

After all this, it was time for breakfast, and it was exceptionally good. Hot coffee in flasks, proper jam in pots, not those infuriating plastic things you spend so much time trying to get into whilst your coffee cools (even more). It was all rather fun with a party of Chinese who were going to Marseille for the day. A couple of them spoke a bit of English and another could speak French. There was also a French lady who told us she lived in Aix and was working in Tarascon (the *patron* later told us she was a circuit judge). She was very elegant and charming – she said she loved London for the shopping to which I answered with the French equivalent of 'crumbs'.

We were on our way just after 9am and Dahb found a good way out of town via the prison and the abattoir. But then there was a huge new bridge over the Rhône with huge new roads. On the roundabout there was a vast lorry *carrying* a bit of bridge, and the driver of an enormous HGV very politely waited for me (I wrote TGV but I'm sure that's not right).

Gradually the roads got smaller, and we entered St-Étienne-du-Grès via back roads and turned up the hill past a *chaussée deformée* sign (road full of bumps). Buses were forbidden and no wonder. Soon, in a lovely village suburb, the tarmac ran out and it was *accès reglementé* which we later discovered was because of fire risk – motorists had to check they were allowed to go through. We were now on a rough track, in fact Grande Randonnée no 6, otherwise known as a footpath. The views were fabulous. There were Swiss-style signs saying how long it took to walk to Les Baux – one said two hours and 12 minutes. What happens if you want to stop and redo your shoelace? Are you all*owed* to take longer? What if you get there too early?

As we went on, the signs ran out (except for those pointing out the *citernes* – water tanks for the fire service) and it was pretty difficult to tell which direction to take. Eventually we reached the top and caught our first (2013) sight of Les Baux so at least we now knew where to go. There was a sign on a fence saying *Danger Taureaux* and I fervently hoped that those little black bulls were on the other side of a well-maintained enclosure. Very eventually we found a tarred road and, wiggling around a bit, emerged on the D27 where lots of camper vans were parked. The landscape was stunning – no other word for it. We went down, which was a bit annoying as we could see we would have to climb up again, and I took a fine photo of the village, its cars and its grockles. In the car park we tethered the Bromptons by a hedge with other bicycles for company (there were a lot of hire bikes around) and went up some steps to the village which was the only way of getting in. Our Tarascon *patron* had recommended the La Reine Jeanne restaurant, but it was chocka, so we looked around and in a back street found a very nice place with a lovely terrace and views, fabulous views, actually, and extremely comfy chairs in the shade. We had salads, rosé and coffee and felt very pleased with ourselves.

We then did the touristy bit, and Les Baux-de-Provence really is an amazing place, even if such a honey pot for the grocks. It is situated on a bare rock spur with vertical ravines on either side, and although on the map it looks as if it is in the Alpilles it is actually detached from them. It was once a very busy place as bauxite was discovered there in 1822 (hence the mineral's name) but now that is no longer mined in France the village has very few residents. The guidebook says it was once a proud fief and if you start repeating those words they sound rather silly. Or you do.

A lot of the village was accessible only if one paid to go into the château, which we didn't, mainly because there were so many people. But there was plenty to see in the back streets, including an extremely pricey *chambre d'hôte*. We wondered what it was like to live there – was the peace that reigned in the evening worth what went on in the day? Probably depended somewhat on whether you were trying to sell anything.

We had had enough, so we picked up the bikes and swooped down towards St-Rémy-de-Provence, a lovely gradient after a steepish start. Unsurprisingly we felt warm and sleepyish. We took the Vieux Chemin d'Arles into town through a *route barrée*, a quiet way in although the centre seemed rather busy. We considered Hôtel Gounod where the composer had written his opera *Mireille,* but it was somewhat costly, so we went to Turismu for a list of hotels and a street map. We looked at all of them then decided to go back through the old centre, which was lovely, and try the one we'd seen on the way in, Hôtel Cheval Blanc. The hotel seemed closed, but we found an open door and a young man who said he was sorry, but he had only a room for three. As it was only 70 euros we said please could we have it even though there were only two of us (four if you count the Bromptons but they never do). He had to dash up to reception on the first floor to check this was all right, which it was.

We paid, in advance, a very nice young man who said the wind was dropping the next day and the temperatures rising. I suppose it must therefore have been windy, though I don't seem to have made a note of it. The bikes had a little room to themselves (free), and we had a very pleasant room which we exited PDQ and went to the café next to Hôtel Gounod for a very welcome drink. Then we did the old town which was really attractive. There were many felines to be seen and Dear Diary says, 'Cat on frog (pic)'. A *crêperie* in a tiny *cul de sac* produced an excellent meal, but the waitress's accent was impenetrable. We made it back to the hotel before lock-up time which was 10pm. On the hotel fire instructions *gagner la sortie* (make for the exit) was translated as 'win out'.

We woke to the sound of birds and rubbish lorries and the smell of baking. There was a white-legged tabby in the garden with a guilty expression. Breakfast was on the terrace and the coffee, although in an open jug, was hot on arrival and we covered it with a saucer. Passing the hospital where Van Gogh was cared for when he was having a difficult time, we cycled up to the ruins of the Roman town, Glanum, and I took a rather good photo of the mausoleum which was a startling white against a perfect blue sky. Much better than the one in the guidebook in which the sky was rather muted and the building positively mucky.

We went back to town as Glanum wasn't open yet (because we were there) and coaches were arriving for the opening at 9.30am and it looked as if it was going to be rather crowded. Going on through La Galine, Molièges and La Crau and after crossing a motorway and a railway line, we had to get over the Durance river to get into Cavaillon. There was a bike lane which wasn't separated from the horrendous traffic, but we got there in one piece if at 12.32 just after Turismu had closed for lunch. We thought it was a good idea and there were plenty of cafés so were soon tucking in. A woman at the next table was considerately holding her ciggy away from her companion with the result that the smoke curled itself into *our* noses.

Pottering in the old town we thought it generally not a very thrilling place though there were some interesting buildings and a fine cathedral. Turismu reopened at 2pm and we got a hotel guide for the area, and thought we'd head for Robion in the Luberon where rumour had it there was a *chambre d'hôte*. The Cavaillon photo shop didn't have our type of camera battery, but the Turismu lady said we should try a big shop on the east side of town which was sort of on our way out. We followed a signed cycle way, then some quiet roads along a cycle way signing to Apt. We found a huge supermarket which had no camera batteries.

We were confused by a cycle sign seemingly pointing the wrong way and landed on a main road but were soon on a quiet road again and heading for Robion. Before we got there we found *a chambre d'hôte* called Mas la Renaissance in the countryside which looked very pleasant, and which had one room left so we grabbed it. It was run by a nice young French couple, David and Stéphanie, and her pa was gardening for them. There was a black poodle and a 7-month-old 'crumpled' puppy. I'm not sure what I meant by this. Perhaps he had just got up and hadn't yet ironed his clothes or perhaps he was one of those Japanese wrinkled dogs.

Our room had a wonderful view of the Luberon. There are two Luberons: the Montagne du Luberon (a mountain range midway between the Alps and the Med with Robion just on the edge) and the Parc Naturel Régional du Luberon. I mean, they're the same thing really though there is a Petit and a Grand Luberon just to keep everyone confused. All these are in the Vaucluse *département*. We absolutely love it round there and I'm not going to waste much time in describing it because if you haven't been there, you really should go.

Dinner was at 7.30pm so we showered and wandered onto the terrace thinking drinks might be forthcoming as they called it 'Place du Pastis' but nothing happened for quite some time. We sat around writing cards and diaries, etc. to the sound of bagpipes playing *Scotland the Brave* over a field towards the next village. The player had trouble hitting the top note and it was all rather funny (rather like the Chinese episode of the Goons where the pianist keeps hitting the wrong note) except for the absence of alcohol. Finally, Dahb did the obvious thing – ask – and we were offered a choice of Kir or beer. Not being very fond of Kir we chose the latter, but it was a 1664 which isn't very interesting. However, there were crisps as well and soon the meal arrived. It was truly excellent as it should have been as David ran cookery courses on the premises. There was an omelette and vegetable tower, chicken, aubergine *brochettes* (skewers), a mashed potato tower (he liked his towers) and a carafe of fragrant rosé. Pud was raspberries, raspberry ice, and meringue – Eton mess, I suppose, and quite delicious.

As we drank our coffee, four people and a Dachshund with an extra-large head arrived. I mean his head was rather large, not that he had two of them. One was a Dutchman (now I realise it looks as if one head was a Dutchman – honestly, I give up) who lived in Belgium and had limited English and no French, which is rather unusual for a Hollander. He said they had left at 5am tomorrow (I told you his English wasn't very good) and they had arrived at 4pm. We said goodnight and crashed out before 10pm – it was still light. We slept solidly until woken by the rubbish lorry at 5am.

Friday 14th June started cloudy, but there was an excellent forecast. At breakfast we chatted to the Dutchman, his dog and his wife, who did speak English (that's right, the wife *and* the dog!). We had the meal in the lovely house and excellent coffee in a flask, hooray. After breakfast we discovered David and Stéphanie didn't take credit cards, so Dahb popped into Robion where there was a cash machine (a couple of kilometres at most). After paying, we continued on the cycle way to Apt and discovered that a white arrow meant Apt and an orange one Cavaillon, which would have been useful to know the day before. We took the old road to Oppède-le-Vieux which wasn't a designated cycle track, but which was untarred and thus traffic-free. We passed some fields with a sign saying it was an organic farm, with lots of small strips of different crops e.g., barley growing between vines. There were some woolly pigs – *cochons de Luberon*, although they were Hungarian, it said. They were guaranteed *pucés* which we suppose meant free from fleas rather than riddled with them, and they were traceable by GPS. We were passed by a Danish couple and a huge dog on a lead. There was a leadless dog mooching around which we assumed was theirs, but it followed us then turned left to our right so presumably wasn't Danish after all.

We rejoined the cycle route and went into Oppède by a no-entry-except-for-cycles road, which was satisfying. Oppède was once partially abandoned but has come to life again and the old square is surrounded by restored houses. We met some cycling Australians who were with Walk Inn, a softy tour company. Climbing up to the church, which was being rebuilt, we were rewarded with incredible views of Mont Ventoux and the Montagne de Lure. Oppède is topped by a château, but it was in such a ruinous state people weren't allowed up there. We descended by a different route, and in the square looked for the restaurant we'd eaten in in 1991 (a non-Brompton holiday) on a circuit from Bonnieux with crashing storms all round but miraculously missing us. It was now only a *chambre d'hôte* but there were other restaurants that might not have been there before. By the public loos there was an extremely soppy cat which invited tummy tickling then went in for the attack, the same trick our Polly plays at home. Tickle my lovely soft tummy – ooh, I've changed into a ravening wildcat!

We went down from Oppède and picked up the lovely road again, soon arriving in Ménerbes. This is where Peter Mayle was living when he wrote *A Year in Provence*. He made no attempt to hide where he was living and was visited by so many people he had to move. When we went there the first time in 1991 it was very quiet, but this time it was busy. I seem to remember it was very wet on the first occasion.

We found a wine and snack bar with a shady terrace and marvellous views, and enjoyed delicious salads, a glass of white Luberon, and one of Côtes de Ventoux (made mostly from the Clairette grape). We then had a bit of a hard slog to Bonnieux – typical, just after lunch, not much shade, mostly cyclable, if tough, so we couldn't even get off and walk. But it got us there, and there was a good deal of downhill near the end. We could see Lacoste, but we didn't branch off this time having already been there, in fact having spent a considerable period holed up in a café because of the rain. It's a lovely place like all the others but its chief claim to fame is that the castle (now ruined though partially rebuilt) belonged to the Marquis de Sade (1740-1814) who wrote naughty books and did naughty things.

As we approached Bonnieux there was a fabulous view of it spreading out up to the church, and of Mont Ventoux (you can hardly miss Ventoux in this area). We wound round and up, passing the track leading to our campings of 1992 and eventually arriving in the main street where an exhausted fluffy pussy was curled up in a shady flower bed. In the square, also shady, we saw the lovely restaurant where we had had at least one meal. I think this one deserved the accolade of best in France as we were still in the process of sitting down when the very friendly waitress plonked a bottle of icy water on the table. Now we sat and enjoyed excellent ice-creams.

As we went back to our bicycles we saw a vintage car driving off but luckily not with two Bromptons on the back seat. That would have been truly annoying. We continued along the cycle route to Apt and reached it during rush hour which made the last bit before the centre a bit tricky. A driver shouted rude things about *vélos* – I'm not sure what his problem was unless it was because we were going faster than he was by using the pavement. As we approached the market square we saw Hôtel le Palais and knew we had to stay there, so attractive and ramshackle did it look. It was delightfully quaint and run by a young couple, the wife speaking excellent English. They were very nice, and the tariff was reasonable, so we booked two nights. There was a beautiful black and white cat called Mozart; I took a lovely photo of him sleeping by a table set for breakfast, waiting for his coffee. Our room was lovely and light and looked onto a private garden, totally quiet and secluded. I think the Bromptons were stabled in a cupboard.

The rest of the day passed in the usual way; shower, out, walkabout, drinks (free packets of crisps!), more walkabout, dinner, which was delicious, and the Côtes de Ventoux *pichet* of blanc eminently quaffable. We were lucky to get a meal in that restaurant as it was Friday, and it was shut Wednesday evening, Saturday evening and all Sunday. It was also very popular with many northern European and French people eating and others queuing in the hope of joining them.

Chapter 19
Provence yet again part 2
Tackling Mont Ventoux

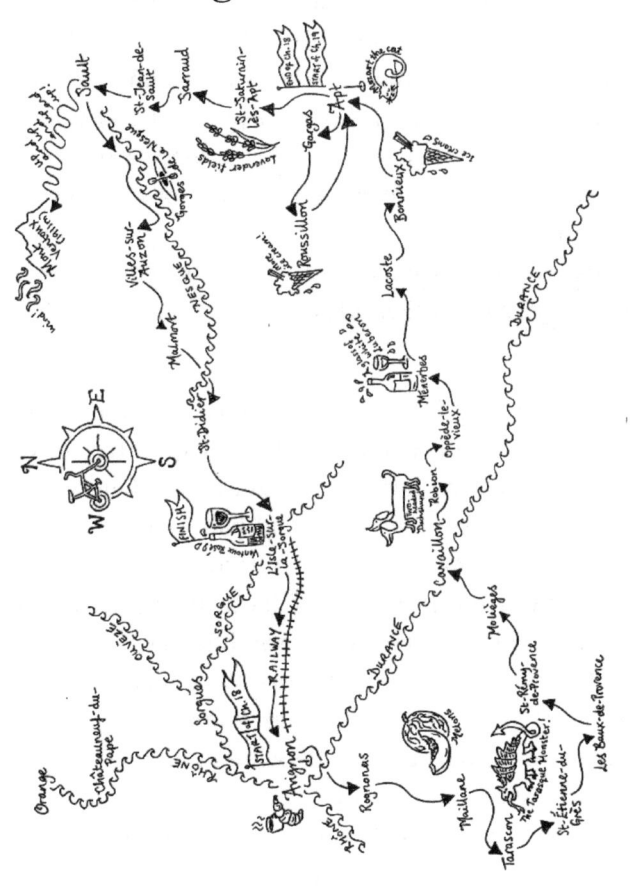

The next day, June 15th, was market day in Apt. We woke to complete silence, but out in the square it was buzzing. After breakfast and trying not to trip over Mozart's feline reincarnation who was sleeping on the floor, we went to have a look. It was a huge Provençal market and there were lots of wonderful stalls. We bought a very jolly yellow tablecloth for 10 euros (*la nappe d'Apt*) and goodies for our picnic. Down the street there was the Bob Flowerdew of Provence, or maybe even of France, who was selling seeds he had collected himself from his own plants. I had a lovely chat with him and bought some of his lettuce seed including one called *Sanguiné* – green with splashes of red. I was so sorry when I'd used them up and am hopeless at saving my own seeds, but there seems to be an English equivalent with the less gory name of 'Freckles'.

We also found a camera shop for charging our battery which took a while and was hugely expensive, so we didn't set off until after coffee time. But before long we had gone over the Passerelle du Midi and had found a cycle route to Forcalquier, which we weren't trying to go to, and also one to Rustrel (ditto), neither of these being particularly well marked. This was the old railway line to Cavaillon and soon we turned off to Gargas, at least we hoped we had. We did get there and discovered it was a fairly new town that had grown up in connection with ochre mining. We had beer on a café's shady terrace in the company of some wonderful dogs, one fully splatted out on the cool tiles looking rather like a tiger rug. We read the *météo* in a paper – it was going to get hotter and hotter, with 35 degrees forecast for

Carpentras, 30 km to the north-west. It was going to be a bit cooler higher up and dry until Thursday when there would be a 50% chance of *orages* (storms).

We found a signed route to Roussillon, which we did want to go to. In fact, revisiting it was the day's main purpose. We had our picnic near a bus shelter, leaning against a parapet. We continued up, passing some snoozing cyclists on a shady bench (good idea but no more benches), and had to climb to Roussillon, quite hard work in the heat and a bit busy. But we got there and left the bicycles just outside the village, grockles everywhere. We had some fabulous ice-creams in a café, then walked in the old village. The views were amazing and hooray, there was a *table d'orientation* at the very top.

We left the grocks to it and swooped back down the same road towards Apt, where there was a signed cycled route. After some quiet roads we reached the rail path again, coming out right in the centre by Turismu. Back at the hotel our nice hostess telephoned the hotel in Sault for us, booking Sunday and Monday – this was Hôtel le Signoret, the one we'd been to a few years ago. We went for a beer opposite Turismu and detected a slight air of disapproval of Dahb's 50cl glass.

Our hotel served food Saturday to Wednesday, so we ate there on tables right out in the square. It was delicious, but I must say Guillaume was a bit scatty on the service side. I mean, he was a bit slow bringing the wine! He kept forgetting the bread and would dash off saying *merde!* before forgetting it again. All very amusing. No sign of Mozart who was no doubt sleeping off a very busy day.

We aimed to leave at 8.30am on the Sunday but were a little delayed because of shopping. We saw Mozart scampering over the road to the square, probably tired of waiting for breakfast. Off we went along the way we'd come in the night before, then we took the Rustrel cycle route, leaving it for St-Saturnin which was nestled on the south side of the Vaucluse plateau. There was a quite purple lavender field which was fairly early for mid-June and was probably the hybrid *lavandin*. We had lemonades at a *Logis* and showed Madame the picture of Mozart waiting for breakfast, as we were laughing about it at the time. She said her cat would be doing something similar somewhere.

Then we started a *very* long climb to Sarraud which was about 6km due north, the views gradually opening, amazing ones of the Petit and Grand Luberon. We could also see Roussillon, Gordes, Oppède and Bonnieux. The flowers were wonderful, and we found a splendid picnic spot under a pine tree (we certainly needed the shade). Continuing upwards, we saw orchids and remembered our tubby headmaster, and just before 4pm reached the top (Col de la Liguière, 998m). Of course, we could see Mont Ventoux, its summit being about a thousand metres higher than we were.

Then we started a huge swoop down, hunting for bars. There were none to be seen, though possibly there was something in St-Jean, which we bypassed. In the valley we crossed a bridge with a wonderful view of Sault. We took a small road straight up (the main road goes round and round), and found our hotel, Le Signoret, which was not surprisingly in the same place it had been when we stayed before. We think it had expanded somewhat, however, and was much busier than before.

Before going there, we had drinks at Bar La Promenade where Dahb had a large beer with no recriminations. We asked for some water and were given a huge bottle and two glasses. The bar was full, mainly with French people, and the waiters were very jolly. Four aged cyclists (no baggage) passed our Bromptons staring as if to put them out of countenance.

We found our hotel greatly changed but our room on the second floor was nice enough, although there was no soap and only one shampoo, already opened. Walking around Sault we found it seemed bigger than before and even lovelier than we'd remembered. We found a shop of lavender goodies and treated ourselves to two small and fragrant bars of soap.

We found Place du Marché and the entrance to Hôtel du Louvre which had been closed in 2006 and still looked impossible to get into from the promenade. We had a drink on the terrace of Bar le Siècle which was pleasant and shady but when Dahb asked for a carafe of water it appeared to be rationed and he was given one glass of it. Hôtel du Louvre's restaurant was shut on Sundays, but we thought we'd try it the next day if it wasn't shut on Mondays.

We went back to Le Signoret for dinner on its terrace which was somewhat smarter than before. We enjoyed our meal as usual though it was quite chilly – we wore jerseys and I went for soup which I think of as a winter thing. We noticed that it was definitely cooler on the north side of the Vaucluse plateau. We washed down the meal with an excellent carafe of Côtes de Ventoux rosé from a local vineyard. There were English people behind Dahb, a French party by the wall and bilingual Belgians to our side. It was all very friendly and pleasant.

The next day we popped up Mont Ventoux.

We are not the only Bromptonists to have gone up Mont Ventoux but there aren't many and we haven't heard of any elderly girlies. We certainly didn't see any other Bromptons on the day. But then, we've seen only two Bromptons in the whole of France. They could have been hidden, of course. The Australian we met in Oppède-le-Vieux told us that you and your bike could be taken up in a van and then cycle down, which I think is rather caddish and I hope no Brompton rider would even consider it.

Why Mont Ventoux? Because it's there? Or should that be: why *not* Mont Ventoux? After all, this limestone *massif* is not really very high at 1911m and remember we once cheerfully went over the Sommet de Lure (1826m) before breakfast, though admittedly breakfast that day was at 4pm and I was probably grumbling like billy-o. It certainly deserves the name '*massif*' as it is about 25km long east-west and 15km north-south. Its geographical isolation makes it visible over great distances, as I keep mentioning. It is known as the 'Giant of Provence', and I read somewhere that it is also known as the 'Beast' which I find rather beastist and hubristic and clearly a word used by the type of person who 'conquers' mountains. I remember reading a Mary Stewart book where there was a mad murderer who went round killing people who talked of conquering mountains. The beautiful heroine survived because she had said she had thought it was a shame that Everest had been 'conquered' (the book was set in 1953). The madman said she was different and therefore spared her, but near the end he was going to kill her anyway for some reason by tipping her out of a boat on the loch, but luckily the hero rescued her in the nick of time.

As its name suggests there is nearly always a wind blowing on the mountain, particularly at *Mistral* time. The temperature at the summit is on average 11C lower than at the foot (the *météo* we'd read the other day telling us it would be 35 in Carpentras had forecast 14 degrees for Ventoux). Rainfall is twice as heavy, and in winter the temperature can drop to minus 27C. From December to April, it is usually snow-capped above about 1300m. Polar species of vegetation flourish at the top. The mountain was once tree-covered, but from the 16th century deforestation went on to supply shipyards in Toulon. Since the mid-19th century replanting has been carried out and, in 1994, Ventoux was classified as a Biosphere reserve by UNESCO.

Three weeks before this Provence holiday, I sat looking at the maps, thinking that if we were going to do it, we should get on with it as we were both in our 60s, nor were the Bromptons in the first flush of youth. We had been close on several occasions, and in 2006 had rather enviously watched those American ladies set off to traverse it on their tandem, but somehow didn't think of doing it ourselves. That day already seemed hard enough to us, from Vaison-la-Romaine to Sault (50km and a climb of over 400m), passing along the north side of Ventoux. We weren't particularly looking for greater challenges.

So now we thought, let's give it a whirl. From Sault, which we were happy to visit again, to the summit was 26km and we had to climb only 1180m or so. We would stay two nights in Sault so that we could travel baggage-free, though we would be sure to take our heaviest item, the pack of bike tools that we might well need and certainly would if we left them behind. We would take plenty of water and a picnic, and if we were lucky, there would be a café somewhere on the way for a lemonade (none of our regular midday beers on this occasion, not on the way up anyway) but we wouldn't rely on it.

The only condition we made for ourselves was that the weather had to be absolutely perfect and, sure enough, the morning dawned fabulous, like all the rest of the holiday. We intended to make a really early start, but the hotel didn't serve breakfast until 7.30am and we didn't want to miss that, so after shopping for our picnic, at about 8.15am we were heading over the plain towards Mont Ventoux, past fields of what we assumed was *épeautre*, the cereal local to Sault, and a very fragrant lavender farm. The town is at 750m, but we had to drop nearly 100m to cross the plain, an unwelcome addition to the total climb. At the start of the ascent there was a sign saying *route barrée* but there were plenty of cyclists going up, and indeed plenty of cars, including a black Belgian vehicle being driven *right* behind a cyclist. We met one or two wives who were driving as support to their husbands, but you wouldn't catch this one doing it. Tricky anyway when you haven't got a car with you.

We were soon into beech forests but there were many clearings with marvellous views. Some of the inclines were too steep for us. We could have made much more effort but remembered that we were on holiday; much was cyclable, though. Past the hamlet of Le Ventouret (alt. 1010m), our map informed us we were starting a scenic bit. As we neared Le Chalet-Reynard (1440m) about midday (normal beer time), we saw a dilapidated sign for a café, like many we have seen in France where the café has long gone. But we turned a corner and there was a huge café and shop, *teeming* with cars, bikes and people.

So we had our lemonades, and chatted to an Englishman staying in our hotel who had already been up and was now on the way down – his wife was one of those in a supporting car. Then we started *the* climb. This is the point at which the Tour de France would join the road in July, having come up from Bédoin (alt. 330m and 21.5km from the summit). It was now steeper, so we needed to push more, but it still wasn't *very* steep and quite comfortable for pushing. We stopped for our picnic and ate it with an incomparable view in front of us – the summit and its observatory. The terrain was getting barer and barer but there were still hordes of cars and bikes. We didn't cycle so much now, though Dahb claims that he could have pedalled all the way. A Frenchman sitting by the side of the road looked at our wheels and said (in French), 'Why?' and I said (in French), 'Why not?' That shut *him* up. He was very nice and friendly.

We passed the memorial to Tom Simpson who collapsed and died during the ascent of Mont Ventoux in the 1967 Tour de France. He was 29 years old. On post-mortem he was found to have mixed amphetamines and alcohol – what a waste of a life and all in the name of sport.

We reached the Col des Tempêtes (1841m) and our first view of the French Alps was truly amazing. It is well named, too; we stepped towards the edge, and it was howling.

Now the terrain was really bare and white, but the tiniest of alpine flowers were poking through. There were warnings of *troupeaux* – what on earth could sheep or goats eat up there? We sternly passed the pre-summit bar and arrived at the top to a chaotic scene of cars and bikes, and lorries resurfacing the road, presumably ready for the Tour in July. With some difficulty we found the summit stone and took a photo of it being read by the Bromptons. We learned about the observatory and an intrepid Jesuit who nipped up there in the 18th century, in the name of scientific discovery. However, the Italian poet Petrarch claims to have pipped him to the post, in 1336.

Well, we'd done it. 6 ¾ hours including stops of an hour in total, but we didn't hang about in those crowds. After exclaiming at the fantastic views and taking some more photos, we shot down to the nearby bar, which was a haven of peace. Over what we considered to be a well-earned beer, tucked into the lee of a wall as it was a tad breezy up there, though far too sunny to be inside, we talked to a very pleasant Dutch couple who couldn't quite believe we'd been up by Brompton. The lady said, "May I ask how *old* you are?" There was a definite you-are-surely-old-enough-to-know-better inflection to her voice, but they were great fun and suitably impressed.

What can I say about the descent, except that the sun was still out, the views were still there, there were fewer cars, and the gradient was gentle enough to be able to cruise down with just a little pressure on the back brake? In half an hour we'd reached the lower café where naturally we had to have another beer, and where another Dutch couple wanted to know how old we were. An elderly Englishman, resident in France, asked me if we'd gone up "on those", and on my answering in the affirmative insisted on shaking my hand.

In another hour, we were on the plain below Sault and there were still cyclists going up the mountain, perhaps just nipping up after work. It was rather upsetting to have to climb up again to the town when it was definitely shower and dinner time, but we couldn't do anything else. We were soon there, clean and out for a delicious meal outside Hôtel du Louvre. Amazingly I didn't fall asleep in my soup which I've been near to doing at times.

So what *is* all the fuss about? Getting from Apt to Sault the day before was harder than our trip up and down the 'Giant'. But here's the rub: when the Tour de France cyclists hurtle up to the summit, they are doing the 21.5km climb from Bédoin at the end of a 240km day, the profile of which can be seen on the Tour de France website and looks more like a week's Brompton trip. They must be feeling exhausted by the time they start the climb from the lower café, and I can't believe they'd be drinking in the views in the relaxed way we did. Of course, there is a huge amount to admire in the Tour de France but for appreciating the French countryside and the friendliness of the natives and other tourists (a folding bike tackling mountains is a superb conversation opener) there is probably little to beat a Brompton. Well done, Modestine! I think I can detect a certain smugness in her demeanour since that day, and sometimes wonder if I've heard a boastful chuckle from her corner as I pass. She does live in our box room with the wine …

Tuesday June 18th dawned another perfect day. We said *au revoir* to Sault and went down the hill below the Promenade, heading south-west across a lovely valley with lots of flowers. We climbed up a gorge, stopping at Belvedere de Castelleras which looked over the Rocher de Cire (872m). There were hordes of people including some Dutch racy-type cyclists and Americans cycling and being escorted by a minibus. It was all a bit much, but luckily, they had come up from the way we were going so it was quieter on the way down. Then there were quite a lot of cyclists near the bottom, starting to go up when it was very hot. We were almost too hot going down!

We were freewheeling down the magnificent gorge of the Nesque and had got down to about 350m when my back tyre went flat. Dahb tried to pump it up but to no avail but we were only one or two kilometres from the village of Villes-sur-Auzon, so I balanced my rucksack in his front pannier and freewheeled into the village while he and Modestine walked. It was now late lunchtime, and we found a lovely restaurant, La Nesque, with a shady garden behind and were soon tucking in and imbibing some of the local beverage. We sat next to a pleasant couple from Leicester who annually cross from Hull to Zeebrugge and drive down over three days with a caravan to Ville's municipal campsite where they meet the same crowd of holidaymakers each year. They said that until a week ago they had had the heating on in their caravan. I think that if we had gone up Mont Ventoux a week earlier we would have frozen, though it's unlikely that we'd have gone.

Finding a shady bench near the square, Dahb mended the puncture. I explored the village and telephoned a *Clé Vacances chambre d'hôte* right next to us as there was no response to my knocking on the door. The call was answered by a M. Bertrand who said he indeed had a room in La Sarrasine and came round to see us. He was charming and showed us to a lovely room in his lovely house, the Bromptons being tucked up in his garage. The room was huge, and the bathroom tiled and cool which was perfect in such hot weather.

After cleaning up a bit, especially Dahb, we sat outside the next-door café Le Soleil, sipping beers in the shade and watching life from our comfy armchairs. Then we walked around, taking the circular road following the line of the ramparts. We saw one *brasserie* with 'yoof', another *brasserie* (closed), a pizzeria (closed), a take-away pizzeria (closed), a *Maison de la Presse* (open), and a minimarket (open). There was also a very attractive church –we probably didn't try to go in so will never know if it was open or closed. We had visited Villes on an earlier occasion but really couldn't remember anything about it.

We went back to restaurant La Nesque which was – phew – open, unlike Le Soleil which was closed when we went back hoping for a nightcap. Back at the ranch our *patron* was sitting outside with a dog, and we arranged breakfast for 8am. He told us that rain was forecast for the morrow, so we dug out our waterproofs which had been gradually making their way to the bottom of our luggage.

It was dry first thing, but cloudier. We had breakfast sitting outside on the pavement and Monsieur brought us a flask of coffee – hooray. He pointed out several houses that belonged to English people and when we asked what he thought about that he said it was fine as they were nice English, as we were, and made the effort to speak French, as we did. There was an absolutely heavenly house, La Maison Rose, pink, as the name suggests, and I really wanted it. We wandered down the *impasse* (cul de sac) behind it and there seemed to be space for growing vegetables behind, so we made a note to buy the house next time we were passing.

Monsieur had gone shopping, so we let ourselves out through the garage and dropped the key back through the front door hoping we hadn't forgotten anything vital. Feeling we'd like to return to Villes-sur-Auzon one day, we went out with a fabulous view of a lovely valley but there were threatening clouds and thunderclaps and then *rain*. We hurried into our waterproofs which were to hand, then after five minutes the rain stopped. We kept the anoraks on long enough to dry them (about five minutes), then took them off again. That was it.

We kept crossing the Nesque which was dry in parts, and bypassed Venasque (where we had been refused a drink some years before). We went to the centre of Malemort where I'd managed to get my hair cut in 1991. Our little road ran out at a 'private/beware of the dog' sign, probably because we were using a superannuated map. We asked someone who said the track *might* be all right, but decided to take the safe option and return down an extremely steep hill to Malemort, the steepness being compensated for by the stunning views of Ventoux. We headed for St-Didier where we found a restaurant opposite the *Mairie*, on a busy but entertaining road, and had excellent salads. The old village was through an arch under the church and was beautiful. I've said that before – we'd been there before.

We left the village and climbed up to the upper outskirts of L'Isle-sur-la-Sorgue which reminded me of the upper outskirts of Cannes. Down we went to the inner outskirts which were busy because it was rush hour, but there were very good cycle routes to the centre. We found ourselves in Place de la Liberté where there was a huge church and a closed Turismu. There was a list of hotels with phone numbers but no addresses.

We thought we might find some on the surrounding quays, so we went round and found some signs to hotels, the first of which was closed. But we soon found Hôtel la Gueulardière with its Bistro de Pétrarque. I like to think he ate there after his quick trip up Mont Ventoux in the 14th century which must have made him a bit peckish. We got a splendid ground floor room with plenty of space for the bicycles. We had our own table and chairs outside and it was a lovely, slightly ramshackle, old-fashioned sort of set-up, just what Tiggers like. We had landed again.

We decided to join Petrarch for dinner but went for a potter first. The old town is surrounded by the arms of the river Sorgue and this waterpower enabled it to be a very active industrial centre for a long time, with weaving, dyeing and tanning going on as well as paper, grain and oil mills. There were ten water wheels, and some can still be seen turning. It is all quite delightful. We found the station and checked the train times for Avignon and after beers somewhere or other returned to the Bistro and had a delicious dinner and some Ventoux rosé. All very satisfactory once again.

There was a huge market the next day and we enjoyed a pre-breakfast peruse and identified some presents to buy later. Breakfast was in the hotel bar which was very *fin de siècle*, its walls plastered with drawings and maps. Coffee was fresh from the machine but served in open jugs; we had to be a bit persistent about getting food as they didn't seem to have thought of that one.

We talked to some Belgians who told us to look in the *Grande Salle* where, as part of the restaurant, there was a museum of teaching materials which was quite amazing. We paid and left, leaving the cycles in an *impasse* just off Rue de la République while we went shopping. First we had a beer stop by the river and made a list (I don't know what we'd been doing all morning, but it was beer time, honest) and then went to get what we wanted. We found another quayside place for lunch and had the most amazing salads. I don't go much for photographing food, being too busy eating it, but this was an exception as my salad was so pretty if ephemeral.

Then we went for the 2.10pm train to Avignon, getting stuck in the ticket queue behind an old lady who wanted a cheap ticket to Brussels and who seemed to be gradually beating down the ticket seller. We were feeling a bit hot and bothered, knowing we needed to fold the bikes, then realised we could use a machine – for the ticket, not for folding. Now that would be an advance. We had to walk across the track to the platform. The TER arrived on time and dropped us at the Avignon town station half an hour later. We partly reassembled the bikes, checked the times of the TGV shuttle at the Poste, then went to the same hotel and even the same room. We paid in advance as we were going early, and went up to our favourite *salon de thé* for a shady coffee by which I mean we drank it on the shady terrace, not that there was anything shady about the coffee except where we were drinking it.

Then we walked via the Palais des Papes to the Roche des Doms where there are lovely gardens with, guess what, wonderful views of Mont Ventoux and also the Vercors and the Alpilles. We could see 'Ch of Chng du P' according to the typed version of my diary (the original scribble might be more informative if I could find the book). We also gazed at Villeneuve-lès-Avignon which is Avignon New Town, 13th century or so, and on the other side of the Rhône, looking amazing. We thought we'd like to stay there another time, especially if we were heading west to Languedoc. The weather was a bit murky, but it was a pleasant temperature and the thermometer at the chemist by our hotel read 26 degrees which was exactly what it had been when we arrived.

We walked along the walls to the famous Pont d'Avignon but couldn't get onto it without paying. When I was working in Avignon with the BBC Singers I'm sure it was free. A few of us wanted to dance on the bridge singing the song, then couldn't remember whether it went *Sous le pont* or *Sur le pont*, so did both. After which it was time for drinks. Dahb and I did a lot more exploring and had beers and dinner near our hotel. A karaoke session was starting up as we left and Dahb was told in no uncertain terms that he was not to join in. He loves karaoke but I haven't yet had to hear him – I dread the day.

I thought for a moment my diary read 'Packed tiny bath and bed, immense racket', but a second look revealed 'Packed comma tiny bath and bed, immense racket from below till about 2.15am when sudden hush till about 5 when delivering, cleaning and rubbish collection started, and rooks and jackdaws in trees outside'.

We left the hotel at 8am for the shuttle to the station, and the rest is (unrecorded) history.

Chapter 20 (Conclusion)
Some travels *not* on a Brompton and what next for Modestine?

So! Since 1993 we have travelled with our Bromptons in the Cévennes and several other regions. We have visited old provinces such as Artois, Dauphiné and Quercy, and we have visited most of the 22 former administrative regions of France.

We have cycled, we have walked, pushing the bicycles, we have taken roads, we have taken footpaths, we have found neither but still got through somehow. Apropos of pushing, the noble doctor often pushes both cycles at once saying it's just as easy as pushing one. The trouble is I have a problem keeping up even though I'm just walking.

We have been at sea level (Charentes, Var), we have tackled many a *col*, the highest being the Montagne de Lure, and we have spent a wonderful day on the gentle Giant of Provence. We have experienced temperatures of 35 degrees, and near freezing (this is just the holidays in summer). We have been to some places twice, more places once and have many a nook and cranny still to explore. As I write we are contemplating another trip to Provence in early July, later than we would normally go but late enough to see the lavender in bloom (it is usually just coming out as we're leaving). If it's very hot, we might then retreat into the French Alps and see how high we can get and cool off. If it's freezing we can always stay on the plains. If it's hot and hideously touristy, as it might be being French holiday time, we can always hop on a train and go somewhere less well-known and further north. Such is the flexibility of Bromptoning.

We have always got there by train, or occasionally bus. Only once have the Bromptons travelled by car in France (not *to* France and apart from a dash in a taxi to catch a train), when we met French friends who have a house in the Jura. We arranged a rendezvous, and the bicycles (and us) were given a lift back to the house.

We have had some holidays in France on our big bikes, and several in the UK. We had a lovely two weeks in Portugal where friends were living for a while. We flew to Faro with the bicycles and travelled to Figueira da Foz where they were renting a very smart apartment. We had a wonderful Corsican holiday, starting from the same friends who were then very considerately living near Gatwick. When we picked up our bikes on our return, my front fork was quite badly buckled, and we decided not to fly again if we could help it. We also nearly lost our car. I volunteered to go and get it but when I showed the docket to the shuttle bus driver he said there was no such parking point as squiggle squiggle (doctor's writing).

He asked me what our car looked like. When I proffered the information that it was a Morris Minor with a door on top, he said he knew exactly where it was, and I was to hang on (as he shot off at high speed). We now drive a little black Yaris with a very discreet cycle rack on the towbar and I can't believe the employee of the airline company would have found that one. In case you're wondering, the door was to provide a flat surface on which to tie the cycles.

In my introduction, I mentioned our holiday in the Auvergne when we had to cycle (on our big bikes) most of the way from the Channel port and then turn round and head back again. But I have also written of a Brompton holiday in that magnificent region. We have been to Normandy several times, taking the boat from Portsmouth usually to Ouistreham, and returning from there or Cherbourg or Le Havre. We have cycled twice in Brittany, sailing to St-Malo on one occasion and Roscoff on the other.

We have often cycled in Wales, once through a snowy Easter. We had a sun-drenched fortnight in Northumberland and another one in Ireland of all places; this luck was counterbalanced by an extremely soggy week in the Yorkshire Dales. There was our 'Middle England' holiday, when we took the train to Lincoln and spent a few days cycling home again through several counties. We are very fond of the Chilterns and have had a couple of trips there. Once we took the train to and from Reading, and on the return journey took our chance with the train (plenty of room on that occasion). Nowadays you have to book in advance, which is a little restricting, and so for our second Chiltern trip we booked a room in a Great Missenden pub for a couple of nights, drove us and the bikes there and did two big circular trips, which worked well.

We also like Shropshire and once took the train to Ludlow and after cycling for a few days turned up at Church Stretton for the return journey. Again, it worked well but now we'd have to book tickets for the cycles, and we don't always know when we'll get to a station – I remember getting a puncture on the Long Mynd. So, the next time we drove to Ludlow and our B&B was happy for us to leave the car while we headed off into the wilds of Salop. We also explored the Severn Estuary by leaving our car near Stroud – it's always a relief to see it still there the next day! I think if we go off to the West Country again, which I hope we will before long, we'll get ourselves organised and use the train. We should, after all, use 'God's Wonderful Railway', GWR, when we can.

But what next for Modestine and me, her friend? And what about electrified Bromptons? We intend to visit France on our velocipedic donkeys for many years to come and there are many more regions (in the informal sense) to explore. Of course, we love the south of France, who doesn't? But we are also very taken by the north and there are plenty of corners we would like to visit either again or for the first time. Good weather helps, but it doesn't happen only in the summer. The Pays d'Auge in what used to be Haute-Normandie is wonderful in late summer or autumn if the sun is shining, with bright red apples on the orchard trees and large contented cows grazing beneath them.

We cycled on our big bikes to the Bay of the Somme and up to Trouville and Montreuil-sur-Mer (one of our favourite towns) in October and there were some quite wet days. I had a very painful throat infection, and my medical attendant did admit at one stage that a sodden progress by bicycle wasn't the usual treatment. But cold French beers helped, and we had lunch in the sun at Trouville and I didn't die and didn't have to be put out for the vultures, which are not to be found in Picardy, as far as I know. I have already mentioned the danger of proceeding too slowly in the south.

Since putting together this book we and the Bromptons have been back to Provence to see the Verdon gorges, and had a trip centred on Vichy, taking in the *départements* of Puy-de-Dôme, Allier and Loire. We have been back to the Jura and have travelled to the far south-west to visit Pays Basque. We were all set to revisit Brittany when the world was struck by Covid-19 and what holidays we could manage in 2020 had to be taken at home. On two occasions we did long day trips on our Dawes – we have posh big bikes nowadays – and three days in Rutland which is a lovely county. Now in 2021 we wonder if we'll get to France, or more importantly get back; perhaps in the autumn and if not, it should still be there next year.

It would be nice to return to the areas we went through when we first tried to get to the Auvergne. Not the very flat bits, though – the flat areas tend to be quite boring and monocultural, and it's very tiring doing a lot of cycling on the flat. Getting off the saddle and walking for a bit can be quite restful.

It's a long time since we've been to Brittany and we haven't seen much of the Pays de la Loire, and the Poitou bit of Poitou-Charentes remains unknown to us. There's more of Normandy to see; perhaps we could combine a Breton trip with visiting our friends in Briouze, a pleasant market town in Orne. The eastern part of Rhône-Alpes might be a bit hilly (Savoie and Haute-Savoie) but why not? It's only a question of how far one can go in a day.

There are so many places we haven't visited that I'm now beginning to wonder if we've been anywhere at all.

About electrification: one of us is now 70 (guess who) and the other not far behind, and our Bromptons are nearer 30 than they like to admit. They recently spent a few days at Warlands of Oxford and came back fully serviced and with various new bits, so they are much rejuvenated and decidedly frisky. The same cannot be said of their riders but we are hanging on in there and are not yet in need of any new bits ourselves. Although we travel more slowly than of yore and therefore get through fewer kilometres, we still feel happy about using our own power to get up hills, whether cycling or pushing. There's little to beat the feeling of achievement at cresting a hill or mountain and the satisfaction of freewheeling down. The ride down Mont Ventoux was out of this world, and knowing we had a bed and that there were several places for dinner added to the perfection.

But it is good to know electrification has arrived and that when the day comes when we feel we need help, it will be there and we can carry on with our cycling holidays. Whether Modestine will carry the battery as well as me and my luggage, I don't know. I haven't discussed it with her. She might well ask me to find a younger Brompton for such a task but really, having spent all that money on her spa holiday I think she should be all right. I should imagine by then there will be plenty of places hiring out e-bikes and we could always just choose to go to a region and do that. But that is surely well in the future. Our holiday formula has served us so well for so long that we hope there will be many more travels with a Brompton, wherever.

Acknowledgments

Where did it all begin? At Swindon Scrapstore (www.scrapstore.co.uk) where as a volunteer I wrote a short history of the charity. I showed it to my friend Viv Cripps, who at the time was publishing Millrace Books: beautiful little hardback volumes that are still available if you look for them. After reading my Scrapstore book and a sample chapter of Travels, she commissioned me to write the latter. Books such as mine are only completed as quickly as 'research trips' (aka holidays) are undertaken, and she wound up the company before I could finish. However, she cheerfully took on the role of mentor and Chief Reader of the Opus and I am so grateful for her expertise and support. We are old friends, our husbands being schoolfellows, and doubtless many glasses will be raised to the success of the venture. Actually, they will be anyway...

Of course, Travels could not have been written had not Andrew Ritchie designed the Brompton, so I raise another glass to him (any excuse). Let's raise another to Dave Henshaw for his marvellous and comprehensive book Brompton Bicycle. I would like to thank The Map Shop in Upton upon Severn for their unfailing helpfulness and alacrity in producing French maps for us. We so enjoy the

Michelin Green Guides and all the information therein. Warlands cycle shop in Oxford sold us our Bromptons and have kept us on the road with crucial servicing when needed.

Cranthorpe Millner must have another glass raised to them (this is good: I'll pop another bottle in the fridge). They responded to my submission with such promptitude and enthusiasm, a beacon of light in the grey days of the hunt for a publisher. This started with Catherine, whose sort-of-automatic-but-personal reception of my submission was cheery and, well, personal, then went on to involve Kirsty, Shannon, Ros, Sian, Donna and Vicky (in no particular order as the wine is kicking in). They know who they are and how supportive they have been.

I think a mention is due to Covid-19 as lockdown provided the opportunity for many things, and not having to rush out every five minutes to play my viola (sadly neglected during that time but still speaking to me) did mean I just got on and finished the book.

There might/might not be more information on my social media sites (Facebook, Instagram etc) and my website: https://suebirleytravelwriter.blogspot.com/. My friend Mark Woodman has been a terrific help in setting this up and scanning old photographs for the book. Some of our meetings take place in the pub, surrounded by noisy people (that's just our table), with varying results.

Where would I be without my dear friend, author Nicola Pryce (https://nicolapryce.co.uk) who fed, watered and encouraged me at her lovely Somerset home, giving me lessons on social media? Her Cornish novels provided much needed relaxation when my own book process threatened to pull me down.

Nearly there now: Becky Ripley, please come forward! Becky not only produced the beautiful covers and the exquisite pen and ink drawings, but offered much welcome advice on other aspects of the book from her experience as BBC producer and presenter.

Last but by no means least, as everyone who knows him would agree, I must thank Dahb or David, husband of 47 ½ years (grief, I need another drink). Well, if Modestine knew a good snack when she saw one, this doctor knows a good camping site even if some of his routes prove to be a little, er, informal.

About the Author

Sue Birley was born in the English Lake District and now lives in a Wiltshire marsh. She was educated at Keswick School, St Thomas' Hospital, the Royal Northern College of Music, the universities of Oxford and Reading and the Open University. Her research work on Anglo-French politics provided the launch pad for writing this book. Indeed, most of her qualifications have proved useful though she has yet to sing for her supper or provide first aid. She takes along a doctor for the latter purpose.

BV - #0004 - 140422 - C6 - 197/132/20 - PB - 9781803780276 - Matt Lamination